Murder in Manchuria

MURDER IN MANCHURIA

The True Story of a Jewish Virtuoso,
Russian Fascists, a French Diplomat, and
a Japanese Spy in Occupied China

SCOTT D. SELIGMAN

Potomac Books
An imprint of the University of Nebraska Press

Library of Congress Cataloging-in-Publication Data
Names: Seligman, Scott D., author.
Title: Murder in Manchuria: the true story of a Jewish
virtuoso, Russian fascists, a French diplomat, and a
Japanese spy in occupied China / Scott D. Seligman.
Description: [United States]: Potomac Books, an
imprint of the University of Nebraska Press, [2023] |
Includes bibliographical references and index.
Identifiers: LCCN 2022056840
ISBN 9781640125841 (hardback)
ISBN 9781640126039 (epub)
ISBN 9781640126046 (pdf)
Subjects: LCSH: Kaspé, Semyon, 1909-1933. |
Kidnapping—China—Manchuria—Case studies. |
Murder—China—Manchuria—Case studies. |
Jews—China—Manchuria—History—20th century. |
Manchuria (China)—History—20th century. | BISAC:
TRUE CRIME / Murder / General | HISTORY / Jewish
Classification: LCC HV6604.C6 S45 2023 |
DDC 364.15/409518—dc23/eng/20230706
LC record available at https://lccn.loc.gov/2022056840

Set in Linotype Electra by A. Shahan.

And in that bloody duel between the greedy, grasping, obstinate Slav and the newborn energies of the occidentalized Mongol, the Jew paid his full quota for the doubtful privilege of his domicile . . . *the worst of stepmothers that have ever nursed the Children of Israel.*

RABBI SHEVEL LEVIN,
the city of Harbin's first rabbi, as quoted
in the *Hebrew Standard*, November 2, 1906

———

Harbin was great for the Jews until it wasn't.

DARA HORN,
People Love Dead Jews, 2021

Contents

Illustrations

FIGURES

MAPS

Introduction

When Semyon Kaspé and Lydia Shapiro parted on a street in the city of Harbin near midnight on August 24, 1933, after a night of music and merriment, neither could anticipate the dark sequence of events the coming months held in store. The macabre aftermath would set the Manchurian Jewish community on edge, arouse worldwide opprobrium, and leave behind a mystery that was never fully solved.

The tragedy that began that night in China's "Wild East" pulled in an improbable cast of Jewish merchants, Japanese military men, White Russian thugs, French diplomats, Chinese judges, and even an Italian spy-for-hire. It was a watershed event in the history of the so-called Empire of Manchukuo, a piece of northeast China forcibly carved off by the Japanese Army in 1931. The fate of Semyon Kaspé would help unmask Manchukuo as the Japanese puppet state it was. And it would herald the exodus of thousands of Russian Jews who had called the land home for several decades, helping to foil a grand Japanese plan to keep them there.

The story of Semyon Kaspé is the stuff of Harbin lore. Histories of the city unfailingly take note of it, and the preservation of many of the storied, turn-of-the-century buildings in which Semyon and Lydia lived and played helps one imagine even today how it unfolded.

The first time I heard about the Kaspé family was when I visited Harbin with a group of friends from the Beijing Jewish community in the late 1990s, although I didn't learn the whole story at the time. On that trip, we made a special effort to locate the historic sites of Jewish interest. I learned that in its heyday, Harbin had been home to some twenty thousand Jews, nearly all of whom disappeared in the run-up to the Second World War or not long after it. But why they had come and where they had gone was a mystery to me, and there were none of them left to tell the story.

We lodged at the Moderne, an iconic, turn-of-the-century hotel built in 1913–14 by Semyon's father Josef, a Russian Jewish entrepreneur. Across the street, we enjoyed bowls of what turned out to be very authentic borscht at the ornate Huamei Restaurant that had once been the Jewish-owned Mars Restaurant. And we made pilgrimages to two imposing buildings—one a hostel and the other a social club—that had once been synagogues, and visited the former Jewish Gymnasium, where we interrupted a class of its current students, Chinese children of Korean extraction. One could still clearly make out the six-pointed Stars of David in the building's fenestration.

Not to be missed was Huangshan, the site of the largest extant Jewish cemetery in East Asia. Located on the outskirts of the city, it is the repository of Harbin's remaining Jewish gravestones, which were removed from their original location in the city center between 1958 and 1962 to make way for new construction, though it is not the location of the actual graves. One can view Semyon's somewhat eroded tombstone there today.

In my experience, to study Jewish history too often means to visit places where Jews *used* to live but no longer do. For me, this has included parts of the former Soviet Union and Eastern Europe and several cities in East Asia and on the subcontinent. The list also includes my home town of Newark, New Jersey, which boasted a flourishing Jewish community of about sixty thousand souls when I grew up there in the 1950s and 1960s. The magnificent old synagogue buildings still stand, most reincarnated as African American churches. The cemeteries in which many of my forebears rest are also still there. But today, Newark probably counts fewer than a thousand Jewish residents, the rest having long since fled to its suburbs.[1]

Newark's Jews came primarily from the Russian empire, and they thrived in the city for about a century, give or take a decade or two, before moving on. But Russian Jews just like my paternal grandparents who headed east rather than west and wound up in Harbin enjoyed a much shorter window there—about half the time. And unlike the Newarkers, who were, in the main, upwardly mobile and financially able to pack up and leave for suburbia, the Harbin Jews departed because they were more or less driven out.

I never foresaw that I would someday learn enough about the Kaspés to write a book about them and others who called Manchuria home in the early twentieth century, still less one centered in the very Hotel Moderne in which I had stayed. In the process, I would learn the full story of the Harbin Jews, from the arrival of the first Jewish man in 1899 to the death of the last Jewish woman in 1985, and understand how the tragic story of Semyon Kaspé contributed to the exodus of the community. And I would take a stab at solving the nearly century-old mystery of who was ultimately responsible for the young man's fate.

Harbin's first Jews, like my grandparents, arrived at their destination at the turn of the twentieth century. But nearly all were gone by 1949 when the Communists took over China. For a short interval during those five decades, they felt safe from the oppression and violence that had plagued them in Russia. Eventually, however, Russians and their hatred caught up with them, and the arrival in 1931 of new Japanese overlords, who quickly joined forces with the Russians, made things for the Jews immeasurably worse.

This is the story of the event in that short history thought by many to be the harbinger of the end. Although the exodus had already begun a few years before it occurred, the Kaspé case persuaded many that remaining was no longer prudent, and that, like so many other times in the history of our people, it was time to move on.

Researching this story posed an unusual set of challenges. First, mirroring the various ethnicities represented in Harbin, relevant materials exist in Chinese, Russian, Japanese, French, Hebrew, Yiddish, and English, not all of which are languages I understand. I have relied on linguistic help from people mentioned in the acknowledgments section as well as from Google and Deepl, machine-translation websites that do a remarkably good job of bridging the language divide.

Second, as a historian I have a strong preference for primary materials. In this case, however, owing in part to the fact that certain archival documents are inaccessible to me and that others were not preserved, I have had to rely a bit more on secondary sources than is my wont.

As with my other works of narrative nonfiction, the characters depicted in this book have not in any way been fictionalized. They really existed, and the events really occurred at the times indicated, although I have occasionally been forced to make some educated guesses when sources disagreed, or when I did not entirely trust them. All dialogue that appears between quotation marks or in block form was recorded at the time or in a memoir, though in a few instances I have condensed material or added italics to make for smoother reading. And no thoughts have been attributed to people who left no records of them, nor have feelings or motives been ascribed to them that were not made explicit by their actions.

A Note on Language and Currency

With a few exceptions, Chinese place and proper names have all been rendered in *hanyu pinyin*. I have, however, used "Harbin" and "Manchukuo" instead of the technically correct, but seldom-encountered, "Haerbin" and "Manzhouguo," and I have employed a few European place names, like "Port Arthur" (modern Dalian) and "Manchuria," which were in popular use at the time of the action of the book and appear frequently in the source material. I've also left Chiang Kai-shek undisturbed and have not Romanized his name into the far less familiar Jiang Jieshi.

In general, I have made the Russian names easier for English readers by favoring shorter endings like "y" over the more cumbersome and less user-friendly "ii," "yi," and "iy." Mostly, I have used the spellings that appeared in the contemporary sources. I have also used Romanized versions of the original Russian names of Harbin's streets, reserving their modern Chinese names for the glossary and gazetteer that appears at the end. Japanese names are presented in Western order—given name before surname—and not the way they would have been rendered in Japan.

In the original materials, sums of money were expressed in both dollars and *yen*, which generally referred to Manchukuo *yuan*. Before 1935, when it was pegged to the Japanese yen, the Manchukuo yuan (sometimes also referred to as the *gobi*) was valued at 24 grams of silver. In 1933, 20 U.S. cents could buy one gram of silver. Modern-day equivalents cited in the text have been based on this exchange rate.

Dramatis Personae

Kaspé Family and Friends

L. Gurevitch (?–?) Comanager of the Hotel Moderne, who negotiates with the kidnappers on behalf of Josef Kaspé.

Josef Alexandrovich Kaspé (1878–1938) Russian Jewish entrepreneur and father of Semyon Kaspé, who owns the Hotel Moderne and several theaters in Harbin.

Marie Semyonova Zaitchik Kaspé (1883–1941) Wife of Josef Kaspé, who moves to France with her two sons in 1926.

Semyon Kaspé (1909–33) Promising young pianist, who is kidnapped in his native Harbin in mid-1933. Nicknames: Senya, Senitchka.

Vladimir Kaspé (1910–96) Brother of Semyon Kaspé, who goes on to an illustrious career as an architect. Nicknames: Volodya, Voloditzka.

Abraham Josevich Kaufman (1885–1971) Physician and leader of the Harbin Jewish community.

Lydia Abramovna Chernetskaya Shapiro (1905–83) Lady friend of Semyon Kaspé, who is with him when he is abducted, and through whom Kaspé's kidnappers initially communicate with his family.

Abraham Pevsner (1891–1964) Josef Kaspé's nephew and comanager of the Hotel Moderne, who negotiates with the kidnappers on behalf of his uncle.

Japanese

Kenji Doihara (1883–1948) Imperial Japanese Army intelligence officer instrumental in the Japanese invasion of Manchuria.

Osamu Eguchi (?–?) Chief of the Criminal Affairs Division of the Harbin Police, who compiles the charges against Semyon Kaspé's kidnappers.

Koreshige Inuzuka (1890–1965) Japanese Imperial Navy captain, who advocates resettling Jews in Japanese-controlled areas of Asia as part of the "Fugu Plan."

Michitarō Komatsubara (1885–1940) Chief of the Tokumu Kikan, or Special Services Agency, in Harbin from 1932 to 1934.

Morito Morishima (1896–1975) Japanese consul general in Harbin from 1928 to 1935.

Saiji Maru (?–?) Procurator of the High Courts of Manchuria.

Konstantin Ivanovich Nakamura (?–?) Chief adviser/interpreter for the Japanese Gendarmerie, or Kempeitai. Nickname: Kostya.

Fukasi Oi (?–?) "High adviser" to the Railway Police who orders the arrest of several of Semyon Kaspé's kidnappers.

Nikolai Nikolayevich Yagi (?–?) Adviser to the Criminal Affairs Division of the Harbin Police.

Norihiro Yasue (1886–1950) Japanese Army colonel charged with executing Japan's plan to invite fifty thousand German Jews to Manchuria in the mid-1930s.

Chinese and Manchus

Aisin-Gioro Pu Yi (1906–67) Last emperor of China and an ethnic Manchu recruited by the Japanese to serve as chief executive, and ultimately as emperor, of Manchukuo. Nickname: Henry.

Chiang Kai-shek (1887–1975) Military man and leader of the Republic of China intent on unifying the nation under the new nationalist government.

Zhang Zuolin (1875–1928) Former bandit and soldier turned warlord who dominated Manchuria in the early twentieth century.

White Russians

Panteleimon Ignatievich Bezruchko (1893–?) One of the Russian partisans who abduct Semyon Kaspé.

Konstantin Galushko (?–1933) One of the Russian partisans who abduct Semyon Kaspé.

Nikifor Pavlovich Kirichenko (?–?) Head of the Russian partisans who abduct Semyon Kaspé.

Dionisy Grigoryevich Komissarenko (?–?) One of the Russian partisans who abduct Semyon Kaspé.

Nikolai Andreevich Martinov (?–1966) Municipal Police inspector, who helps plot the kidnapping of Semyon Kaspé.

Nikolai Mitronovich Nikiforov (?–?) Head of the criminal department of the Municipal Police, who proves useless in investigating Semyon Kaspé's abduction.

Konstantin Vladimirovich Rodzaevsky (1907–46) Head of the Russian Fascist Party and editor of *Nash Put*.

Alexei Yelievich Shandar (1894–1994) One of the Russian partisans who abduct Semyon Kaspé.

Yakov Kirillovich Zaitsev (?–?) One of the Russian partisans who abduct Semyon Kaspé.

Oleg Volgin (1912–?) Pseudonym for a young Russian man assigned to the Hotel Moderne to learn Semyon Kaspé's routines. His real name is unknown.

Europeans

Albert Henri Chambon (1909–2002) Vice consul of France in Harbin from 1931 to 1933.

Fotopulo (?–?) Greek spy who reported on Semyon Kaspé's comings and goings.

Louis Osmond Ferdinand Reynaud (1884–1943) Consul of France in Harbin in the early 1930s.

Amleto Vintorino De Chellis Vespa (1884–1945) Italian spy-for-hire pressed into service by the Japanese to conduct intelligence work after their invasion of Manchuria.

Murder in Manchuria

Prologue

Semyon Kaspé was young, handsome, dapper, talented, and full of joie de vivre. In the summer of 1933, the world was at his feet.

A promising career as a concert pianist lay ahead of him. A recent graduate of the Paris Conservatory, he had pleased the French music critics, who had praised the vigor in his fingers and wrists and the "frankness of pace and brashness in movement" of his technique. In the few months since he had returned to Asia, he had performed to great acclaim in the bustling cities of Shanghai and Tokyo and delighted audiences in his hometown of Harbin, a city with a robust music scene, with his interpretations of Mussorgsky and Chopin. And on the horizon, a rare opportunity beckoned: a concert tour of the United States.[1]

Semyon had grown up in privilege in Harbin, a major city in northeastern China, a region known to foreigners as Manchuria. His Russian-born father, Josef, like many veterans of the Russo-Japanese War, had settled there in the first years of the century. A pillar of the local Jewish community, Josef Kaspé had built several businesses there. The crown jewel of his holdings was the fashionable Hotel Moderne at 113 Kitaiskaya Street in the city's waterfront Pristan district. It included an opulent jewelry store that dealt in Fabergé eggs and other Russian valuables. He and his wife, Marie, had given Semyon and his brother, Vladimir, the best primary and secondary education the city had to offer. In 1926 their mother had packed the two boys up and taken them to Paris to complete their studies.

Since his return in mid-1933, Semyon, twenty-four, an eligible bachelor, had been the toast of the town. Although the bulk of Harbin's population was Chinese and Semyon had studied their language, he spent little time among them. His life was lived within the expatriate community, replete with its concerts, recitals, dinners, parties, and romance. And

1

he had taken up with a young woman whose background was similar to his own.

He had probably known Lydia Chernetskaya in childhood, as she was, like him, the child of a local Jewish businessman and a talented musician. Four years older than he, she had also lived in Europe. But unlike him, Lydia, now Lydia Shapiro, was married, and she was already the mother of four. However, she had recently left her husband, which had occasioned her return to her father's home in Harbin.

But the Harbin of 1933 was not the city they had known in their youth. Much had changed since Lydia's departure in 1921 and Semyon's five years later. Whether Manchuria was even a part of China anymore was now very much in doubt. On a pretext, the Japanese Army had seized control in 1931 and, after taking Harbin the following year, proclaimed the establishment of the independent republic of Manchukuo. Japanese troops occupied the country and Japanese officials controlled the levers of government. Corruption was rampant and so was crime.

Among Harbin's sizable Russian population were tens of thousands of White Russians, sworn opponents of the Bolsheviks, the lion's share of whom had fled Russia for their lives after the October Revolution. Some among them had established the Russian Fascist Party. Well organized though underfunded, it was deeply antisemitic, its members blaming Jews for fomenting the revolution that had led to their enforced exile from Mother Russia and their impoverishment. They had become especially belligerent under the new Japanese administration, were strongly suspected of torching Harbin's main synagogue, and were almost certainly behind several recent kidnappings of local Jews. The Jewish community had begun to feel especially vulnerable.

Semyon was surely aware of the danger; his father certainly was. The elder Kaspé knew he was a target. He had been excoriated in a right-wing Russian-language newspaper for supposedly dealing in "ill-gotten" goods; it was even alleged, preposterously, that these included the Romanov family jewels. The paper had also improbably branded this successful businessman a Communist, an accusation for which it provided no evidence. He now seldom left the Moderne, where he and his son were living, and when he did venture out, it was with a posse of bodyguards in tow.[2]

Semyon didn't share his father's sense of vulnerability. He often went out to friends' nighttime parties and regularly drank at the American Bar on Konnaya Street, often in the company of Lydia. But although he wasn't willing to forgo social life, he did accept his father's offer of a car with an armed chauffeur.[3]

Not that it did him much good.

On the evening of August 24, 1933, he had a date with Lydia. Another couple joined them for dinner and a musical evening at the Moderne. When the party ended just after midnight, he did the gentlemanly thing and escorted her home. Lydia lived not far from the Moderne, and Semyon ordered his driver to see her to her father's house.

Of Semyon and Lydia, however, only she would make it home safely that night.

1

Tug of War

Between the late nineteenth century and the end of World War II, the vast land of Manchuria had the misfortune of being coveted by three countries. One of them, China, the one that arguably had the strongest historical claim to it, was weak and ultimately unable to protect it from the designs of the other two. The region fit handily into the strategic plans of both Russia and Japan to expand their spheres of influence—plans that would be difficult to execute without suzerainty over the area. As a result, Manchuria's sad destiny was to be fought over, invaded, and colonized.

The region, which consisted of the three modern Chinese provinces of Liaoning, Jilin, and Heilongjiang and parts of today's Inner Mongolia, was, at four hundred thousand square miles, quite a bit larger than Texas. More than twice the size of Japan, it bordered on Russia to the north and east, Mongolia to the west, the rest of mainland China to the southwest, and Korea to the southeast. Its traditional Chinese name, Guandong, "east of the pass" in Mandarin, signified the lands beyond Shanhaiguan, the easternmost pass of the Great Wall of China, where the wall meets the sea.

Largely unspoiled, the Manchurian terrain was rich in natural resources, including vast virgin forests, abundant arable land, and extensive deposits of coal, iron, and precious metals like gold and silver. But it was also quite frigid, especially in winter, when Siberian winds forced temperatures in its northern reaches as low as -58°F and the ground froze to a depth of four feet. The south was more temperate. The fertile fields of southern Manchuria produced abundant harvests of soybeans, sorghum, maize, and wheat. And Port Arthur, on the Yellow Sea, was an ice-free harbor.

Beginning in the late seventeenth century, Manchuria had been controlled by Beijing. After its own native Jurchen people, later known as Manchus, breached the Great Wall, overthrew China's Ming Dynasty and established the Qing Dynasty in 1644, there was no question about its status as a part of the Chinese Empire. But it was a special part. For most of their reign, which lasted until 1912, the Manchu emperors kept their sparsely populated, sacred ancestral homeland as unspoiled as they could. They discouraged ethnic Chinese from migrating there, although they couldn't prevent a considerable illegal inflow of Chinese farmers, whom Manchu landlords hired to work their fields. In the 1860s, however, that restriction was lifted and by 1900, Chinese made up the vast majority of Manchuria's seventeen million people.[1]

China's humiliating defeats at the hands of European powers in the two Opium Wars of the nineteenth century, which forced it to grant them special trading rights and pried its ports open to foreign commerce, had exposed its vulnerabilities. Not long afterward, during the waning years of the Qing Dynasty, central control over China's hinterlands weakened.

At the turn of the twentieth century, two wars were fought over Manchuria. What became known as the First Sino-Japanese War began in 1894 when China and Japan clashed over Korea, traditionally a Chinese client state. Within months, Japan defeated Chinese ground troops and destroyed the Chinese navy, and its soldiers pursued Chinese troops across the Yalu River, which divided Korea from Manchuria. Japan took control of Port Arthur and chased the Chinese through southern Manchuria and into Shandong Province before the war was over.

The 1895 treaty that ended that war marked a humiliating defeat for China's Qing Dynasty and cemented Japan's status as a major power in Asia. China was forced to open several ports to Japanese trade, pay a large indemnity and cede control over various lands on its mainland's periphery, including Korea, Taiwan, the Pescadores archipelago and southern Manchuria's Liaodong Peninsula.

Japanese control of this peninsula, however, alarmed Russia. Russia also had designs on Port Arthur, which sat at its tip. The czar's Pacific fleet was based in Vladivostok, whose port froze up in cold weather for as long as half a year. Port Arthur would offer him year-round access to the Sea of Japan and the ability to project power into the Pacific. Conspiring with Germany and France, two other European nations active in China at the time, Russia forced the Japanese to withdraw.

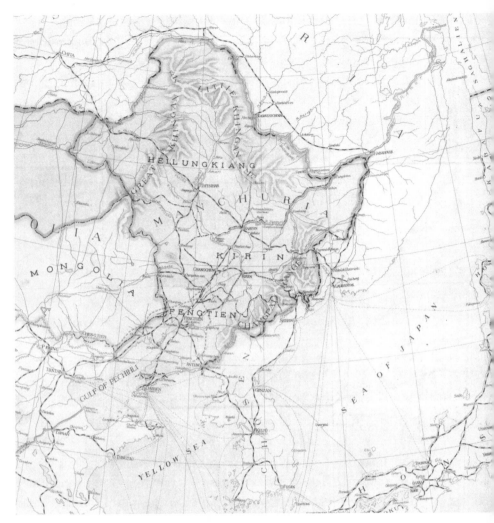

MAP 1. Detail from a 1928 South Manchuria Railway Company map showing Manchuria's geographical relation to Russia (with Siberia at top), Mongolia (left center), Korea (Chosen, bottom center), and Japan (far right). Library of Congress, Geography and Map Division, Washington DC.

It was a grievance Japan would nurse for a long time, made all the more galling when Russia itself then seized control of the region. In 1896, Russia entered into a strategic alliance with the shell-shocked Qing government to prevent further Japanese encroachment in the territory. In exchange, Russia was granted a concession to build a railroad through the heart of Manchuria that would complete its trans-Siberian line by linking it to Vladivostok on the coast. Russia would exercise political control in a swath of territory on either side of the rail line.

Building the line through Manchuria instead of Eastern Siberia shortened the route by 560 miles, saving money and time, and Russia moved in men and materials rapidly to begin construction of what became known as the Chinese Eastern Railway. A year-and-a-half later, it signed an additional agreement to lease the Liaodong Peninsula, develop Port Arthur for its Far East fleet and merchant marine, and build the South Manchuria Railway, a 550-mile southern spur to the port from Harbin.

With the completion of the railroad in 1902, Russia became the dominant player in Manchuria. This rattled Japan, which proposed a deal: it would not challenge the czar's dominion over Manchuria if Russia guaranteed not to move into Korea. But negotiations broke down, and in early 1904, the Japanese navy staged a surprise attack on Port Arthur. It damaged and blockaded the entire Russian fleet in the opening salvo of what became known as the Russo-Japanese War.

Japanese ground forces once again moved through Korea into Manchuria, though this time it was the Russian army that they beat back. When Russia finally sued for peace after eighteen months, it was forced to turn over Port Arthur and the South Manchuria Railway to Japanese control.[2]

The defeat did not signal the departure of all Russians from Manchuria, however. Russia retained control of the Chinese Eastern Railway zone, and those Russians already in Manchuria remained. After the war, in fact, their numbers swelled as decommissioned soldiers like Josef Kaspé, who saw little benefit in returning to Mother Russia, chose to settle there.

After 1912, when China's Qing Dynasty collapsed, the new Republic of China that replaced it nominally inherited Manchuria, which, in addition to its indigenous population of Chinese and various Manchu tribes, was now home to a large complement of Russians and Japanese as well as Koreans and other minorities. But the internationally recognized Chinese government in Beijing was too weak to exercise any control over Manchuria. Zhang Zuolin, a former bandit and soldier turned warlord was the *real* law in the region, and despite being Chinese, he struck a

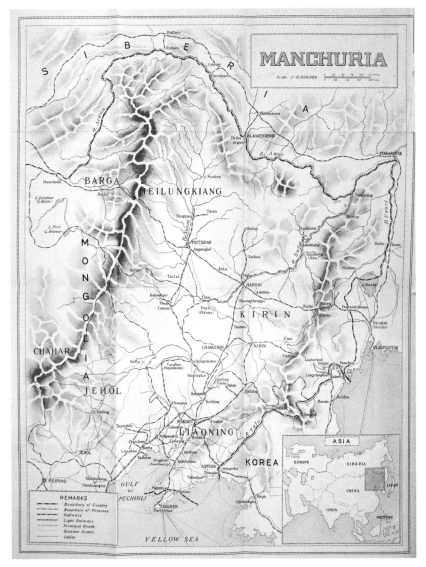

MAP 2. This 1932 map shows provinces and rail lines in Manchuria. The line running diagonally from Manchouli (Manzhouli) on the Russian border (upper left) to Vladivostok (center right) represents the thousand-mile Chinese Eastern Railway, an extension of the Trans-Siberian Railway constructed between 1897 and 1902. The South Manchuria Railway, the 550-mile spur that runs from Harbin (center) to Dairen (Dalian), or Port Arthur (center bottom), was built in 1906. Percy Thomas Etherton and Hubert Hessell Tiltman, *Manchuria: The Cockpit of Asia* (New York: Frederick A. Stokes, 1932). Courtesy of Roy Delbyck and Dan Cohn.

sweetheart arrangement with Japan. In return for Japan's military and financial support, he protected her interests.[3]

Japan would not for long remain content with the status quo in Manchuria, on whose agricultural products and vast mineral wealth she had come to depend. Before too much time had passed, she would move to possess the region in its entirety.

2

Harbin — Cosmopolis in the North

It was in more or less the geometric center of Manchuria, at the point where the tracks crossed the Sungari River, that Russia set up the headquarters of the Chinese Eastern Railway. And that is where — and *why* — the city of Harbin was established.

Innumerable Chinese cities have storied histories dating back thousands of years, but Harbin is not one of them. Before 1898, the location — about 350 miles west of Vladivostok, 520 miles north of Port Arthur, and 650 miles northeast of Beijing — was the site of a small rural settlement. The constant danger of flooding from the river made it a problematic location for a city, but proximity to the water made it a good logistical bet for the Russians. The Sungari was a tributary of the Amur River (called the Heilongjiang in Chinese), which was accessible from the Sea of Japan. This meant men and materials could reach the area, which lacked usable roads, relatively easily by water. That is, they could do so between April and November when the Sungari was navigable; access was impossible when it froze in wintertime.[1]

Building and administering a railroad required importing construction material from Russia, Europe, and the United States, since there was no local manufacturing infrastructure. Maintenance shops, switching stations, depots, and storehouses all had to be built, as did hospitals and schools to support the families of the planners, surveyors, engineers, technicians, clerks, construction workers, security guards, and civil servants who came. Fully twelve thousand Russians had arrived in Harbin by 1900, as well as tens of thousands of Chinese recruited for railway construction jobs.[2]

Because the city was located in the railway right-of-way, which was about one thousand miles long and thirty-one miles in width, it was completely under Russian control. China retained no authority there.

Harbin was not only the headquarters of the railway; it was also the hub of the Russian military presence, the center of Russian commercial and industrial development, and the headquarters of the Russian-run legal system, such as it was, whose jurisdiction was limited to the railway corridor. Only Russians and Chinese were permitted to own land there.[3]

Although the city was located in China, one would never have suspected that from its layout or its architecture. Nowhere to be seen in Pristan, Harbin's commercial center, were the narrow, random lanes, the winding alleys, and the Buddhist temples with their graceful, upturned eaves that one saw all over China. Harbin had been laid out on a grid by Russian city planners, and it featured public squares and parks, visual axes and broad boulevards, many as wide as 140 feet.[4]

With its soft curves, huge central archway and triangular plaza, the imposing art nouveau railway station, which opened in 1899, would not have been out of place in a European capital. The bulbous, onion-domed cupola of the massive, 175-foot-high St. Sophia Orthodox Cathedral, built in 1907, dominated the local skyline and served as a constant reminder of the city's Russian soul. And the commercial buildings on Kitaiskaya Street, ornate stone and concrete structures with thick walls and double windows (which were sealed tight in the frigid winter and opened only from the beginning of May until the end of August) all bore signs in Cyrillic. Downtown Harbin looked for all the world like a Far Eastern version of St. Petersburg, and the city was, indeed, sometimes compared to the Imperial Russian capital.[5]

A short stroll through Pristan confirmed the multiethnic, cosmopolitan nature of the place. Rickshaws traversed the cobblestone streets alongside horse-drawn Russian *droshkies*—open carriages—and motorized jeepney taxis. The delicatessens dealt in red and black caviar and the kiosks sold *booza*, a slightly alcoholic Russian drink made of fermented sorghum, buckwheat, or barley, but also offered baklava. Chinese street vendors hawked *bingtang hulu*, candied hawthorns the Russians called *takhuli*, as well as dumplings and barley soup. And in the winter months hawkers warmed their fingers over charcoal stoves, the aroma of sweet grilled sausages and garlic permeating the frigid air.

Japanese women in kimonos visited shops with Russian-language

FIG. 1. An undated postcard of the St. Sophia Orthodox Cathedral, which dominated the Harbin skyline. Author's collection.

displays, as did babushka-clad Russian matrons and Chinese women in *qipao*, high-necked, tight-fitting dresses with slitted skirts. Inside the shops it wasn't unusual to see a Russian shopkeeper calculating discounts on a Chinese abacus or a Chinese merchant haggling with foreigners in a local patois the Russians called *moya-tvoya*—pidgin Russian sprinkled abundantly with Chinese words.

Recreation included swimming, sailing, and rowing on the river, and, in winter, skating and sledding on the ice. There were all kinds of sports, including horse racing. And of course, there were parties, dances, concerts, movies, lectures, and a wide variety of social clubs. Philanthropic organizations collected money for the poor and displaced. Perhaps because there was always poverty in Harbin and it was always visible, it was a very charitable town.

Harbin boasted no fewer than twenty newspapers. Its Russians had their choice of nine dailies. The Americans and the Brits, numbering no more than three hundred, nonetheless read two, or three if you counted one that was part English and part Russian. In addition, there were six Chinese and two Japanese dailies, plus one in Yiddish for Jewish residents.[6]

Jews had begun to arrive in Manchuria at the turn of the century. When efforts to persuade Russian merchants to relocate to Manchuria got off to an anemic start, it occurred to Count Sergei Yulyevich Witte, the czar's finance minister and an old railway man himself, that Russia possessed a very useful tool for encouraging commerce and economic development in the railway zone, and, in so doing, cementing her hold on the region. It was her Jews. Thanks to his efforts, the government offered them an incentive to settle there. It was a wise move; one result was that Harbin became a boom town, and eventually a highly diverse international enclave and trading center.

The opportunity to relocate to Manchuria had its distinct attractions for Russian Jews. Within the confines of the Russian Empire, there was much discrimination and even violence against them. They were restricted to geographic areas like the Pale of Settlement, a western region of the empire that included modern-day Belarus, Lithuania, and Moldova as well as much of Ukraine and Poland. Jews were subject to special taxes, banned from some professions, and subjected to school quotas. Jewish boys could be conscripted into military service at age twelve and forced to serve for decades, usually as cannon fodder, never as officers. Plus, Jews were the all-too-frequent targets of violent pogroms—genocidal attacks, often religiously motivated—that killed or injured many and were sometimes even sanctioned by the local authorities.

In legalizing Jewish residence in Manchuria, the czar offered Jews willing to settle there freedom from these restrictions, as well as from worsening economic conditions in Russia itself. To the Jews of the Pale, Manchuria was very far and very remote—less so for Siberian Jews—but it offered deliverance from persecution and the opportunity for a better life. It was Russia without pogroms. Many Jewish entrepreneurs and professionals thus decided to make the long trek and settle there. They were permitted to live anywhere in the Russian right-of-way, which included Mukden, Dalian, and several smaller settlements like Hailar, Qiqihar and Maoershan. But most picked Harbin.

By most accounts, the first Jew to arrive in Harbin was a railway engineer; he and his wife came from Russia in 1899. Not long after, Harbin played host to its first *minyan*, or prayer group, which required a quorum of ten Jewish men. There were forty-five Jews by 1900 and three hundred by 1902, when the Harbin Jewish Community was officially established. Most lived in small, one-story houses on four streets in the Pristan waterfront district: Samannaya, Magazinnaya, Polizeiskaya and Artilleriyskaya. Although Pristan also had a sizable Chinese population, it was sometimes referred to as "Jew Town."[7]

Josef Alexandrovich Kaspé, the patriarch of his family and father of Semyon, was one of those early arrivals. Born in Chernikov in the Mogilev region of Byelorussia in 1878, he made his way to Manchuria in the ranks of the Russian army during the Russo-Japanese War, one of some thirty-three thousand Russian Jews who fought for the czar. Whether his service in a cavalry regiment was voluntary is unclear. Although Jews were routinely conscripted against their will in imperial Russia, some believed that showing patriotism by volunteering to serve in a popular war could help them win the rights they were routinely denied.

However willing Josef might have been to serve, he apparently did a good job of it, because he was honored for his service with the Cross of

St. George. It was an award for "undaunted courage" in the lower ranks of the service, received before he was demobilized at the age of twenty-eight in 1906, after Russia's ignominious defeat in the war.[8]

Manchuria was hopelessly far from his home, but what was so advantageous about going back to the Pale? For more than two decades, Kaspé's fellow Jews had been voting with their feet. By the turn of the century, hundreds of thousands had already sought their fortunes abroad and many more would follow. The Russian-controlled zone in Manchuria had much to offer, and staying on and building a life there had its attractions. It promised growth and opportunity rather than stagnation and repression. By the time Kaspé arrived, Harbin already had a nascent Jewish community. And the many Jewish soldiers who, like him, opted to stay on after the war soon swelled their ranks.[9]

Unfettered by arbitrary restrictions, Jews became pioneers in exploiting Manchuria's natural resources and played an outsized role in Harbin's commercial development. Jewish industrialists created logging, mining, fur trading, and sugar processing enterprises and plowed capital into distilleries, flour mills, and soybean mills. Jewish developers built Harbin's first commercial buildings, apartment houses, banks, and hotels, and Jewish furriers, restaurateurs, hoteliers, pharmacists, butchers, bakers, tailors, haberdashers, milliners, jewelers, booksellers, brewers, and confectioners set up shop in the new city. Many of these entrepreneurs were extremely successful, and Kaspé was one of them.

Blessed with a talent for business, he initially set up a watch repair shop, but before long he began buying and selling jewelry. By purchasing jewels and gold from refugees in need of cash and selling them at a profit to the growing ranks of wealthy residents of the town, he was able to build what was described as "the finest jewelry business in the Far East," and by 1913 he had amassed sufficient capital to buy, together with a partner, a plot of land on Kitaiskaya Street (Russian for "Chinese street") in the busy Pristan district. It remains downtown Harbin's main shopping area to this day. The ambitious Kaspé had big plans for the lot.[10]

Another early arrival destined to play a leading role in the life of Harbin's Jewish community as well as the Semyon Kaspé story was Dr. Abraham Josevich Kaufman. Born in a small town in Ukraine, he was a grandson of the founder of Chabad, a Hasidic movement established in the eighteenth century. Educated in Perm, Russia, he completed his medical training in Switzerland in 1909. He reached Harbin in 1912 and remained there for the next thirty-three years.

Kaufman helped establish the Jewish hospital and became its medical director. An ardent Zionist, he was a regular whirling dervish when it came to Jewish causes. There were few local Jewish organizations he did not lead at one point or another. He raised funds for local and regional Zionist organizations, edited *Evreiskaya Zhizn* (Jewish Life), a weekly Russian-language magazine, and in 1919 became the chairman of Harbin's Jewish community, a position he held almost continuously until 1945. The recognized spokesman for Harbin's Jews, Kaufman was a gifted and inspirational orator. He also played an important regional role, first as vice-chair of the National Council of Jews of Siberia and the Urals, and later as chairman of the National Council of Jews of East Asia.[11]

From the start, Jews felt comfortable in Harbin. "It appears to be the only place in Russia where the numerous nationalities live in peace together," the *Hebrew Standard*, a New York–based weekly, reported giddily in 1909. Jews participated freely in local government; twelve of forty members of the city council in that year were Jewish. The community set up a *chevra kadisha*, or burial society, to ensure that even the destitute among them received proper religious interments in the new Jewish cemetery, which opened in 1903.

Before long, they had recruited a rabbi, a *shochet*—a kosher slaughterer trained in Jewish law—and a *mohel*, a ritual circumciser, all necessities for any orthodox Jewish community. A *mikveh*, or ritual bath, was opened for women. The community also looked after the Jewish soldiers sent to Manchuria in 1904 to fight in the Russo-Japanese War, providing them with kosher food, clothing, and cash. They also welcomed them at their religious services and even provided proper burials to those who fell on the battlefield.[12]

A continuous stream of immigrants swelled the ranks of the nascent community, driven by deteriorating economic conditions and pogroms in Russia. Lydia Shapiro and her family landed in Harbin in 1905, fleeing the worst pogrom Odessa had ever seen. After Russia's defeat in the war with Japan that same year, Josef Kaspé and his wife also settled there, together with many other Jewish soldiers. And even more refugees made the journey in the wake of the First World War and the October Revolution of 1917, some on their way to other parts of the world, others determined to put down roots.

As it grew, the Jewish community built two synagogues—an imposing building on Artilleriyskaya Street consecrated in 1909 and a second on Diagonalnaya Street that opened in 1921. The latter could accommodate eight hundred and host community meetings as well as religious services. Elementary and secondary schools were established, as well as a library, a Talmud Torah—a religious school—and Kaufman's hospital, which treated Jews and non-Jews alike. Jewish clubs abounded. And shortly after the Russian Revolution, when even more Russian Jews passed through, many of them penniless, a soup kitchen, a free clinic, and a home for the aged, all funded by donations, were added.[13]

Life for Harbin's Jews was largely without drama for the first two decades of the century, although as early as 1912 signs of homegrown antisemitism on the part of the Chinese began to emerge. As the new government of the Republic of China renegotiated an earlier trade treaty the Qing government had signed with Russia, the Chinese Chamber of Commerce in Harbin urged Beijing to "raise the Jewish question." It suggested that "in each article providing the Russians with privileges, we must include a note that that article does not apply to Jews. Only in this way, we will succeed in limiting the rights of the Jews."[14]

Just over a decade later, in 1922, the Harbin government, under Chinese control after the overthrow of the Qing Dynasty in 1912, passed an ordinance prohibiting the use of Yiddish in public places. The official explanation was the need to keep any Bolsheviks among the local Jews under surveillance. The press attributed the law to pressure from members of the "Black Hundred," an ultranationalist, antisemitic group of Russian monarchists who wanted to restore the Romanov dynasty, but it may well also have had to do with xenophobia on the part of the Chinese officials. The measure was not strictly enforced, but it did impel local rabbis to deliver their sermons in Russian, and in several instances Chinese police broke up meetings of Yiddish-speaking Jews.[15]

Харбинъ, — Синагога.
Charbin, — Synagoge

FIG. 2. The "Main Synagogue" on Artilleriyskaya Street, consecrated in 1909. Public domain image. Author's collection.

Dr. Kaufman protested the ordinance in the name of the Jewish community, but in 1926 things only got worse. The Chinese authorities suddenly refused to ratify the status of the Jewish Communal Board of Harbin and ordered it to cease functioning. This stripped it of the power to tax its members and issue vital records for births, marriages, and deaths. The authorities also refused to legalize the Zionist Society for Jewish Resettlement in Palestine, insisting it was a political rather than a philanthropic body. By mid-1927 the policy was reversed, but at a price. The Jewish Communal Board was forced to eliminate from its charter all references to secular cultural activities. Its powers were limited to religious and charitable activities, taxing local Jews to fund them, recording life events, and issuing vital records.[16]

The Jewish population reached its peak of about twenty thousand in the mid-1920s, which is about when the dark clouds began to loom on the horizon for the Jews of Harbin. The large influx of anti-Communist White Russians who fled the newly established Soviet Union swelled the ranks of Manchuria's Russian population. Many settled in Harbin because they wished to; others remained because they were unable to get papers to go elsewhere. And many of them disliked Jews.

Among them was a group of dispirited people who had lost everything in the Revolution, who blamed Jewish people for their misfortunes, and who were hell-bent on extracting revenge. These disaffected Russians posed a far greater threat to the lives of Harbin's Jews than did the Chinese authorities. To people like Kaspé, it began to seem as if the perpetrators of the pogroms they believed they had left behind in Russia for good might soon once again find ways of making their lives miserable.

3

White Russians and Antisemitism

One reason the Russian population of Manchuria increased so rapidly in the 1920s was that Mother Russia was in such turmoil. The country experienced World War I, the Russian Revolution, and the civil war between the Soviet Red Army and the anti-Bolshevik "Whites" that followed it all within the space of a decade, as well as a typhus epidemic from 1918 to 1922 and drought and famine in 1920–21. The triumph of the Bolsheviks prompted a mass exodus. Many officers in the Imperial Russian Army, officials in the czar's government, and White Russians now feared for their lives. Other exiles were simply formerly wealthy people who had lost everything or did not wish to live under communist rule.

For many émigrés, Manchuria was merely a waystation on a journey that ended in Tianjin, Shanghai, Hong Kong, or elsewhere in Asia, but for at least one hundred thousand, and maybe as many as 150,000, it was a mecca of sorts. After all, parts of it, like Harbin, looked, felt, and spoke Russian. Though some arrived with little more than the clothes on their backs, others brought wealth, professional knowledge, and experience, enriching the community. In the second decade of the twentieth century, Harbin's Russian ranks peaked at about 120,000, and the city became home to the world's largest Russian diaspora community.[1]

On December 15, 1921, those who had left Russia without permission after 1917, and Josef Kaspé and others like him who had lived abroad for more than five years, were summarily stripped of their Russian citizenship by Moscow unless they applied for Soviet passports. Kaspé and his family did not, though many in the railway corridor did, especially in 1924, when extraterritoriality—exemption from the jurisdiction of local law—ceased for Russians. The Soviet Union now managed the Chinese Eastern Railway jointly with China, and it forced all non-Soviet Russians out of the railroad's administration. Some twenty thousand railroad employees applied for Soviet citizenship to save their livelihoods.[2]

Others sought citizenship in the Union of Soviet Socialist Republics for patriotic reasons or just to avoid being stateless, and as a result there were now more Soviet citizens in Harbin than stateless Russians. They were officially subject to the jurisdiction of the Republic of China, but practically to that of Zhang Zuolin, the chief warlord of Manchuria, and his corrupt minions, who had no particular love for Russians.[3]

Among the stateless were many who were deeply anti-Bolshevik. Although they and the Reds shared a common language and culture, read the same newspapers, ate the same food, sent their children to the same schools, and went to the same concerts, operas, ballets, and plays, members of the two factions distrusted one another. The Whites suspected the Reds of infiltrating their organizations and spying for the Soviet government, while the Reds were wary of "radishes"—those who *appeared* red but were white on the inside—who held Soviet passports but were secretly anti-Communist.

Harbin's Russians ranged from the very wealthy to the destitute. Writing in 1923, American travel writer Harry A. Franck described railway officials and people who had fled Russia early enough to have brought their wealth with them as living in grand style, with private watchmen— usually ex-soldiers—guarding their spacious, opulent homes. They were greatly outnumbered, however, by the poorer refugees:

> Along all the principal thoroughfares of Harbin squatted scores of white beggars, women and children among them, appealing to Chinese as well as to European passers-by. In the market-places of this and of other towns along the Chinese Eastern Railway I saw many a Russian covered with filth, sores, and a few tattered rags, a noisome receptacle of some kind in his hands, wandering from stall to stall pleading with the sardonic Chinese keepers to give him a half-rotten tomato or a putrid piece of meat.
>
> Barefooted refugee children roamed the streets, picking up whatever they could find, including some of the nastiest of Chinese habits. Former officers of the czar, and wives who were once the grace of

any drawing-room, speaking French with a faultless accent, lived in miserable pens with only ragged cloth partitions between them and their teeming neighbors, eating the poorest of Chinese coolie food, some of them unable to go out unless they went barefoot.[4]

Where Russians had once despised and abused the local Chinese population, it was now they who were cleaning the toilets and selling their favors. Some worked under Chinese taskmasters or pimps or became concubines of powerful Chinese officials. Former officers in the czarist army became bootblacks in Harbin. Deep resentments among the disaffected found expression in their politics. Some refused to give up the improbable dream of overthrowing the Communists and restoring the prerevolutionary order—if not the Romanov dynasty itself—and worked toward its realization in any way they could. They joined organizations like the Brotherhood of Russian Truth, which sent agents into the Soviet Union in order to destabilize it.

In the mid-1920s, Harbin gave birth to its own homegrown, anti-Communist organization. Student exiles attracted to Italian-style fascism as an alternative to communism formed a movement to unite their classmates against the Bolsheviks and disseminate anti-Soviet propaganda. Borrowing Benito Mussolini's uniforms—black shirts and wide waistbands—they built a nationalist political association that ultimately evolved into the Russian Fascist Party. Its tentacles eventually spread to the United States and some twenty-six other countries with sizable populations of Russian émigrés, but its center of gravity always remained in Harbin.

Konstantin Vladimirovich Rodzaevsky became the group's leader and spokesperson. Born in 1907 to a bourgeois family in Blagoveshchensk, a rough-and-tumble Siberian frontier town six hundred miles north of Vladivostok, Rodzaevsky had joined the Communist Party youth organization as a child and by 1925 had made his way to Harbin. There he enrolled in the Juridical Institute, the local law school where, under the influence of two stateless, anti-Soviet professors on the law faculty, he became an admirer of Mussolini for the latter's struggle against communism and socialism in Italy, and a sworn enemy of the Bolsheviks. And when several of his classmates formed the nascent Russian Fascist Organization, he was all in.

FIG. 3. Konstantin Vladimirovich Rodzaevsky, leader of the Russian Fascist Party, 1934. *"Russian Fascists in World War II,"* Wikimedia Commons.

Five feet eleven inches tall and weighing only 140 pounds, Rodzaevsky was outgoing and charismatic, but also impetuous. A passionate ideologue who was more tactical than strategic, he managed to get himself expelled from the institute shortly before graduation for leading an anti-Soviet demonstration on campus. Because of his energy and his organizational skills, he rose quickly through the group's ranks. In May 1931, when it held its first congress and assumed the moniker of the Russian Fascist Party, it appointed the twenty-four-year-old Rodzaevsky party secretary. He established satellite groups in other Manchurian towns and smuggled anti-Soviet propaganda into Russia. And he helped draw up the party's manifesto, which predicted the early demise of the Soviet Union.[5]

He edited *Nash Put* (Our Way), the party's official organ, which never missed an opportunity to disparage local Jews. In its pages, Rodzaevsky had accused Josef Kaspé of Communist sympathies and suggested he was dealing in jewels looted from wealthy Russians. He, too, was poised to play an important part in the tragedy that was soon to befall the Kaspé family.

Rodzaevsky and his compatriots were always more focused on opposing communism than on projecting a clear vision of what a post-Soviet Russia might actually look like. But what *was* crystal clear was not only the group's opposition to communism, but also its deeply antisemitic character. This was not the religious antisemitism of the Russian Orthodox Church; it was, rather, a political form of Jew-hatred. Rodzaevsky and his fascists blamed Jews for the October Revolution and railed against both "Jewish state capitalism" and "Jewish-Bolshevik internationalism." Whatever became of Russia after the Bolsheviks, as far as they were concerned, it would be a place where Jews would be unwelcome.

As author John J. Stephan recounted:

> A party slogan urged: "Against the Jewish fascism of the USSR! For the Russian fascism of the RFP [Russian Fascist Party]!" Elaborate pedigrees of Soviet leaders were compiled with the same meticulous care exercised by Himmler's SS researchers. Cartoons lifted from Julius Streicher's Jew-baiting *Der Stürmer* and republished in RFP pamphlets depicted Kremlin leaders with exaggerated Semitic features. Special attention was called to Jews within the Soviet Communist Party. . . . The OGPU [the Soviet secret police] was called a "Zionist nest." Lenin was stigmatized as a "half Jew." Even Stalin, a Georgian who could hardly be accused of philo-Semitism, came off as a "concubine of American capitalists and Jews."[6]

Almost from its beginning, the Russian Fascist Party looked to Japan as a natural ally. Japan had participated in a losing fight against the Bolsheviks in Russia's maritime provinces, and the Japanese remained deeply anti-Soviet and fearful of Russian ambitions in Manchuria and Korea. An alliance with Tokyo could be mutually beneficial, especially if the Japanese decided to take on the Soviets again. And when Japan occupied Manchuria in the same year the Russian Fascist Party was officially born, there was reason to hope such an alliance might actually come to pass.

4

The Kaspés

Between 1913 and 1914, Josef Kaspé oversaw the construction on his Kitaiskaya Street lot of his flagship Hotel Moderne, a three-story, art nouveau complex that included a European-style luxury hotel, a restaurant, a café, a patisserie, a seven hundred–seat theater and, of course, his jewelry shop. Designed by a noted St. Petersburg architect, it was not the first hotel to be built in the town, but it was the first to meet European standards. It was also certainly the toniest, its iconic turret towering majestically over the thoroughfare below. Inside, there were spacious drawing rooms and a banquet room called the "White Hall," as well as a billiard room, a bar, and a barber shop.

The Moderne opened its doors to great fanfare in 1914; standing-room-only performances began at the theater that fall. After renovations in 1921–23, it boasted thirty-nine rooms with private baths and fifty-six without. The choice suites were on the second floor, just above the main entrance. Kaspé eventually acquired full ownership of the property when his partner departed Harbin. Nor was this his only venture. By the late 1920s, he also owned the Palas and Orient theaters in addition to the one at the Moderne. His theaters presented plays, operettas, concerts, and, of course, the latest movies from Hollywood. Fred Astaire and Ginger Rogers were immensely popular in Harbin in the 1930s, and the city even had a Shirley Temple fan club.[1]

Important banquets and weddings of the prominent were held at the Moderne, especially those of the Jewish community. It was the site, for example, of the communal celebration commemorating the 1917 signing of the Balfour Declaration that pledged British support for the establishment of a national home for the Jewish people in Palestine. And everyone passing through Harbin who was anyone, of any nationality, stopped there.

Lord Willingdon, a British politician who had held high offices throughout the British Empire, stayed at the Moderne with his wife in 1926 on their way back to Britain after he had been named governor-general of Canada. Yamamoto Manjirō, a Japanese social critic who wrote under the pen name of Hasegawa Nyozekan, lodged there in 1928 and Soong Ching Ling, the widow of Chinese president Sun Yat-sen and sister of Madame Chiang Kai-shek, was feted at a banquet there in 1929 on her way back to China by train from Soviet Russia.[2]

Russian fare was the hotel's specialty. *National Geographic* contributor Lilian Grosvenor Coville described the "steaming tureens of Russian borscht, a soup which is a meal in itself" served up by "bewhiskered Russian waiters" in the dining room. "An individual portion contains half a pound of meat floating in a sea of cabbage and sour cream. And the guests must also have Russian shashlik, pieces of mutton roasted on a skewer, and many other Russian dishes."[3]

Like Josef Kaspé, Marie Semyonova Zaitchik, five years his junior, had been born in Cherikov. They were probably married there sometime in the first decade of the twentieth century. What is known is that she joined him in Harbin in 1905 and bore two sons there, Semyon in 1909 and Vladimir the following year.[4]

Vladimir's interests drew him to architecture, but Semyon showed unusual musical ability as a very young child and began to study piano at the age of eight. His parents indulged his interest by sending him to the Shanghai School for Boys for a year to study with Russian musicians Josef Yasser and Boris Lazareff. On his return, he was enrolled at the Harbin Commercial School.[5]

Founded in 1906 for the children of Chinese Eastern Railway employees, the school was considered the best in the city. Instruction was in Russian, and the curriculum mirrored that of most Russian schools: mathematics, science, history, and foreign languages were all taught. At Harbin Commercial, however, Chinese was also an obligatory subject. Because of its excellent reputation, its graduates had little trouble gaining admission to the best universities in Europe and the United States.[6]

Many well-to-do Jewish families in China sent their children abroad for further study after graduation, and this was the Kaspé family's plan for

FIG. 4. An aerial view of Kitaiskaya Street with the Hotel Moderne in the foreground. Wikimedia Commons.

their sons. Soon after Semyon's graduation in 1926, he, his brother, and his mother all departed for France, leaving their father in Harbin. The plan was for the three to take up residence in Paris, where Semyon and Vladimir might complete their education. By the middle of 1927, both boys had enrolled in the École Alsacienne, a venerable private academy that offered a classical secondary education in Latin and the sciences.

Although a year apart in age—Semyon was seventeen and Vladimir a year younger—they both entered the second cycle of the *classe terminale*, which meant they would receive their baccalaureate diplomas in a year's time. Although they were a bit younger than their classmates, they were judged by the school to be good students.[7]

Vladimir went on to study architecture at the École des Beaux-Arts and Semyon entered the Conservatoire de Paris, where he studied piano under Isidor Philipp, a French pianist, composer, and teacher of Hungarian Jewish descent. Philipp, himself a graduate of the Conservatoire, had studied with Camille Saint-Saëns and Théodore Ritter and was a friend of Claude Debussy. Something of a legend in musical circles, he was much beloved by his students, many of whom went on to fame and success.

Under Philipp's tutelage, Semyon made steady progress, and in early 1930 began performing publicly in Paris. He played a recital for the American Women's Club on a Sunday afternoon in February in what was essentially a dress rehearsal for a June 2 debut piano concert at the Salle Chopin, a performance hall in the Salle Pleyel, where Saint-Saëns and Anton Rubinstein had performed their debut concerts, and Frédéric Chopin himself—Semyon's favorite—had performed his last.[8]

That night, young Kaspé played Bach, Beethoven, Schubert, Schumann, Mendelssohn, Chopin, Liszt, and Prokofiev to decidedly mixed reviews. *Le Figaro* praised his technique, adding that "all he needs is to assert himself with more conviction in Chopin, in particular, where one appreciates precise rhythms and a nice sound, if not enthusiasm." And the verdict in *Comœdia* was that he possessed "brilliant virtuosity and a sonority that does not lack a certain sparkle," but that his interpretation could have been more thoughtful and less dry.[9]

Semyon took the criticism to heart. It was a full year before he gave another public performance. In the spring of 1931, once again at the Salle Chopin, he played Bach, Chopin, Debussy, Mussorgsky, Durand, and Dandelot. The newspaper *L'Intransigeant* observed that he had made progress. "Here is the young Semyon Kaspé who comes back to us after a year's silence during which he seems to have made good use of his time. He has lost none of his vigor." Writing in *Excelsior*, a critic praised his "excellent technical precision," but advised the young pianist to "make a point of moderating his impulses and disciplining his game."[10]

Semyon gave a series of radio performances in July. After a third concert in 1932, his reviews had become something closer to unalloyed praise. "Mr. Semyon Kaspé has already done a lot to soften a native harshness. . . . He not only has rare vigor in his fingers and wrists, but also a frankness of pace and brashness in movement, which gives his performances an original accent," wrote *L'Intransigeant* in 1932. And *Comœdia* applauded "a refined mechanism and a real musical sense" in pieces he played by Alexander Tcherepnin, Nicolas Nabokov, and Sergei Prokofiev.[11]

FIG. 5. Semyon Kaspé at the piano. *Rubezh* (The frontier), December 9, 1933.

FIG. 6. Semyon Kaspé, ca. 1932. Author's collection.

By now fluent in French and English in addition to his native Russian, Semyon graduated from the Conservatoire in mid-1932. He continued his radio concerts through the end of the year, when he would return to Harbin. He went alone; his brother, Vladimir, had begun service in the French military and their mother remained in Paris.

One factor in his decision to return might have been the assassination in May of that year of Paul Doumer, the president of the French Republic, by Russian fascist Pavel Gorgulov. Despite the fact that Gorgulov was deeply antisemitic, his act made all Russians in France, Jews included, feel less secure. But the decision to go home may also have been his father's. Josef Kaspé, well acquainted with the music scene due to his ownership of several theaters, had begun to make plans for an East Asian concert tour for Semyon.

It was clear to all that Semyon Kaspé was a major talent, and that he had a bright future as a concert pianist. What no one could know at the time was exactly how short that future was destined to be.

5

Lydia

Upon his return home from Paris, Semyon met—or, more likely, renewed his acquaintance with—Lydia Shapiro. Born Lydia Abramovna Chernets-kaya in Odessa in 1905, she had been brought to Harbin by her parents at the age of six months in the wake of the worst pogrom Odessa had ever experienced. With more than four hundred Jews killed and some sixteen hundred Jewish homes and businesses destroyed, it was the handwriting on the wall for thousands of local Jews. Most who left in the wake of the rampage went west to the Americas, but Lydia's parents, Abram and Anastasia, opted instead to head to Harbin, where other Jewish Odessans had preceded them.

Abram, who had worked as a barge hauler on the Dnieper River, initially found employment as a laborer on the Chinese Eastern Railway, but before long he went into business for himself. He eventually established a reinforced concrete factory that did a brisk business during the city's building boom. His grandson Michael recalled years later being told that the Chernetsky name had been stamped on many of Harbin's sidewalks during this era.

As a result of Abram's business acumen, the family lived comfortably and employed several servants to see to their needs. Although Lydia lost her mother in 1921, she kept up her grades, excelling in her studies at the Russian girls' school she attended, the Gymnazia Generezova. She also studied piano, and by the time of her graduation at sixteen was considered a prodigy.

Lydia's father decided to send her abroad for further study, and she departed in 1921 for the University of California at Berkeley. Her true interest was in a career in music, however, and so she left the United States after one semester and enrolled in the Berlin Academy of Music,

FIG. 7. Lydia Abramovna Chernetskaya Shapiro. Courtesy of Daniel McDonald.

where, with financial support from her father, she continued her study of piano under the tutelage of classical pianist Leonid Kreutzer, also a Russian-Jewish émigré.

It was in Berlin that Lydia, a diminutive beauty at five feet two inches tall with brown hair and grey eyes, fell passionately in love with a cellist named Constantine Shapiro. Eight years her senior, he was also a Russian-born Jew. His family had been prominent during czsarist times and he was well educated, so after the October Revolution he and his elder brother had fled Russia for Germany. When Lydia was introduced to him in 1925, he was the first cellist in the Frankfurt Opera Orchestra. Marriage followed within a matter of weeks, and in 1926, after her graduation at the top of her class, the couple relocated to Paris. They remained

FIG. 8. Lydia Shapiro and Semyon Kaspé, 1933. Courtesy of Isaac Shapiro.

there only briefly, however, heading next to Palestine, where Lydia gave birth to their first two children, twin boys, in Tel Aviv.

Theirs was a world of recitals and performances with orchestras and chamber music groups. But earning a living as musicians in British Mandate Palestine was challenging, to say the least. Within a couple of years they gave up and decided to try their luck in Harbin. There a third son was born, but Harbin, too, proved only a brief stop. From China the couple went on to Japan. There, at the age of twenty-five, Lydia gave birth to their fourth son, all the while juggling the rearing of her growing brood with a career as a concert pianist. The family engaged a governess to help shoulder the tasks involved in raising the boys.

But all was not well in Lydia and Constantine's relationship. She was more successful than he in the music world and became the family's principal breadwinner, engendering resentment on his part. Their son Isaac recalled his father as "verbally and physically abusive" and given to criticizing his wife, including about her musical ability. This may provide a clue to her bold decision, in the summer of 1931, to leave him. With four young sons aged six months to five years in tow, she returned to Harbin to live with her father. And there, her son Isaac recalled, she was pursued by several young men in the city.[1]

When Semyon Kaspé returned to Harbin in 1933, Lydia had already been back for two years. It's likely the two had known each other as children, as both were piano prodigies with parents prominent in the local Jewish community. If not, they might have become acquainted in musical circles during Lydia's brief sojourn as a newlywed in Paris, which coincided with Semyon's time there. But now that Semyon had returned, he set his sights on Lydia and the two began dating. Theirs appears to have been a serious relationship, despite the fact that Lydia remained married to Constantine and was a mother of four.

The couple kept company that summer, until the evening of August 24, the night before Semyon was to travel to Dalian to give a concert. That night, he invited Lydia to a party at the Moderne. Just after midnight, as they left the gathering and boarded his father's vehicle, the skies opened up and torrential rain pelted the city.

The superstitious might have called it a bad omen.

6

Invasion

The Manchuria that Semyon Kaspé had left in 1926 was not the one to which he returned in 1933. Two years earlier, it had acquired a new landlord.

The Empire of Japan had long coveted a bigger share of the Manchurian pie than it had been left with after the Sino-Japanese and Russo-Japanese wars. After the latter, Japan had gained control of Port Arthur and much of southern Manchuria, including the South Manchuria Railway. But there was more to be desired. The Japanese economy had been in poor shape even before the Great Depression ravaged it, and Manchuria possessed agricultural products, minerals, and industrial raw materials the country lacked, as well as a vast expanse of land on which it might resettle some of its overflowing rural population.

To secure its holdings in Manchuria, Japan already kept a large army—the Guandong Army—there, and it had struck a sweetheart arrangement with Zhang Zuolin, the region's chief warlord. But just as the Japanese had once worried about the czar seizing control of Manchuria, they now feared that the Soviets might seek to avenge Russia's defeat and try again. And although the decaying Qing Dynasty had not been much of a threat before its fall in 1912, Chinese generalissimo Chiang Kai-shek now seemed to be making progress in his effort to unify the new Republic of China. Gaining dominion over Manchuria, which had slipped from central government control, was on his agenda. In 1928, after Zhang Zuolin's men took a drubbing from Chiang's nationalist forces, Japan decided to cut bait on the warlord.

In an action masterminded by a Japanese military man named Kenji Doihara, a former adviser to Zhang, the Guandong Army bombed a train on which Zhang and several of his aides were passengers, resulting

FIG. 9. Manchurian warlord Zhang Zuolin. Wikimedia Commons.

in Zhang's death. The warlord's son, Zhang Xueliang, stepped into his father's shoes, but to the further dismay of the Japanese, the younger Zhang soon joined forces with Chiang Kai-shek's nationalists.

Doihara, who had been involved with China since 1913, was the Guandong Army's indispensable man. He spoke Mandarin, was steeped in the ways of Chinese politics, and was well connected throughout the region. A stout man with a little black mustache, he was jocularly referred to in Western circles as "Lawrence of Manchuria." To the American government, he was a "super-spy, agent provocateur and manufacturer of incidents."[1]

To many Japanese, asserting sovereignty over the whole of Manchuria was their manifest destiny. But it was not Tokyo that lit the match that sparked the occupation of Manchuria. It was, rather, rogue officers of its Guandong Army who forced the Japanese government's hand.

Also the work of Doihara, who had been appointed head of the Mukden branch of the Tokumu Kikan, or "special agency," the army unit responsible for military intelligence, the plan involved staging another explosion on September 18, 1931, along the South Manchuria Railway near an encampment of Zhang Xueliang's troops. It didn't do much damage, but it didn't need to. Blaming the Chinese for the supposed terrorist act, the Japanese army quickly "retaliated" by destroying the nearby Chinese garrison.

The conflict quickly metastasized. Japanese reinforcements from neighboring Korea entered and occupied Manchuria. The Chinese forces were no match for them, and Chiang Kai-shek ordered Zhang Xueliang not to resist. For its part, the Japanese government, even though not responsible for initiating the action, had little choice but to support the invasion, which was quite popular at home.

Harbin was the last major city in Manchuria to be occupied. It, too, was taken by means of a ruse planned by Doihara, the "manufacturer of incidents," who was now reassigned to head the Harbin Tokumu Kikan. Japanese troops closed in on the city from the south and west in -30°F weather. Japanese agents, including a man named Konstantin Ivanovich Nakamura, worked inside the city, together with Konstantin Rodzaevsky, head of the Russian fascists, to create disorder in Harbin. They planted grenades at several Japanese properties in the town, causing a riot in which a Japanese and three Koreans were killed. This provided the pretext the army sought to justify intervening to "protect" the local Japanese population.[2]

Soviet Russia made no effort to defend the city. Nor were Generalissimo Chiang Kai-shek's troops in any position to do so. As a result, it took only seventeen hours for Harbin to fall to the Japanese on February

FIG. 10. Kenji Doihara. Wikimedia Commons.

5, 1932. The city's White Russian inhabitants "cheered lustily from the housetops" as the troops marched in, according to *Time* magazine. Many took to the streets waving Japanese flags and shouting "Banzai!" meaning "ten thousand years." Young Russian flower girls met the marching soldiers and some ten thousand White Russians paraded through the city, hurling insults at the Chinese. Of all the various nationalities that made up the diverse population of Harbin, it was clear which, apart from the local Japanese, was happiest to welcome the conquerors.[3]

With the capture of Harbin, the Guandong Army consolidated its control over the whole of Manchuria. It had taken just five months. Martial law was declared and within days, on the ludicrous pretext that it had not *invaded* China, but merely *intervened* to aid the local populace in realizing its fond wish for independence, the army established a puppet government of Chinese and Manchus to rule over the three northeastern provinces that made up Manchuria—Liaoning in the south, Jilin in the middle, and Heilongjiang in the north. On March 1, that council proclaimed the establishment of Manchukuo (pinyin: *Manzhouguo*)—"the Manchurian state"—independent of the Republic of China. And that autumn, the government of Japan extended full diplomatic recognition to the new jurisdiction.

The army, which was running the show in Manchukuo, calculated that the new state might gain some semblance of legitimacy by the appointment of a figurehead with an arguable claim to leadership. They settled on recruiting Aisin-Gioro Pu Yi—the last emperor of China's Qing Dynasty, who was, of course, an ethnic Manchu. Known in foreign circles as "Henry," Pu Yi had occupied China's "Dragon Throne" beginning in 1908, but been forced to abdicate just after his sixth birthday in 1912, shortly after the Chinese Revolution. He had been expelled from Beijing's Forbidden City in 1924 and had relocated to Tianjin, where he lived a life of ennui.

The delicate errand of coaxing him to return to the land of his ancestors was entrusted to the redoubtable Doihara, who was dispatched to Tianjin. A vain man, the former boy emperor had never given up hope of being restored to the Qing throne, and Doihara played to his ego. Eventually, Pu Yi agreed to head the new puppet state in his ancestral homeland, and he was smuggled out of Tianjin in the trunk of a car and taken by ship to Port Arthur.

Not long after he entered Manchukuo, however, the naïve Pu Yi realized he had allowed himself to become a virtual prisoner of the Guandong Army, and was in no position to make demands of his captors. But he was soothed into doing their bidding when he was told that Manchukuo might become a monarchy and require an emperor of its own, and that because Japan had designs on *all* of China, it was even possible the Qing Empire might someday be restored. On March 1, 1932, Aisin-Gioro Pu Yi was installed not as emperor but as the chief executive of Manchukuo. Even he would be drawn into the tragic series of events that were soon to befall Semyon Kaspé.

7

Two Toxic Elements

Having seized control of Manchuria, the Japanese turned their attention to administering and financing it. Part and parcel of this effort involved dreaming up ways to fleece the region's well-to-do of their wealth and property. Jews were especially attractive targets. Their accumulated wealth and their real estate holdings—like Josef Kaspé's Hotel Moderne, for a prime example—would be very useful to fund the occupation.

The Japanese also awarded monopoly concessions to various syndicates, mostly criminal, which paid heavily for their privileges. Exports, narcotics, poppy cultivation, opium dens, prostitution (there were 172 brothels in Harbin alone), and gambling houses were all to be regulated. And as time went on, they thought up more activities to control, like the sweeping of chimneys and even the taking of ice from the Sungari River.

Enforcement would be the work not only of the civil and military authorities, but of hired guns. The key problem was making sure most of the proceeds from these enterprises ran upstream to the government and did not simply wind up in the pockets of the soldiers, police, and bureaucrats, among whom corruption was not only rampant, but more or less expected.[1]

To this end, it was urgent that security forces be organized and staffed. In Harbin, order was kept by no fewer than *eight* organizations. Some were ostensibly military and others civil; some took orders directly from Japan and others reported to the resident Guandong Army or the new Manchukuo government. Their jurisdictions overlapped and they did not coordinate with one another. They included the Japanese Intelligence Service, or Tokumu Kikan; the Japanese Gendarmerie, or Kempeitai; the Japanese Consular Police; the Manchukuo Gendarmerie, the Manchukuo State Police, the Harbin City Police, the Harbin Criminal Police, and the Railway Police. Competition and mistrust among these agencies would figure prominently in Semyon Kaspé's story.

It would hardly have been feasible to staff the entire civil service with recruits from Japan, nor would it have bolstered the Japanese narrative that Manchukuo was self-governing. So after their takeover, the Japanese by and large kept in place the officials they had inherited. Each local government entity, however, now answered to a Japanese "adviser" who controlled everything.[2]

Many such advisers were local hires. And selecting from Japanese already resident in Manchuria who could speak the local languages severely limited the slate of choices. Japan had never sent its finest citizens to live in Manchuria; many of its early settlers were hiding out or fleeing, for one reason or another, from their previous lives. Those who arrived immediately after the takeover were not much better. Many had criminal records. There were drug dealers, pimps, and smugglers. By one estimate, the lion's share of the Japanese in Manchukuo were involved in underworld activity of one sort or another. But a criminal record proved no barrier to a sinecure in the new government, especially if one could speak Chinese, Manchu, or Russian.[3]

A good example was Konstantin Ivanovich Nakamura, the man who had worked with Rodzaevsky to create the mayhem the army had used as a pretext to enter Harbin. Nakamura had lived in Korea and Manchuria for some twenty years before the Japanese occupation. By one account he was an ethnic Korean, but he used a Japanese surname and a Russian given name and he had embraced Russian Orthodoxy. Nakamura lived in Harbin with a common-law Russian wife and was fluent in the Russian language. Known by the Russian diminutive moniker "Kostya," he had once owned a photo studio, but more recently operated a barber shop in a Harbin suburb that was, in fact, little more than a front for a brothel.

That is, when it wasn't being used for the sale of morphine, opium, and heroin.

An enthusiastic consumer of vodka and pornography, Nakamura was also a pedophile. His own wife had caused his arrest in 1924 for molesting her twelve-year-old daughter by a previous marriage, and he regularly employed underage girls as prostitutes. The Chinese authorities had never taken action against him because he had enjoyed extraterritoriality, which meant that only the Japanese government was empowered to discipline him. And Japanese officials had never shown any particular interest in doing so.

In 1926, a Russian client went into his barber shop for a shave, only to be drugged and relieved of five hundred dollars. The man complained to the Japanese Consulate, but the diplomats refused to punish Nakamura. Nor did they take any action when he was caught keeping a twelve-year-old girl as a prostitute.[4]

Not only did Nakamura never face Japanese justice; the aid he provided the Japanese Army in its takeover of Harbin in 1932 resulted in his recruitment by the Kempeitai, the Japanese gendarmerie, to serve as an interpreter and adviser. Since he had extensive knowledge of the Harbin underworld and close ties to the White Russian community, his services promised to be very useful. And if he used his new position to enrich himself on the side, no one really cared much unless he attracted too much attention.[5]

Nakamura would play a pivotal role in the fate of Semyon Kaspé in the months following August 4, 1933. So would Nikolai Nikolayevich Yagi, who had also lived in Harbin for many years. A Japanese who had made his living as a narcotics trafficker in the 1920s and had ties to the Russian underworld, he, too, had joined the Orthodox Church. He was hired in 1932 as a "high adviser" to the municipal police department, which put him in effective charge of the foreign section of the force, where he oversaw a staff of Chinese, Koreans, and Russians. The international population and multilingual character of the city made a diverse police force a necessity. It was said that Yagi had paid for his appointment, which was commonplace. In fact, he had ponied up $50,000 to the Japanese military mission to get the job, secure in the knowledge that it would offer him myriad shady opportunities to earn back far more. And within two years of his appointment, he had indeed parlayed his position into some $300,000 in cash and several valuable properties.[6]

Like Japan, Russia had never sent its best and brightest to Manchuria, apart, perhaps, from the professionals initially dispatched to design and administer the railroad and Jewish businessmen like Josef Kaspé. Many local Russians who arrived penniless were uneducated, and some had criminal records. But the Japanese also found room for them in government service, both civil and military. People who had lived at the bottom of society under the Chinese now suddenly found themselves elevated to positions of power and authority that many were all too eager to abuse, often in cruel and inhuman ways. They constituted a veritable rogues' gallery of willing collaborators with the new Japanese masters of Manchuria.

Among the Russian members of the Harbin police force the Japanese inherited was a man named Nikolai Martinov, who would also become deeply involved in the Kaspé affair. Born in Samara on the Volga River in European Russia, Martinov had joined the socialists at the age of fifteen, but soon became disillusioned with them and left the movement. He worked as an accountant, studied mechanical engineering, and eventually joined the army, but he opposed the new Soviet regime and joined the White movement. He participated in numerous battles and was wounded and arrested more than once by the Red Army, but he managed to escape each time.

Martinov arrived in Harbin on crutches in 1923 by way of Vladivostok and Korea, and worked, variously, as a school janitor, a bus driver, a porter, a guard, a shop assistant, and a milkman in the intervening years. He had also organized a Russian detachment under the command of Marshal Zhang Zuolin.

From Harbin, he provided food, supplies, and weapons to his fellow partisans in Russia, even after he had secured a position as an inspector in the Harbin Police Department's Criminal Investigation Division. He was both inherited by *and* hired by the Japanese after their conquest of Manchuria. While continuing to work as a police inspector, he was also engaged by the Japanese military mission as a special agent.[7]

In 1932, Martinov had shot and killed a former czarist colonel. During his trial for the offense, he claimed his weapon had discharged accidentally and was given a suspended sentence and a fine by the Chinese judges who tried the case. Many suspected the judges had been instructed as to the verdict by the Japanese authorities, but there is no extant evidence of that.[8]

Some Russians, like Konstantin Rodzaevsky and his Russian fascists, could be more useful *outside* of government as long as they could be effectively controlled. They could be employed to spy on the resident Soviet citizens, and could spearhead operations within Russia intended to destabilize the Bolshevik government. They could also take on dirty work and allow the Japanese to achieve their goals with apparently clean hands.

And the Japanese even occasionally found uses for resident foreigners who were neither Japanese nor Russian, but who possessed local knowledge. Among them was an improbable Italian spy-for-hire by the name of Amleto Vespa.

Born in L'Aquila in central Italy, Vespa was a small, bony man with dark red hair and blue eyes. He had gone abroad at the age of twenty-two, avoiding conscription into the Italian army. He had spent several years in America, where he picked up English, and eventually made his way to Siberia, where he worked for a time as a laborer on the Trans-Siberian Railway and learned to speak Russian. He had also lived in Mongolia, Manchuria, Korea, and China, and worked as publisher of a small newspaper in Russian and Italian, and as an importer.[9]

In 1920, Vespa had secretly entered the service of warlord Zhang Zuolin as head of the latter's security services. He was especially effective at foiling the smuggling of arms, many of which were Italian-made and destined for bandits in Manchuria. When the Italian diplomatic mission in China, angry at the disruption of this lucrative trade, threatened to have him deported, he immediately took out Chinese citizenship in order to deny his native land jurisdiction over him.[10]

As he described his responsibilities for Marshal Zhang in his memoir: "My assignments were many and varied: to gather political information, to keep an eye on the agents of other nations, to hunt bandits, smugglers of arms and narcotics, white-slave traders who exported thousands of young Russian women refugees from the revolution, to keep a check on Soviet and on Japanese activities."[11]

After Zhang's assassination by the Japanese army in 1928, Vespa shifted his focus to business. He built and managed the fashionable Atlantic Theater, a silent moving-picture house in Harbin, and as a fellow theater owner he knew Josef Kaspé personally. At the very end of 1931, an attempt

FIG. 11. Amleto Vespa, 1927. Amleto Vespa, *Secret Agent of Japan*
(Boston: Little Brown, 1938).

was made on his life. The plot was discovered and a suspect was arrested
and extradited to Shanghai. But this sort of thing was par for the course
in Vespa's line of work. "After my return to Harbin as Zhang Zuolin's
agent, outlaws of all sorts, racketeers, smugglers, white-slave traders and
the underworld gentry declared war against me as openly as I had done
against then," he wrote later.[12]

One didn't make a lot of friends in the espionage business.

Shortly thereafter, the Japanese made Vespa an offer he couldn't refuse.
It was actually less an offer than a command. As he recalled it, in early

1932 he was summoned to the office of Kenji Doihara, then head of the Harbin Tokumu Kikan.

Doihara didn't beat around the bush. "Several times, in the past, the Japanese military authorities have proposed that you should leave the Chinese service and join ours," Vespa recalled him saying. "You have always refused. But today things have changed. I am not inviting you, I am *telling* you that from now on you are going to work for the Japanese." He made it clear that the alternative would be death—his own, and those of his wife and two children. "I am making you no offers, Mr. Vespa," he continued. "I am giving you orders and I have told you why."[13]

The next day, Doihara introduced Vespa to his successor, the new chief of the Tokumu Kikan. The man, whose name Vespa claimed never to have learned but in any case never revealed, was not shy about giving his new charge a remarkably candid description of Japan's real goals for Manchuria:

> We Japanese are a very poor people, and we could not afford the luxury of paying the expenses incidental to our occupation of Manchuria. In one way or another, therefore, the Chinese of Manchuria must foot the whole bill. That is our principal task. . . .
>
> If we had openly declared that we officially occupied Manchuria, the thing would be easier and no one would have a word to say about it. But we have officially declared for our own good reasons that the new Manchurian state was formed as the result of a revolution of the people themselves, and that the Japanese are here only as advisers. Hence we must see to it that the Manchurians pay us, but it must be done in such a way that no one will be able to accuse us of *making* them pay, or receiving any money.
>
> Our system consists, first, in secretly granting monopolies to trustworthy individuals; second, in compelling, indirectly, the rich Chinese and Russians—and especially the rich Jews—to part with considerable portions of their wealth and . . . this must be done so cleverly that they will never know that it is the Japanese who do the compelling and get the fruits of it.

He went on to describe the need to engage a corps of Russian refugees willing to work underground for the Japanese. "We need Russian names to cover up our activities," he told Vespa. "We need men who are not necessarily over-intelligent, who possess ambition . . . capable of tackling any sort of job. They must know how to handle their knives and revolvers well, and how to keep their mouths shut."

These men would be granted "full liberty" to deal with the Soviets in Manchuria as they saw fit. And they would also be useful in the plans the Japanese had for local Jews. "In spite of the fact that they are all Russian origin, many of [the Jews] have been able, more or less legally, to become naturalized citizens of other countries," Vespa's new boss went on to say. "Whenever you see a foreign flag in front of an establishment you may rest assured that it hides one or more Jews. Of course we cannot attack them directly and openly, especially those who belong to a nationality with extraterritorial rights. But indirectly we will have to make things tough for them."[14]

That a Japanese official would have been so candid with a foreigner he was meeting for the first time is frankly hard to believe, and it bears pointing out that Vespa's memoir, though always illuminating, is thought by some not always to be entirely reliable. One tendentious element is his deep disdain for his Japanese overseers, which can be found on nearly every page.

Manchuria was not the scene of Japan's first encounter with either White Russians or Jews. Between 1918 and 1922, during and after the Russian Civil War, some seventy-five thousand Japanese soldiers had been sent to Siberia and Russia's maritime provinces to support White Russian forces in their struggle against the Red Army. It was during that same intervention that the troops had their first experiences with Jews, of whom some twenty-five thousand lived in Siberia. Several thousand of them actually fled to Manchuria during and after the conflict. White Russian generals welcomed the opportunity to indoctrinate the Japanese with anti-Jewish attitudes.

Still, there was no tradition of religious or social antisemitism in Japan, and no official policy of discrimination against Jews. What colored Japanese attitudes toward Jews was mostly a myth. The twenty-four-chapter *Protocols of the Elders of Zion*, the infamous Russian antisemitic forgery that alleged a global Jewish conspiracy for world domination, was given to Japanese army officers and soldiers and subsequently translated into Japanese. Many Japanese accepted its lies and stereotypes at face value.[15]

There was, however, also Japan's earlier experience during the Russo-Japanese War, when German-born, Jewish-American financier Jacob Schiff, resentful of Russian mistreatment of his fellow Jews, singlehandedly facilitated crucial loans to finance the Japanese military. This act persuaded many Japanese that Jews were, in the main, wealthy and able to project considerable political and economic clout internationally. But the *Protocols* suggested that they were not to be trusted.

Vespa's unnamed supervisor, who espoused strong personal anti-Jewish sentiments, had said it all very succinctly. Manchuria was to pay for its own colonization, and one important source of capital would be its Jews. The Japanese would use the reactionary Russian émigrés to bilk them—people of wealth like Josef Kaspé—for what they were worth. But it all had to be done covertly; to be seen to be behind it could spoil Japan's plans for gaining international recognition of its new puppet state, and for attracting foreign investment to it.

The fusion of two toxic elements—Japanese imperial overlords and reactionary, antisemitic Russian fascist émigrés—would cause an explosion that laid waste to the hitherto idyllic world of the Kaspés.

8

An Unholy Alliance

Josef Kaspé's Hotel Moderne survived a devastating flood in August 1932 when twenty-one days of constant, torrential rain caused the Sungari River to overflow its banks and turn the lower part of the city into a huge lake. Many who lived in the Pristan quarter lost their homes, and hundreds of Chinese residents died of cholera from contaminated water. Food became scarce. Kitaiskaya Street was navigable only by boat. An iconic image shows Kaspé in short pants, posing with several members of the hotel staff, one of whose feet are completely submerged, in the front of the building.

It is worth noting that although the flood inundated Pristan, where most of the city's Jews lived, not a single Jewish life was lost. This was due to the cohesion of the Jewish community, which quickly organized the delivery of food and water to victims. The soup kitchen went into overdrive. Doctors made rounds on boats and members of Betar, the Zionist Jewish youth organization, moved Jewish families in peril to higher ground.[1]

Had the flood occurred a few months earlier, it would have disrupted the May visit of a very important foreign delegation headed by Victor Bulwer-Lytton, a British politician and civil servant. Its mission had important implications for Japan's stated hope of securing international recognition for Manchukuo, whose existence it had proclaimed the previous February.

Lytton's five-member commission had been established in late 1931 by the League of Nations in response to a petition from the Chinese government to investigate Japan's claims about the supposedly independent state it had formed in Manchuria. To fulfill their mission, the commissioners spent six weeks in the region on a listening tour. They visited Japan

FIG. 12. Josef Kaspé, third from left in short pants, in front of the Hotel Moderne with several employees during the 1932 Sungari River flood. Author's collection.

and China before arriving in Manchuria, and on May 9 they began a twelve-day sojourn in Harbin. They were intent on meeting with a broad spectrum of local stakeholders and hearing a wide range of opinions.

Their Japanese handlers were equally resolved to make sure this did not happen.

With so much at stake, Tokyo's representatives choreographed the entire visit down to the tiniest detail. A Manchu honor guard and several

Харбинъ-Вокзалъ

Harbin Teishajō, Harbin.

FIG. 13. Postcard view of Harbin Station. Author's collection.

bands were on hand as the special train bearing the delegation pulled into Harbin Station, as were crowds of hand-picked citizens instructed to cheer enthusiastically. The arrival was marred only by a Korean who attempted to hand an envelope to a delegation member. He was seized, of course, and reportedly buried alive later that day.[2]

Amleto Vespa recalled later that more than thirteen hundred people—Chinese, Russian, Korean, and even a few Japanese who were distrusted—were arrested under cover of darkness by local police in advance of the delegation's visit and incarcerated six miles away, across the Sungari River, for the duration of the group's stay in Harbin. Five hundred local thugs were recruited, issued military uniforms, and detailed to "guard" the homes of wealthy Chinese known to be hostile to Japan; they were told they would be punished for any misdeeds committed by their charges. Local officials in whom the Japanese authorities had confidence, by contrast, were assembled into a "reception committee," rehearsed as to what they should and should not say, and warned not to stray from the script.

After speeches, the commissioners, escorted by the cavalry in armored cars, sidecars, and motorcycles, were driven through city streets festooned with Manchukuo flags and portraits of Pu Yi. The Japanese had produced them for a nickel each and sent gendarmes door-to-door to force local residents, Russians and Chinese alike, to purchase them for two dollars, under penalty of arrest.[3]

The group's destination was the Hotel Moderne, which became ground zero for the senior members of the delegation. Vespa, assigned to pose as a European businessman staying at the hotel, was charged with reporting any Chinese who approached the delegates. He described the place as "in a regular state of siege." Rooms near those of the commissioners were assigned to Japanese and Russian agents who pretended to be ordinary hotel guests. Police agents—each delegate had four assigned to him— filled in as hotel staff members, and secretly noted every movement of their charges.[4]

National Geographic contributor Lilian Grosvenor Coville, who was living in Harbin at the time, wrote that the hotel was surrounded by a cordon of soldiers and police, and that anyone approaching the building had to present credentials to Japanese plainclothesmen posted at the entrance for entry.[5]

The group's movements were strictly controlled, ostensibly to protect its members from harm. And it is true that Harbin had become a dangerous place in the early 1930s. During the very week of the delegation's visit, bandits attempted to kidnap two British bankers playing golf; the daughter of an American automobile manufacturer was abducted and held for a sky-high ransom; and, a short distance from town, a train was wrecked by thieves who relieved a young American passenger of his money and all of his possessions.[6]

But in truth, their Japanese handlers were more focused on protecting the delegates from dissenting voices than from abduction. They wanted to make certain none was ever approached by anyone of whom they did not approve. Concerned over reports that some locals intended to present the commissioners with petitions that contested the bogus Japanese claim of strong local support for the new government of Manchukuo, the authorities assigned some thirty of their own officials as escorts to keep the delegates busy with endless banquets and meetings.

FIG. 14. A 1930s postcard showing the entrance to the jewelry shop at the Hotel Moderne during the Japanese occupation. At the top right, an arrow points to the name "Kaspé" in Cyrillic, written vertically on the side of the building. Author's collection.

All those precautions didn't stop people from trying, however. Vespa recounted that five Chinese and two Russians were shot by Japanese police for attempting to deliver appeals to the commissioners. One of the latter was a student at the Harbin Polytechnic Institute who was protesting not the invasion of Manchuria, but merely the closing of his school. He was killed on the spot in a guest room on the second floor of the Moderne, as was the Russian guard who had failed to keep him at bay. In a memoir, Oleg Volgin—an alias for a member of the Russian Fascist Party assigned by Kostya Nakamura to guard the side entrance of the Moderne—recounted that some two hundred men, mostly Chinese, were arrested simply for loitering *near* the hotel.[7]

Although the Japanese authorities took the mission of the delegation deadly seriously, they actually had little respect for the delegates themselves, deriding them privately as "old women whose main job is to go from one banquet to another." They believed they were successful in their efforts to insulate them, however, and after the group departed they were more than satisfied with the visit. Nakamura even celebrated with an evening of drinking and debauchery. But in truth, the commissioners had managed many conversations with local Chinese who opposed colonization and received some five hundred letters from locals, many via the local diplomatic missions. And in October they issued a stinging, ten-chapter report. Although they assigned some blame to China for the tenuous state of affairs in Manchuria, they found that Japan had wrongfully invaded the territory and declared that it should be returned to China.[8]

This was a major blow to Japan's hopes for diplomatic recognition for the puppet state, and the country not only rejected the commission's findings; it resigned from the League of Nations in protest. Many in Tokyo blamed the Japanese officials in Manchuria for this, accusing them of failing to insulate the commissioners, and some were summarily dismissed from their posts as a result.[9]

According to Vespa, the chief of the Japanese Intelligence Service (Vespa's local Japanese "handler") blamed not the local Japanese, but rather Jews and Freemasons for the actions of the League. The ostensible link between Jews and Freemasonry was right out of the *Protocols*, and there had been two Jews assigned to the Expert and Scientific Delegation attached to the Lytton Commission. Lord Lytton, though not Jewish himself, was said to have ties to Chaim Weizmann through the marriage of one of the latter's relatives.[10]

Vespa's chief insisted,

> It is the Jews and Masons who make the League's decisions; no one else. The League has made its decision; we shall make ours. . . . From today henceforth, the Jews, the Masons and whoever is in sympathy with them, must not be allowed one moment's peace in Manchukuo. Indirectly they must be persecuted, tormented, humiliated, reviled without respite. We must make their lives as miserable as possible. We must show those scoundrels that we Japanese can hit back and hit hard. Starting tomorrow, I have ordered our two Russian papers to start a merciless campaign against the Jews, the Masonic Lodge,

and the Y.M.C.A., which is a Jew-Mason organization. Rich Jews must be kidnapped daily and made to pay, not small sums such as my predecessor asked for, but very large amounts.[11]

The truth was, Jewish kidnappings were already occurring; a rash of them had begun shortly after the Japanese marched into Harbin. There was nothing particularly new about hostage-taking in Manchuria; it had been going on for decades. But in the past, such activities had mostly been the doings of the *honghuzi*, or "red beards," marauding Chinese guerillas who mostly menaced wealthy Chinese. Now, however, White Russians were getting into the act in a big way, sometimes operating independently, sometimes in the service of their new Japanese overlords, who dreamed up creative ways to put them to good use.

Jews, many of whom had become quite prosperous, became favorite targets. The Japanese government saw the local Jews as deep pockets who could easily be separated from their wealth, which in turn could be deployed to fund the occupation, to develop the region, and to bankroll Japan's eventual conquest of the rest of Asia, which was already being planned. And corrupt Japanese functionaries in Manchuria, for their part, viewed them as a convenient means of lining their own pockets.

The Russian fascists loathed all Jews, branding as communists even people like Josef Kaspé who were unabashed capitalists and quite unlikely to have been Bolshevik sympathizers. It blamed them for the revolution that had precipitated their own exile. The fascists had already begun to harass Jews even before the arrival of the Japanese, and were eager to do the dirty work asked of them by their new Japanese masters, whose support arguably rendered them the most influential émigré group in all of Manchukuo apart, of course, from Japanese nationals. When Jews were seized, Japanese gendarmes often looked the other way, especially when they stood to gain the lion's share of the spoils.

In many cases, after money changed hands victims would be returned a little worse for the wear, but a merchant named Meir Koffman was not so fortunate. The former president of the Harbin Jewish community, Koffman was the owner of a large pharmacy. One night in March 1932, just ten days after the establishment of Manchukuo, he was snatched by four Caucasian men and pushed into a waiting automobile.

The police were tight-lipped about whether a ransom demand had been received; they told the press only that they believed both Chinese and Russian thugs had been involved. The next day, however, two Russian newspapers reported that the kidnappers had issued a demand for $30,000 and threatened to cut off their captive's ears if it was not satisfied. They had sent two letters, one of which was signed with the pseudonym "Juan Salvador." It was reprinted in the papers and read, in part: "I did not fulfill my word in respect to Koffman's ears, as I know his friends are trying to collect the amount demanded by me. I withheld sending them in my own interest. If, however, the amount demanded by me is not paid, then his relatives will receive from me the promised surprise. . . . Perhaps they do not wish to see him without his ears."[12] No doubt they did not, but as a practical matter, they were unable to raise the money. Koffman owned property but had little available cash, and his friends weren't in a position to make up the difference. As a result, Koffman, who had initially been kept in a cellar in town but later moved to a small Chinese house on its outskirts, was murdered. That fact, however, didn't stop the kidnappers from continuing to negotiate with his family. Mrs. Koffman ultimately paid them $18,000 for her husband's release. But not only did she never see him alive again; she never saw him at all. His kidnappers had tortured him in life and dismembered him in death. His body was never found.[13]

Even more brazen was the seizure of I. Sherel de Florence, the son of a local Jewish merchant, who was abducted by six armed men in plain view of two hundred witnesses as he exited one of Harbin's synagogues on Yom Kippur, the holiest day of the Hebrew calendar. His captors initially demanded $100,000 from the Jewish community for his release, and to show that they meant business, exploded a bomb outside the home of Dr. Salomon Rabinovitch, the community's president. The two sides eventually came to terms at about $25,000, and after 105 days in captivity, Sherel de Florence was released.[14]

Occasionally the motive was not financial, nor was kidnapping the chosen tactic. A Jewish official of the Chinese Eastern Railway, Yecheskiel

Alter, who refused demands that he resign his position to clear the way for a White Russian to be appointed in his place, was shot dead in his home as his helpless wife looked on in August of 1932.[15]

The seemingly endless string of antisemitic violence and brazen acquisition of Jewish wealth and property under Japanese rule deeply alarmed Harbin's Jewish community. Many of its leading lights therefore took extra precautionary measures, like hiring armed bodyguards and carrying guns. Josef Kaspé, for one, had begun to take great care whenever he stepped out of the Moderne, which, these days, was seldom. He also had thick steel bars installed on his family's ground floor apartment there and engaged several armed bodyguards.

But armed escorts offered no protection from the authorities. As non-Soviet Russians living abroad after the October Revolution, the Kaspé family was stateless, and hence more vulnerable than those with foreign passports to possible hostile government actions such as arrest, exploitation, or expropriation of property. That is likely why, before Semyon left Paris, he applied for, and was granted, French citizenship, which his mother and brother did as well. This meant that if he got into trouble, he could seek the protection of the French Republic through the good offices of its diplomats abroad.

Semyon's naturalization also helped his father. Soon after the young man's return, his father arranged to have most of his assets transferred to his sons' names as a means of protecting his hotel and his other holdings from expropriation. By some accounts, the Japanese authorities had already attempted to persuade him to sell his interest in the hotel, but even though he rebuffed them, he knew they had other ways of getting people like him to come around.[16]

Josef knew the new Japanese authorities would think twice before making a move on a property that flew the French flag, as the Moderne now did. Even after the Lytton Commission issued its scathing report, Japan still held out hope that some nations might recognize its newly created puppet state, and, in so doing, legitimize its occupation. Many in Japan saw the invasion as a rightful action taken in self-defense rather than a violation of international law and felt that foreign acceptance of an independent Manchukuo was a matter of Japan's national honor.

Then, too, foreign recognition would facilitate the new state's ability to attract investment. Thus it was vital to this endeavor to maintain cordial relations with the United States and European powers. The Japanese had especially high hopes for France, and hoped to drive a wedge on the issue between the French on one hand and the British and Americans on the other.[17]

Although Japan's overarching control of the levers of power in Manchuria was in many ways inhibiting, normal, day-to-day activities did not cease under its reign, and there was nothing to stop Semyon from going ahead with his plans to perform in China and Japan and, after that, spend a year in the United States. After impressing Harbin audiences, he was soon off to Shanghai to make his local debut at the Embassy Theater there. Warmly received, he followed it with an appearance with the Shanghai Symphony Orchestra, then under the baton of Mario Paci, an Italian conductor credited with helping introduce classical European music to China and training some of China's first pianists. The concert, which included six solos and two encores and which was broadcast simultaneously on the radio, brought down the house.[18]

From Shanghai it was on to Japan; Semyon visited that country twice in the spring of 1933 to give concerts. By June he was back in Harbin, however, his talent as a pianist broadcast to all who could receive a signal from the Dalian Broadcasting Station.[19]

But Semyon's American concert tour was not to be. Despite all of his father's precautions, the family would come to grief beginning late on the night of August 24, 1933.[20]

9

Kidnapped

Just as Semyon and Lydia arrived at her home at 109 Pekarnaya Street, only a few blocks from the Moderne, several men—all Caucasian—jumped on the running boards that extended along the side of the vehicle, drew revolvers, and pointed them at Semyon's chauffeur. As one grabbed the driver's gun and took over the wheel, another forced himself into the back seat with Semyon and Lydia. The former kept his cool as they were blindfolded, but Lydia was so terrified that the man in the back seat felt obliged to soothe her: he told her she had done nothing wrong and promised she would not be hurt.

The driver sped to the Novy Gorod district, south and east of Pristan, where, at the intersection of Strelkovaya Street and Bolshoi Avenue, Lydia and the driver were released. Semyon, however, was spirited away in a waiting second car, which headed for a small house in the Staryi Gorod district, southeast of Novy Gorod.[1]

The next day, exactly what had transpired the previous night was anything but clear. The newspapers that reported on the kidnapping differed on many crucial details. *Zarya* (Rays of Sunlight), a Russian-language paper, counted only two kidnappers, identified them as Russians, and reported that they had told Lydia to warn Semyon's father to prepare a ransom of 300,000 yen, or about $1.4 million in 1933 dollars, equivalent in purchasing power to close to $30 million today.[2] The *Hull Daily Mail* wrote that the abduction occurred in front of Lydia's home and that the bandits had driven Semyon's car a distance before releasing Lydia. The *Nottingham Evening Post* identified Semyon as a polo player rather than a musician, and both *Le Petit Parisien* and *Le Matin* put the ransom demand at 500,000 dollars, not yen. And according to the *New York*

Herald's European edition, Semyon's chauffeur had drawn his pistol to protect his passengers before he was overpowered.[3]

The Japanese-owned *Manchuria Daily News* placed the kidnapping on Kitaiskaya Street at 12:30 a.m., portrayed Semyon as traveling not just with a lady friend, but with a "bevy of belles," and related that the kidnappers had left the girls unmolested, even as they had seized Semyon. He, the paper reported, had offered no resistance. And the paper put the ransom demand at three million dollars.[4]

In the absence of hard facts, the rumor mill went into overdrive. Many pointed fingers at the Russian Fascist Party, which had already published attacks on the elder Kaspé in its house organ, *Nash Put*, asserting that the silver, enamelware, precious stones, porcelains, and Fabergé eggs on display in his jewelry store had been confiscated from the Russian upper classes by the Soviets after the October Revolution and were hence not Kaspé's to sell.[5] Others alleged that the Japanese were responsible: that Josef Kaspé had refused their offer of a million yen for the Hotel Moderne and that this was simply plan B to pressure him into yielding. Still others blamed Soviet agents, alleging that after the October Revolution, Josef had been given the czar's crown jewels to resell, that he had never paid for them, and that this was his creditors' way of collecting their due. In this far-fetched scenario, Semyon was ostensibly being held in the basement of the Soviet Consulate. Still others placed the blame on unnamed Jewish enemies of Kaspé.[6]

Whoever had done it had crossed a line. Kidnappings of Chinese were not unusual, nor were those of stateless Russians, including many Jews who had never applied for Soviet citizenship after the Russian Revolution. But there had seldom been an abduction of a citizen of a Western country. And the ransom demanded was nothing short of outrageous.[7]

On August 26, resident French consul Louis Reynaud sent a dispatch about the incident to Auguste Wilden, France's minister in Beijing, with a copy to the Foreign Ministry in Paris. He summarized what he had been able to glean about the abduction from Josef Kaspé, who had already requested his assistance, and from conversations with the police, with whom Kaspé had also been in touch. He numbered the kidnappers at five and confirmed that they were not only white but presumed by the police

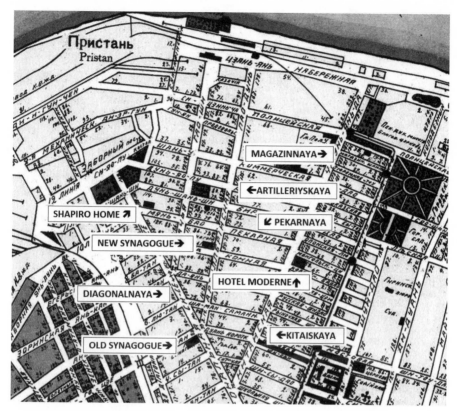

Map boxes: Пристань / Pristan, MAGAZINNAYA→, ←ARTILLERIYSKAYA, SHAPIRO HOME ↗, ↙ PEKARNAYA, NEW SYNAGOGUE→, HOTEL MODERNE↑, DIAGONALNAYA→, OLD SYNAGOGUE→, ←KITAISKAYA

MAP 3. Detail of a street map of Harbin showing key locations. The original is a Central Intelligence Agency Russian-language map published in 1947. Library of Congress, Geography and Map Division, Washington DC.

to be Russian. He also noted that the police were especially disconcerted at the news because they believed they had put an end to the rash of abductions earlier in the year when they had killed Ataman Woliewski.

Woliewski, an underworld kingpin of Polish origin who had fled to Harbin after the Russian Revolution, had led a gang that had terrorized the Jewish community for two years. The police suspected his band had been responsible for the three major kidnappings in the past two years: Jews Sherel de Florence and Meir Koffman—the former head of the Jewish community, who had also been murdered—and a gentile wine dealer named Tarasenko. Woliewski had been killed just in time to thwart his plan to abduct Aaron Moshe Kiselev, since 1913 the chief rabbi of Harbin, and with his death the police thought they had more or less broken up the kidnapping ring.[8]

Reynaud reported that the Kempeitai, the Japanese Gendarmerie, had instructed all the municipal police services to find the criminals and free their prisoner, but that their efforts, including interrogation of those who witnessed the kidnapping, had yet to yield any results. He was certain the abduction had been planned by people who followed young Kaspé's comings and goings, and he nursed the suspicion that Semyon's driver, who had been arrested, had been complicit, even though the man strongly denied any participation in the attack.

Reynaud, who had found Josef Kaspé ailing and distraught when he visited him, noted that due to the prominence of the Kaspé family and Semyon's French citizenship, the incident had especially alarmed Harbin's foreigners, who worried that the local authorities appeared incapable of repressing the banditry that was increasingly being directed at them. He wrote that he had called for a meeting of the local diplomatic corps to discuss practical measures they might all take to ensure greater security for their citizens.[9]

The following day, the *Manchuria Daily News*, an influential Japanese-language daily funded by Tokyo and published in Port Arthur, reported that the police believed Semyon had been taken by someone who bore a grudge against his father or himself. Cited as evidence was the fact that the abductors had made no effort to hold Lydia, whose father was also Jewish and well-to-do, and the impression the police had that Josef Kaspé had many detractors. The paper also reported a false rumor that he had already sold the Hotel Moderne to Japanese interests for $250,000 in gold.[10]

Josef Kaspé, who had been ill even before the kidnapping, informed his wife, Marie, of Semyon's abduction, and so did the French Foreign Ministry. That office contacted her by telephone on August 29 in Paris, where she had remained with their son Vladimir, and at her request telegraphed Harbin for an update. In a follow-up letter delivered to her lodgings at 4, rue Henri Heine, the ministry confirmed that Josef had already received a communication from Semyon himself in which he repeated the kidnappers' demand for 300,000 yen.[11]

FIG. 15. The Consulate of Japan in Harbin. Wikimedia Commons.

On August 30, an arrest was made. The police took a man named Finogenov-Zorin and his chauffeur into custody after a search of the former's garage yielded up a false license plate and a pair of goggles. This was seen as significant because Lydia Shapiro had told police the kidnappers had worn masks, false mustaches, and goggles. But nothing came of it, nor of the report a few days later that police were seeking a man named Treffesky who had recently fled to Shanghai, nor of the arrest of a man named Vaganov, thought by some to have been one of the assassins of the czar, the czarina and the Romanov family. He had been suspected because police had confiscated a Russian army revolver and twenty cartridges concealed in the folds of his wife's dressing gown.[12]

Shanghai's *North China Herald* saw the abduction as evidence of a broader war against Jews being waged by White Russians in the Manchurian cities of Xinjing and Harbin. And it pointed out the obvious contradiction in their insistence on blaming local Jews for the Russian Revolution: "That there were Jews amongst the leaders of the Russian revolution is undeniable, but it is equally true that a very large proportion of Russian Jewry was not in support of the doctrines which the Communists preached, nor were they prepared to live under their domination. To that extent Jews who have fled from Russia have common cause with the White Russians and deserve not persecution but regard as fellow sufferers in misfortune."[13] This article, in turn, spawned a preposterous rebuttal in the form of a letter to the editor signed only "Bona Fide Russian." The writer insisted that "An organized political Anti-Semitism is non-existent amongst the White Russians. All sensible Russian patriots realize too well that heterogenous Russia will be never reborn nationally if they preach racial hatred and animosity. . . . Harbin of present day is a city of international intrigues, and nothing is easier there than to start a rumor or to engineer a plot. To connect the anti-Jewish sentiments and the kidnapping of Mr. Kaspé is certainly a clever piece of work."[14]

Reynaud had assigned the case to his deputy, Albert Chambon, and by September 13, the two had concluded that the efforts of the local police were sorely lacking. Reynaud cabled his superiors in Paris with the suggestion that they petition the Japanese government in Tokyo to press local civilian and military authorities in Manchuria to redouble their efforts to find Semyon. His request was denied, but he did receive permission to appeal to his own Japanese counterpart in Harbin "on an informal and strictly personal basis."

Because the Japanese consul was out of town, Reynaud secured an audience with his deputy, but he might as well not have bothered. The first vice-consul insisted that the Kaspé case was exclusively a matter for the Manchukuo authorities, and that neither the Consular Police nor the Japanese Gendarmerie would get involved because they were

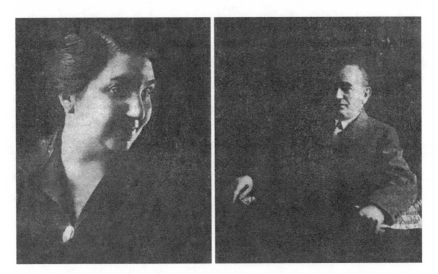

FIG. 16. Marie and Josef Kaspé. Courtesy of Dan Ben-Canaan.

responsible only for the protection of Japanese nationals. To have asserted otherwise would have been to admit that Japan controlled internal affairs in Manchukuo.[15]

Reynaud also met with C. F. Garstin, his British counterpart in Harbin, and told him confidentially that negotiations for Semyon's release were not going well. He reported that although it had not been publicized, Josef Kaspé had agreed to pay Semyon's captors 35,000 yen ($165,000), but only *after* his son had been set free. The arrangement had fallen through, however, and the elder Kaspé had come to believe that the kidnappers had accomplices within the police force. Garstin added that "I am informed that the chief of the local criminal investigation department is aware of the identity of the leader of the gang, but has pledged his word of honor to the Russian from whom he received the information that he would not act thereon."[16]

The authority to whom he was referring was N. M. Nikiforov. He headed the criminal police and had been assigned principal responsibility for investigating the Kaspé case. But his organization was one of *two* local police departments, the other being the municipal police, whose foreign section was under the command of Nikolai Nikolayevich Yagi, the former drug trafficker.[17]

Nikolai Martinov worked for Yagi, who in turn reported to L. N. Goroshkevich, chief of the Criminal Investigation Department of the Harbin Municipal Police. Goroshkevich had also ordered Martinov to investigate the case; the two police forces were rivals, and not only did they not cooperate with each other; they sometimes deliberately set out to foil each other's efforts.[18]

In the opinion of the French Consulate, Nikiforov was inept and even if he had been more capable, lacked the personnel to carry out the investigation. As Chambon described it later,

> He did not even take evidence from Josef Kaspé's driver, who had a direct connection with the kidnapping, and was seriously suspected of being a partner in it. Nor did Nikiforov station policemen in the places where the kidnappers exchanged letters with the Kaspé family. Furthermore, he did not even trace the calls made by the kidnappers in order to locate the place from where they were made, which would have led to the arrest. In sum, he did not take the most basic steps that could have helped find the kidnappers.[19]

A young, energetic career diplomat, Albert Chambon was a graduate of the Paris Institute of Political Studies who had studied Chinese at the National School of Modern Oriental Languages before being sent to China, his first foreign posting. In the three short years he had been in the country, he had worked in the Fuzhou and Shanghai consulates and then the legation in Beijing. He had arrived in Harbin in late 1931, which meant he had witnessed firsthand the Japanese occupation of the city and the proclamation of the establishment of Manchukuo. In the brief time Semyon Kaspé had been back in Harbin, Chambon had befriended the young musician, who was exactly his age. The two young men met often at Semyon's piano recitals and at dinners given by mutual friends.[20]

What Chambon, to whom Reynaud had assigned the case, did not know was that Nikiforov had received a telephone call from one of the kidnappers just two days after Semyon's abduction. "Kaspé is in our hands," the man had told him. "If you remain quiet, you'll get your share. Give us your word that you won't act against us."

Nikiforov had responded that he was not entirely in control; that the

Kempeitai, working under the command of Kostya Nakamura, was also involved. The gendarmerie had two roles: as a conventional military police force and a secret police. This, however, had not fazed the caller. "We're not worried; just give us your word," he had responded. And apparently that is precisely what Nikiforov did, because for the balance of his tenure overseeing the case, he remained useless in the search for Semyon Kaspé.[21]

The task of negotiating with the kidnappers fell to the managers of the Hotel Moderne, Abraham Pevsner, a nephew of Josef's, and a Mr. L. Gurevitch. The two men had been approached by three people offering to find Semyon in exchange for a hefty bounty. One, who worked for the Japanese military, secured an advance payment of 2,000 yen from them but was never heard from again. Another was a medium who offered to conduct a séance to locate Semyon. A third, named Kimstach, claimed he had connections with the criminals. Although he could not provide evidence for this, Pevsner and Gurevitch found him credible and were willing to work with him.

Shortly after his visit, however, Kimstach was arrested by Nikiforov's criminal police. According to Chambon, he had connections to Yagi's operation, and Nikiforov nabbed him lest his rivals get the credit for solving the crime and reap the reward. Chambon sought an interview with Kimstach to find out what he knew, but was denied permission by Nikiforov.

The kidnappers were aware of all this; they clearly had sources who were keeping them well informed of developments. And they let Josef Kaspé know this in a threatening letter delivered to Lydia Shapiro's home. In it, they attempted to persuade him that they would always be a step ahead of him, and that he should cease all efforts to find his son and simply pay the ransom. The letter read:

> Mr. Kaspé,
>   If you want to see your son, pay the money on time and abandon all your attempts to find him. We know for sure that you have been giving money for the search to the police agents, that you have been conducting your own search and promising them, as well as your

friends, a large reward for finding your son and for catching us. We can tell you more—we know them all by name and we are tracking them better than they are tracking us. Stop it; it is a waste of money in the first place, and secondly, you are putting your son's life in danger and you are not safe yourself, no matter how well-guarded you are. Remember, this small trick of yours—not to pay the ransom or trying to approach us with provocations—presents no danger to us. It is dangerous for you and your son who is STILL being kept in good condition.

The deadline for paying the ransom is August 28 at 8 o'clock in the evening.[22] The signal "the ransom money is ready" is known to Mrs. Shapiro. . . .

For every day the ransom is not paid the sum will be increased and the conditions under which your son is being kept will get worse. Pay the ransom and your son will come back, or else. You understand we didn't take him as a joke but to get a ransom, and if the ransom is not paid in full you can blame yourself for your son's death. You will receive additional instructions as to how to get us the money.[23]

On September 25, a full month after the kidnapping, Reynaud reported to Beijing and Paris about the lack of progress in the investigation, which he attributed to inexperience, incapacity, or complicity on the part of the police. He also reported that letters from Semyon himself had been received by his father and by some friends. In them, the young man had urged his father to pay the ransom and call off the police, who, he insisted, were powerless over his captors. At the same time, the kidnappers, through short telephone calls and intermediaries, refused to lower their price. Reynaud again voiced his suspicion that they were working in cahoots with the secret police, "whose venality," he wrote, "is well known."

By some accounts, Josef Kaspé dug in his heels and refused to pay any ransom for his son. Some said this was at the urging of the French Consulate, but Chambon insisted later that he had, on the contrary, counseled the elder Kaspé to pay it, but that the old man was in such "a state of indescribable prostration and incredible stubbornness" that he was not thinking clearly. One way or the other, however, Kaspé was in a bind. He simply couldn't afford the bounty.

Although he was reputed to be wealthy, the Depression had decimated his holdings. His properties had been mortgaged and, in some cases, remortgaged. And because he had not made payments on some of his loans, his credit was poor and he was in no position to borrow the ransom money. Beyond that, he had transferred his assets to his sons, so he couldn't legally sell the hotel without their signatures. And even if he could, the banks would get first crack at any proceeds. Despite it all, he did offer the kidnappers 35,000 yen. It was almost certainly all he could come up with.[24]

On September 27, just over a month after the abduction, having received no indication that a payment was forthcoming, the kidnappers turned up the heat. At ten o'clock the following morning, a messenger arrived at Lydia Shapiro's home with a parcel. She wasn't expecting anything and had no inkling of who might have sent it or what it might contain. And she was shocked when she opened it.

It contained a piece of one of Semyon Kaspé's ears, and a note to his father in his handwriting.

My dearly beloved father,
In the name of everything holy, save me! Am I and my beloved art worth less than money? For God's sake, pay the 300,000 yen quickly if you don't want to receive pieces of my body.

Today I will lose a part of my ear. It will happen in a few hours. I am now sitting and writing this letter and trying to forget everything and not think about anything. I am trying not to lose heart, but I'm afraid I will not be able to keep control of myself. Oh! How terrible all this is.

If you don't pay this money, after the piece of the ear they will cut off the whole ear and then the forefinger. If you don't pay after that, I will be killed if I don't die before that from the torture. Then I will not need my freedom. Will I ever see you, Mother and Volodya again? Or am I to return to you an invalid?

I beg you to save me and end my torture and suffering. Hurry! Hurry!

Your unfortunate son,
Semyon[25]

Chambon recalled later that the effect of this grisly development on Josef Kaspé was the opposite of what the kidnappers intended. "Now that they have cut off part of Semyon's ear, I'll give them even *less* than I offered," he declared. "My son is no longer whole, so I will pay them even *less*." Persuaded that this was evidence of the elder Kaspé's descent into madness, Chambon and Reynaud became convinced that Marie Kaspé should be summoned from France. Josef agreed that she could be helpful, and cabled her to come.[26]

Before she departed, Marie Kaspé paid a call on Henry Cosmé, the Foreign Ministry's deputy director for Asia, with a request. She explained that it was impossible for the family to meet the demand of the kidnappers and asked that the French government guarantee the funds with a Parisian bank, pending the sale of their properties in Harbin. Cosmé informed her—correctly or incorrectly—that regulations prohibited the government from doing this.[27]

For his part, Reynaud immediately renewed his plea with the Foreign Ministry for a formal diplomatic démarche to the Japanese government, and this time it was approved. The French chargé d'affaires in Tokyo was ordered to advise the Japanese government of the importance his government placed on the freeing of one of its citizens. And he got immediate results. The very next day, under orders from Tokyo—which still hoped to secure French recognition of Manchukuo and had every reason to cooperate, or at least to *appear* to cooperate—responsibility for the Kaspé case was officially transferred from Nikiforov to Osamu Eguchi, who was to work closely with the Kempeitai. Now that the case was attracting unwelcome international attention, Tokyo wanted it overseen by a Japanese rather than a Russian.

Eguchi was a safe choice. He had once headed the criminal investigation section of the Tokyo Metropolitan Police. But his appointment had not merely been a reflection of his perceived capability. Amleto Vespa recalled later that Eguchi had paid $100,000 a year to the Japanese military authorities for the privilege of holding the Harbin job.[28]

Reynaud finally secured an audience with Morito Morishima, the Japanese consul, who was more accommodating than his deputy had been. Morishima had reported on the Kaspé case to the Foreign Ministry the previous month. He pledged the assistance of the secret police and, if necessary, of the Guandong Army, in the search for Semyon—a promise he was not really in a position to deliver on.[29]

Reynaud had come to believe that the Russian Fascist Party had played a leading role in the kidnapping, and that it had close links with the Kempeitai as well as the Japanese general staff, both of which, of course, were part of the army. He noted also that several of the party's members were actually *employed* by the Tokumu Kikan—the Japanese Intelligence Service—ostensibly to provide information on Soviet activity in the city. That was the organization run by Amleto Vespa's boss.

For the first time, however, Reynaud reported that "we are on the trail of the kidnappers." He based this on a visit he had received that morning from L. N. Goroshkevich, chief of the Criminal Investigation Department of the Harbin Municipal Police and Nikolai Martinov (Martinov would shortly be taken off the case for unspecified reasons). The pair had also paid a call on Josef Kaspé to assure him his son would soon be freed. After receiving the news, Mr. Cosmé of the ministry immediately informed Marie Kaspé of this development and of his hope that the matter would soon be settled.[30]

His optimism was misplaced.

10

Search

Prior to the reassignment of the matter to Osamu Eguchi, while the inept and possibly compromised Nikiforov was still in charge of the investigation, the French diplomats in Harbin had concluded it was time to take matters into their own hands. While Reynaud was meeting with government officials and representatives of other nations, Chambon engaged as private detectives a man named Golubev, a member of the Brotherhood of Russian Truth but no friend of the fascists, and two other anti-Soviet Russians named Peters and Andreevich. These were men who regularly crossed the border into Russia to distribute anti-Soviet leaflets and carry out acts of sabotage. Chambon charged them with spearheading the Consulate's own search for Semyon and his abductors. He was careful to meet them in secret and outside of the Consulate, however, lest the police become aware that he had retained them.[1]

It didn't take long for the men, who had been offered a cash reward if they solved the crime, to latch onto Semyon's trail. They discovered he had been taken to Ashihe, a village on the railway some twenty-five miles southeast of Harbin. They also believed there had been nothing political about his kidnapping; it had been a criminal act with ransom and nothing else as its goal.

On October 9, the newspapers reported that Nikiforov's men arrested a man named Vasily Ivanov, not as part of the Kaspé investigation, but because he was suspected of having participated in earlier kidnappings. Ivanov allegedly confessed to a role in the abduction of Sherel de Florence the previous year, and implicated another man, Alexei Shandar, who had come to Harbin in 1922.

There is reason to doubt the Ivanov story; some have insisted that he was fictitious, invented by the police for one reason or another. But either because of his confession or for some other reason, Shandar was arrested and, under interrogation, confessed not only to a role in Sherel de Florence's abduction, but also to that of Meir Koffman in March of the previous year.[2]

Shandar named Dionisy Komissarenko, another member of the Brotherhood of Russian Truth, as a member of their gang and, most importantly, Nikolai Martinov as its leader. Martinov was the very officer in Yagi's Municipal Police force who had been asked to investigate the Kaspé kidnapping before being summarily removed from the case. He was subsequently arrested as well.

The *China Weekly Review* didn't miss the significance of the inclusion of Martinov's name on the list: "These arrests have thrown a lurid light upon the activities of certain 'White' Russians in North Manchuria. It has been repeatedly asserted that there were 'White' Russians in police employ there, as elsewhere in China, who are capable of every possible criminal activity. . . . Today it has been made terribly clear that this is absolutely true, that there were actually Russian murderers and bandits in police employ, chosen primarily because of their 'White' political complexion, and enabled to carry on their nefarious activities under police protection."[3]

Although Komissarenko was still at large, Shandar and Martinov were now in custody. The latter two denied any knowledge of the Kaspé abduction, and the police had no particular reason to link them to it until Komissarenko's name came up *again* in the following days when, in early October, a driver paid a call on Manager Gurevitch at the Moderne.

The man reported that several days before Semyon was abducted, two men had approached him with an offer of a million yen if he would lend his car for use in a kidnapping. He had refused, but he identified them to Gurevitch as Komissarenko and his brother-in-law, Panteleimon Bezruchko. Although Gurevitch had not had the presence of mind to take down the name or license number of the driver, he did pass the names on to the police, who immediately arrested Komissarenko. The latter was freed, however, ostensibly for lack of evidence, which Chambon took as further proof of complicity between the police and the bandits.[4]

Chambon's men hatched a plan to visit Ashihe and free Semyon, but they needed $150 for the mission, and perhaps because they had already been burned once, the Moderne managers proved agonizingly slow in coming up with the money. The delay proved costly. By the time they arrived in the town, the criminals had already departed with their captive.

Chambon's investigators did uncover some evidence in Ashihe, though. There was no question that the gang had hidden out there, and the locals confirmed that Komissarenko had been among its members. And so upon their return to Harbin, they hatched a plan to seize him on his next trip back to Harbin for supplies.

Komissarenko, who had grown up near Vladivostok in Russia's Far East and had graduated from a local vocational school, had been running a flour mill when the Russian Revolution broke out. The Bolsheviks had not only confiscated his property; they had also killed two of his brothers, and he therefore nursed a deep hatred for them. In 1931 his family was exiled to Zeya, not far from the Chinese border, and soon after, he and another brother had fled to Harbin.[5]

The kidnapping of Komissarenko was a cloak-and-dagger operation. After Chambon's private detectives found out from their sources which train he would be on, they determined to capture him upon his arrival at the Harbin railroad station. The night before, Chambon received a late-night phone call with the cryptic message "the jackal will be there tomorrow morning at eight o'clock," a prearranged signal that he was to position his car on a shady street near the station at the appointed time. And sure enough, at 8:15 the next morning, two of Chambon's detectives, each with a firm grip on a frightened Komissarenko, forced him into the car.

"This gentleman is Monsieur Chambon. He is the French vice-consul in Manchuria," one of the men told their silent prisoner as they headed for Chambon's home, confident that the police were unlikely to stop a vehicle bearing diplomatic plates. When they arrived, they placed him on the sofa in Chambon's living room and the Frenchman pointed a Colt revolver at his chest.

"You know who I am," Chambon said to him. "I know you are one of those who kidnapped Semyon Kaspé, whom it is my mission to protect. I'll give you three minutes to tell me your name, where you and your accomplices are holding Semyon Kaspé and who ordered you to kidnap him. If you do not answer all these questions, I will shoot you, and my friends and I will throw your body into the Sungari River."[6]

The threat was enough to persuade the terrified man to talk. He immediately began to name names. Assured that he would be released if he signed a confession, he implicated Nikifor Kirichenko, a known Russian Fascist who headed the gang and oversaw all communication with Semyon's family; Alexei Shandar and his brother; and Konstantin Galushko, the son of a deacon of the Russian Orthodox Church. In addition to Bezruchko, his own sister's husband—who had already been named by the driver who had visited Manager Gurevitch—he also fingered Yakov Zaitsev, a former contract killer in Shanghai and Tianjin, and Nikolai Martinov, the police inspector. It was now crystal clear that some of the very same Russians who had earlier seized Koffman, Tarasenko, and Sherel de Florence had also kidnapped Semyon Kaspé.[7] Komissarenko also revealed that the kidnappers had been recruited for their mission by none other than Kostya Nakamura of the Kempeitai, who had masterminded the kidnapping.[8]

Reynaud circulated Komissarenko's confession to all the foreign consuls in town, but he must have had second thoughts when he released the list of names to Eguchi. Doing so actually had the opposite effect of what he intended. Eguchi immediately informed Nakamura, and acting under the latter's orders, the Criminal Police arrested not those men, but rather Chambon's informants, Golubev, Peters, and Andrevitch.[9]

After Komissarenko was freed, Nakamura ordered him to the Soviet border and told him to lie low, but he did not make it there due to the intervention of Colonel Fukasi Oi, a retired military man who led the Railway Police, an entity apart from either of the local police forces in town. Oi, who was widely respected by local Chinese and foreigners alike, knew nothing of any police cooperation with the kidnappers. Tipped off to Komissarenko's flight, possibly by Chambon himself, he ordered his men to arrest the man en route.[10]

As Reynaud wrote to his superiors on October 10, "far more complicated political intrigues and personal rivalries than anticipated at the start of the investigation are delaying the release of Semyon Kaspé."[11]

This was an understatement.

One person to whom the French Consulate had not been able to get access was Semyon's chauffeur, who had been arrested early on. There had to have been an insider who was aware of Semyon's movements and was able to tip off the kidnappers as to where he would be on the night of August 24. According to the *North China Herald*, Josef Kaspé told a Russian newspaper he suspected the chauffeur might have been complicit, in part because he had heard that the man had put up no resistance to the kidnappers, despite the fact that he had been armed. "Go everywhere with my son and do not hesitate to use the revolver if you see that there is any danger," the old man had allegedly told the driver. Yet the man had not fired a shot.

Reynaud wrote his superiors on October 20 that a local newspaper had received an anonymous letter, presumably from the kidnappers, demanding the immediate release of Semyon's driver. Reynaud had raised his possible role in the kidnapping with the Japanese authorities, passing on "some precise information on certain shady establishments he frequented before the incident," and on relationships he claimed the man had had with "suspicious individuals." He urged them to initiate "a new, very severe and meticulous questioning" of the man.[12]

If the letter had indeed been from the kidnappers, their eagerness for the driver's release was certainly reason to believe he might have been working with them, though this was never proven. Two other men, however, *had* been watching Semyon's movements. One was Oleg Volgin, who was working as an interpreter for Nakamura and the Kempeitai; the second was a Greek named Fotopulo, a sometime hash house waiter who spent a good deal of his time loitering in the hotel's lobby. He had made it his business to find out which restaurants Semyon preferred, with whom he associated, when he was likely to leave the hotel, and what routes he usually took.

II

Letters

By letter and by telephone, the abductors kept reminding Josef Kaspé of their demands. And in a plaintive missive dated October 22 that reached his father just before the second-month anniversary of his abduction, Semyon himself wrote:

> After so much suffering, and after the letter written in my blood, I
> have heard that you have done almost nothing for me, and I can
> no longer address you as "Dear Father." You offered the kidnappers
> 50,000 yen,[1] and the same amount to the police. I now realize
> that only my death can convince you, and that as long as you deal
> with the police, you will not free me. Two months of my pain and
> suffering have not persuaded you. I know that you have said, "Let
> them make soup of my son; I won't give a penny more."
>
> Before all this began, I would have spit on the man who told
> me that, but today I believe it completely. You let Mother know
> everything, and you allowed her to come, knowing that she might
> not find me alive. Only a wild animal could do such a thing. I
> assume that it is necessary to tell you about every pain I am now
> suffering, covered in mud and lice, which make it impossible for
> me to sleep. I am shaking with cold and hunger, and undergoing
> indescribable sufferings. I do not know if I can ever forgive you. I am
> sick of writing; I want only to weep.
>
> My kidnappers have made a concession, and agreed to accept
> 200,000 yen, the other 100,000 yen to be paid after my release,
> under terms to be arranged between you in advance. You must break
> off all contact with the police; otherwise, you are leaving no hope
> of my release. All your measures and conversations with the police

are public knowledge, and you nevertheless stubbornly persist in your naïveté. If you continue to refuse, they will turn me over to the *honghuzi* [Chinese bandits], and then you can complete your collection of my body parts. You will then have to negotiate with the Chinese, and you know exactly what that means.

I have been unable to restrain myself. I wept like a child when I thought that "my dear father" was digging my grave with his own hands.

There is a rumor in the city that I am already dead. My letter will convince you that it is untrue. But that does not move you. I know that you are telling everybody that you offered them 150,000 yen, and they would not agree. You could at least have started the negotiations with this sum, but you did not do that, either. Perhaps one day, I will be able to tell you the intimate details of what I have been through, and then I shall look at my poor mother and at poor Volodya and at their sorrow.

Since you have refused the kidnappers, they wanted to cut off one of my fingers today. Only my entreaties and prayers made them relent. Yes, it has come to that. Unfortunately, you will not be able to admire the results of your handiwork.

I cannot write any more. My suffering is over, and my nerves refuse to accept help. I beg you: when they call you, answer the telephone yourself. Do not make excuses; everyone knows you are not ill.

I have nothing more to say to you.

Au revoir,

Senya

The previous regular code will be replaced by a new one.
Papa, you remember our conversation about the trip to Dalian, just before the kidnapping . . . that is to convince you that this letter is genuine, and contains no fraudulent attempt at extortion.

S. Kaspé[2]

The postscript was not written in Semyon's hand, however, and the "code" in question was thought to be an account number at the Far Eastern

Bank, or Dalbank, the principal Russian credit institution in the Far East. Chambon believed the entire letter had been dictated by the bandits.

Josef explained himself in a response dated October 30 that he paid to have published in the local Russian newspapers, since he had no other way to get it to his son. It seems to have been calculated to persuade the kidnappers to lower their demands:

Dear Senya,
You are well aware of our situation, and the state of our business, and I am very surprised that you totally ignore it in your letters. You are perfectly aware that I have never had liquid cash in my possession, and that I have always had debts.

Several years ago, when I separated from my partners in the Hotel Moderne, I mortgaged the house and the store at Hong Kong Bank in order to pay them their share. In recent years, the worldwide depression and inflation have severely damaged my business, especially the movie house. In order to avoid bankruptcy and cover my debts, I took a second mortgage on the properties. To this day, because of poor business, I have not paid the bank a cent on the loan. Furthermore, two years ago, I registered the house and the store in your names, you and Volodya, and you then became the owners of the properties. The house and store have second mortgages on them, and no bank will give money for a third mortgage. Legally, I cannot even ask for one, because nothing has belonged to me since I put all the properties to your names.

Selling the Hotel Moderne is impossible under the current conditions, and even if there were a potential buyer, I could not sell it without you, since the Hotel Moderne is under your ownership.

Even if we sell the house and the store, and after we return the money to Hong Kong Bank, to various people, and to all the public institutions, which is compulsory in the event of a sale, the remaining sum is still smaller than the ransom that has been demanded.

The best proof is those two months of suffering, yours and mine, during which I have been unable to save you.

Dear Senitchka, if you only knew how many sleepless nights and how many terrible days I have been through, trying to find the means of saving you, but to my great sorrow and deep despair, I cannot obtain more money than I have offered the kidnappers.

I am at the mercy of God and the good will of your kidnappers . . . Your dear father[3]

Apparently the kidnappers were well aware of Josef Kaspé's predicament, at least as far as the problem of the registration of his property went. They had earlier deposited a letter at the home of a Russian bank employee that contained Semyon's signed power of attorney permitting the sale of the Moderne, but it never reached the elder Kaspé.[4]

Reynaud wrote his superiors on November 2 that he no longer believed the promises of the Japanese officials in charge of the case and was certain the kidnappers were in bed with them. Komissarenko had told Chambon as much. "Some confidential revelations that were made to me on behalf of subordinate agents of the Japanese police and gendarmerie arouse in me doubts about the sincerity and impartiality of their services, in which, in the absence of evidence to the contrary, we can no longer have more than limited confidence," he reported. "The evil from which the Harbin police has always suffered, seems, in fact, to have spread and contaminated certain elements of the Japanese police."

Chambon also believed the kidnappers had complete knowledge of his *own* actions, which were not undertaken without danger. He worried aloud about "the risk of exposing myself personally to the vendetta of the thugs who really seemed to be perfectly aware of all the official and private steps attempted to obtain the deliverance of their prisoner."[5]

Josef Kaspé was deeply depressed by the situation and Semyon's apparent inability to understand his financial predicament; Chambon remarked that at times the man seemed to "lose the sense of reality." Abraham Pevsner continued negotiating with the kidnappers via telephone or through intermediaries, and despite later accusations that Josef Kaspé had ordered him to play for time, there is no indication he was anything but deadly serious about it. After all, prolonging the negotiations had already resulted

FIG. 17. Albert Henri Chambon. Courtesy of the Chambon family.

in harm to Semyon. Freeing the young man, however it was accomplished, was the only goal. Pevsner had apparently offered them 50,000 yen and promised the same sum to the police if they could free him.

And, indeed, he made progress. The kidnappers were well aware of Komissarenko's capture and they may have felt the net closing in on them. It certainly appeared as though they were running out of time. It was at this point that they moved their prisoner yet again, to a location further from the city. And they lowered their demand to a down payment of 100,000 yen and a guarantee of an additional 100,000 after Semyon was set free. Chambon attributed their willingness to accept less money as a sign of alarm on the part of Nakamura, who feared that prolonging the affair raised the chances of a revelation of Japanese involvement and, consequently, a loss of face for Japan.[6]

A November 11 letter from Semyon, likely dictated in whole or in part by his kidnappers, confirmed the revised terms:

Papa,
I know about the latest conversation of Abraham [Pevsner] with my kidnappers. You have been stubborn for a month about offering 50,000 yen. You have apparently offered the same amount as a reward to the police, and you still claim that you have no access to the immovable property of the Hotel Moderne, because it belongs to me. It all sounds very disingenuous.

My kidnappers are well aware that you have decided to pay 50,000 yen to several policemen for finding me (they know exactly who the policemen are). I have been a prisoner for two and a half months, and you can be sure now that their searches have been completely fruitless. It is absurd to ask Abraham to confirm the situation. No less ridiculous is your declaration that you have no right to sell the properties. They know, as does everyone in town, that you are and have always been the owner of the Hotel Moderne, and if Volodya and I have been made the owners in name, it was only to enable you to make the hotel a French property. You are mocking them if you think you can get out of this cheaply. Do not forget that I will be exposed to more amputations if you continue this way.

They have notified me that they agree to reduce the ransom. They demand 100,000 yen, and another 100,000 yen to be delivered 10 days (or more, if necessary) after my release, which you will have to promise. They absolutely refuse your offer of 50,000 yen. There is no need even to discuss it, or to waste time over it. They demand that you abandon the services of the police, and that you conduct serious negotiations.

My kidnappers wish to finish the matter, and for that purpose consent to any reasonable discount on the amount, but for that, you must act sincerely and openly, and not treat people as if they were naïve.

I repeat: it is better if you answer the telephone yourself. You remember that you answered the telephone one time, and for some unexplained reason, refused to speak (Micha the servant said you were not at home, when you had answered it a few minutes before). Such acts enraged my kidnappers, and led them to cut off part of my ear for the second time. Do not forget that you are continuing to play with fire. My kidnappers intend to finish the whole affair, if possible in the next few days. That is unquestionably why the negotiations have become more urgent, and you must accede to their terms, because they are trying to simplify the terms of my ransom.

If you are considering remaining obstinate, and offering them the same sum again, making up all sorts of stories, and playing the same game (it may be entertaining for you, but not for me, and not for them), then it is best to discontinue the negotiations, and give up any idea of ransoming me and the hope of freeing me. All you have to do is answer the question: yes or no. There is no other way out. If the answer is yes, you will have to come to an arrangement with the kidnappers for the terms of my release. You have the opportunity to free me tomorrow, or the day after. There is no need for me to speak with you about my situation, and all the suffering I am going through.

I heard rumors that Mama would arrive soon, or had already arrived. They told me that she was in Harbin. It requires the greatest cruelty on your part not to allow her to see me, when the meeting could take place at any time.

You propose that the kidnappers give me your letter. That is not essential. They know everything: your plans and your behavior. You can call them directly, or through one of their people. It would be more correct to send me more essential things; that would be more logical.

My kidnappers are presenting you with more reasonable terms than their original demand. They will try to arrive at another reduction, but it depends on you alone, not on anyone else. Finish it quickly. Do not forget that human beings have limited strength.

I hope you are healthy . . .

Semyon[7]

12

Playing with Fire

In the meantime, some progress was made on following Semyon's trail. On November 13, Reynaud was granted a two-hour meeting with Colonel Michitarō Komatsubara, chief of the Tokumu Kikan in Harbin, which was responsible for military intelligence gathering. The colonel promised him the assistance of the Kempeitai and the police. Kostya Nakamura of the Kempeitai, however, later imposed a condition on committing his men to aiding in the search: he would have to be cut in personally on the reward. Seeing no alternative, Chambon agreed to his terms.[1]

Three days later, guided by Komissarenko, a posse consisting of the deputy chief of the Kempeitai, four of his agents, two police detectives, Chambon, and his detectives—who had apparently been set free by this time—set out for Ercengdianzi, a railway station forty-three miles southeast of Harbin. The plan was for Chambon's men and the Japanese officials, who were in full uniform, to hide and for Komissarenko to proceed to the hideout alone so as not to arouse suspicion and thus not trigger the murder of Semyon. It was agreed he might spare Bezruchko, his brother-in-law, who was one of Semyon's guards, but he was to shoot the two others he expected would be there.

Komissarenko led the party to a crude shelter made of branches in a deserted wooded area where Kaspé had been held, but his captors had already abandoned the position. In the rubble of the hut were empty cans and bottles, scraps of newspapers, a vial of iodine, and a blood-stained length of linen, which Komissarenko identified as the bandage used to stanch Semyon's bleeding after his ear had been severed.

They guessed Semyon would likely have been too weak to travel any distance, so they suspected he and his kidnappers were not far away. So although the rest of the expedition returned to Harbin that night,

Chambon's agents remained on-site with Komissarenko, promising to telephone for reinforcements the next day if they were able to locate the new encampment. Chambon summed it up this way in a note to the ministry on November 25: "Despite the assistance of Japanese gendarmes and detectives, and perhaps even *because* of this assistance, our officers were unable to locate the bandits and their victim."[2]

Indeed, Nakamura, who of course knew all about the expedition, had ordered the kidnappers to move on yet again. And, surely anticipating a possible denouement in the near future, they once again lowered the ransom demand, though they rejected the stipulation of simultaneous payment and release of their prisoner on which Josef Kaspé continued to insist. Semyon made mention of the new terms in what he believed would be his last communication with his father. Reading between the lines of his letter, written on November 17 or 18, suggests that the kidnappers were feeling increasingly desperate, and eager to put an end to the situation.[3]

Dear Father,

I appeal to you for the last time, to the father I still love, despite the memories I have since the day I was kidnapped, and despite all your faults.

You are sentencing me to death now; unless you accept the kidnappers' terms within three days of receiving this letter, they will shoot me. This decision will be carried out without pity, despite all my pleas. They told me this today, and all I could obtain was a reduction in the ransom. You must first give 75,000 yen, and another 50,000 yen no more than 10 days after my release. The terms that Abraham offered in his last conversation were completely unacceptable. The money must be delivered first, and only after 48 hours will I be released.

Your offer, thank you, is totally naïve. All the concessions they made to you so far were made in order not to delay my release, and finish the matter as soon as possible. When you imagine that you can make all sorts of offers, you are apparently still trying to mislead my kidnappers with clearly unreasonable demands. Instead of finally reaching a compromise agreement, your proposals are making negotiations impossible. You have reached a point where if you refuse, my death awaits you.

You have subjected me to torture twice, and now inescapable death awaits me. They reach a hand out to me, and pity me, when they see that I am a victim of the cruelty and unreason of my father, while you only insult them, and thereby bring my end nearer. In another few days, I will have been a prisoner for three months. The day of my release is receding, the day of my death approaching.

The last time, they proposed that you pay 75,000 yen, and 100,000 yen after my release. After great effort, I have now achieved a new discount: 75,000 yen before my release, and 50,000 yen after.

It has been decided to grant no more discounts. They are giving you three days to consider, and in the event of your refusal or other excuses on your part, on Wednesday I will no longer be in this world. I have officially committed myself to pay the remaining sum after my release, but I asked that they reduce the amount, since I cannot promise the sum of 100,000 yen. As you see, due to the sincerity of my request, they have reduced the amount by half. Together with the first payment of 75,000 yen, you must attach a letter with the signatures of two guarantors, in which you commit yourself to pay 50,000 yen within the allotted time. In the opposite case, the responsibility will fall not only on you, but on your guarantors. My kidnappers are designing a quick and extreme means of forcing you to pay the required amount. In such a case, you and your guarantors will suffer, because this device will be very painful.

It is easy for you to pay the first sum. The movie house alone, where I have heard a series of war movies was screened, gives you the means to pay, not to mention the hotel and all our jewels, for which you can obtain a great deal of money.

You, father, are an excellent organizer and a brilliant trader. You know that I have always appreciated these qualities. On more than one occasion, you have rescued our business from a critical state, whether because of our partners, or because of fate. Is there nothing you can do to save my life? We have the means to pay the money demanded for me. You should not let a matter of money stop you. You have simply decided to play some kind of game, without recognizing that you are playing with fire. Your game can end in my death. Were Mother and Volodya here, I would have no worries about my fate.

Father, I cannot believe you would permit me to die, and that you would willfully and indifferently be my murderer. If that is the case, then there is no justice in the world. I am convinced that this will not happen, and that in another few days, I will again be a free man. You say that you are fearful now; consider in what state I am. I am totally exhausted from all I have experienced and suffered. In another three long and terrible days, the day of my death may arrive, should you not wish to save me. I beg you to save me. It is possible; for my part, I feel now the same feelings that a person feels who has been sentenced to death.

You are the only one who can grant me a reprieve. Do not cause me any more suffering; agree to ransom me on Sunday. Do not conduct useless and worthless negotiations; do not propose unacceptable terms through Abraham for carrying out the ransom. That means refusal, and death for me. You ask in what state I am. Your question is strange. Do you not understand what I have become, after three months of living under the most terrible conditions: hunger, cold, dampness, lice, sleeplessness, and mud? I have already written a great deal to you of these matters. It would be better to send me more essential things: bread, clothes, *etc.* Mother would not have asked me such a question; she would not have acted in this way.

Father, this is my last letter. Act to prevent your being informed of my death. You will receive no more letters from me. Either they will send you my head, or you will never see my body, and will not know where it is. Remember that Koffman disappeared without a trace.

For the last time, I beg you to save me, and not prolong my suffering. I have three days left, and I so much want to live. Father, think what awaits me, when they tell me of your refusal, and of my death sentence. Then it will be too late. Dear father, do not permit

it. You love me, and despite all the evil you have done me, I love you. Do not prolong my sufferings before my death. Do not kill me.
    Your son,
    Semyon[4]

At the same time, Semyon penned a farewell to his mother and brother, in part, perhaps, as a means of further ratcheting up the pressure on his father. How much of it was included by order of his captors is, of course, unknowable.

Dear Mother and Volodya,
Who would have believed, who would have thought that this would be my last letter before my death? Unless Father releases me within three days from the imprisonment in which I have been held for the past three months, I will be executed. I do not know where you are right now, or what is happening to you.
    You, Mother, are probably planning to go to Harbin, and you, Voloditzka, are already in Paris, after finishing your military service, and you are surely completely preoccupied in the affairs that you love. How pleasant it must be to return to your old life, full of renewed energy. I also felt like that, until now. I wanted to live so much, to use my unrealized strength (unrealized because of my stupidity and passivity) to change and reorganize my life.
    I cannot believe that things are this way, and that all this is only a dream. I am in a very low, cold building. Today is a holiday for me; I have something to eat. I am in the company of strangers guarding me night and day. Today I am writing for the last time. Father, because of his refusal, is sentencing me to death.
    You, my dear ones, must recognize the whole truth. If I die, Father will bear sole responsibility for my death. He has killed me. I curse him, I curse the day he made me, and I beg you to refuse to see him again. You, Volodya, do not abandon our dear mother. As my last wish before my death, I trust you to take care of Mother, and give her all the hugs she deserves. You must build her a home, treasure her in her old age, and not abandon her while she is alive. You will be the only source of support in her life. He who was husband and

father for you can no longer live with you. It will be easier for me to die that way. Try not to think about him, and do not forgive him, as I myself have done. He behaved cruelly to me, and was the cause of my torture. Twice they cut off pieces of my ear, and they disfigured my face and my body. Father knew, and allowed it to happen. Despite everything, I forgive him.

It is dark here. I wrote to my close friends every day, and asked them to urge Father not to let me die. My eyes are trembling; I must finish.

I feel better after having spoken to you. During the entire period of my imprisonment, I was with you. In three more days, I may not be alive. I know well that my father has consigned me to die innocent, because, ever since I was born, I have been unable to meet his expectations.

I loved people devotedly and sincerely, and did evil to no one during my life. How ironic it is to die because of the man I loved so much.

My body will not be returned to you, but will be buried, and not abused. Take my personal effects, my papers, and my music. To Lydia Shapiro, I leave some of my notebooks and music pages as a keepsake.

What can I say to you in my final hour? I have always loved you with all my heart. I leave you everything that is dear to me. I will think of you in my last hour. I am brave, and will not lose my sanity. Establish a memorial in my memory.

Yours, and only yours,
Semyon[5]

13

Arrest

Semyon Kaspé's abductors had anticipated the possibility of one or more of them being arrested. If that occurred, Komissarenko told Chambon's detectives, they had planned to move their captive to a new hiding place further down the eastern branch of the railway near Xiaoling, about forty-six miles southeast of Harbin. After the Kempeitai and police officers returned to Harbin, the detectives spent several days in that area, convinced it was where Kaspé was now being held.

Komissarenko didn't know the camp's exact coordinates, however, because after his coconspirators learned of his arrest they had refused to reveal any additional information to him. But local people reported that four Russian bandits who were not from the area had arrived a week earlier with a rich prisoner, and an employee of the railway recalled seeing a man traveling frequently between Xiaoling Station and Harbin, generally on the night freight trains, whose description matched that of Galushko. By observing the light of a campfire at night, the detectives were able to ascertain the encampment's approximate location.

To rush in and attempt to free the captive would be unwise, however. They did not know how well armed the kidnappers were, and a sudden ambush would surely endanger Semyon's life. So they hatched a plan to seize one or more of the men during a return trip to Harbin for supplies. That way they might learn the exact location of the camp. Since a supply trip was sure to involve a visit to Komissarenko's home, two of Chambon's detectives would hide out there and spring a trap.

Chambon knew they would need reinforcements, however, and so against his better judgment, he turned to the Kempeitai. Colonel Komatsubara, chief of the Tokumu Kikan, had promised their cooperation, but it was Kostya Nakamura who was calling the shots at the Kempeitai, and

Chambon already had good reason to believe him complicit in the kidnapping. Komissarenko had already said as much. Nevertheless, seeing no other option, he asked Nakamura on November 20 to supply several armed Kempeitai officers for the mission. And true to form, Nakamura proved an obstacle. He agreed to support the mission, but only on the promise of a 10,000 yen bribe. And even then he would send only one officer, and arm him with a single pistol.[1]

At six p.m. the following day, Kirichenko, the gang leader, arrived at Komissarenko's house together with Galushko and Shandar. They carried two Mauser pistols each. Lying in wait for them, but hidden, were two of Chambon's detectives and the lone Kempeitai officer.

"Find us warm trousers, with fur lining, and we'll soon travel to the line," Kirichenko ordered Komissarenko.

Komissarenko asked where the men were hiding out.

"It's none of your business," Kirichenko answered. "We'll set a meeting place later. We're in a dangerous situation. The police aren't responsible for these searches; the French Consulate is, and they're the ones we're afraid of. Tomorrow, I'll ask the Hotel Moderne people for the 75,000 yen we're supposed to get before we release Semyon. If they refuse, it's better to kill him and try to escape."

Although Chambon's plan had called for the Kempeitai to take the kidnappers into custody, Nakamura had apparently given the lone officer different orders. He refused to fire his gun and would not permit Chambon's detectives to move against the men, who left Komissarenko's home unmolested. When asked why he had not acted, the officer replied, "First of all, I make only $5 a month. I don't want to risk my life for that amount of money. Secondly, there's no guarantee that the pistols and bullets supplied by the police will work. Finally, I haven't been given any such instruction."[2]

In other words, Nakamura had deliberately sabotaged the entire operation. Even his own man doubted he had been supplied with workable ammunition.

The next day, November 22, Kirichenko called the Hotel Moderne, as he had said he would. The hotel managers were expecting his call and they agreed to the ransom demand, but still insisted that the payment

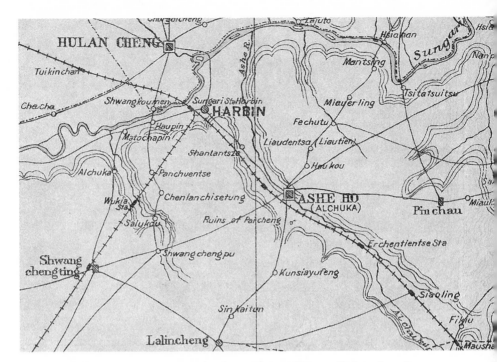

MAP 4. Detail from a map showing the three Chinese Eastern Railway locations southeast of Harbin where Semyon Kaspé was held captive: Ashe Ho (Ashihe), Erchentientse (Ercengdianzi), and Siaoling (Xiaoling). "Kirin, Harbin, Vladivostok," U.S. Adjutant-General's Office, Second Division, General Staff (Military Information Division), Washington DC, April 1905.

and Semyon's release be simultaneous. This, however, was a nonstarter for Semyon's captors, who ceased all communication for several days after that. Their silence was ominous. Chambon now articulated what everyone in Harbin was thinking: "There is more reason than ever to be worried about the fate of Semyon Kaspé."

Early in the afternoon of November 24, Bezruchko recalled later, Kirichenko and Galushko returned to Xiaoling to relieve him and permit him to go back to Harbin. They got off the train just shy of the station and made their way to the hideout, where Kirichenko told the men he now believed their chances of obtaining a ransom were small. He complained to Semyon about how stubborn the Moderne managers were being about payment.

"Your affairs are becoming complicated," he grumbled. "You've cost us a lot of money—almost $800." He was talking about the expense of supplies for keeping Semyon in hiding.

"It's not my fault you kidnapped me," Semyon pointed out. "When you let me go, I'll pay you whatever you want."

"All right, we'll free you tonight," Kirichenko promised. Then he spoke privately with two of his accomplices and mused to himself for a half hour. Finally, after much hesitation, while the others were drinking tea, he pulled his gun out of his pocket. Without a word, he aimed at Semyon and shot him through the throat. The young man immediately fell to the ground, dead. It had been three torturous months, almost exactly to the day, since his capture.

Then the men sprang into action. They undressed Semyon and burned his clothes, together with other items in the hideout, in an effort to leave no trace of him. Then they wrapped his body in the tarpaulin that had covered the hut, borrowed a spade from a nearby farmer, dug a shallow grave at the foot of a rock, and buried him, taking care to cover the grave with earth, stones and snow.[3]

On November 28, the police allowed Komissarenko to return to his home, though he remained under surveillance. They hoped to use him to snare the rest of the gang. With Semyon dead, there was no longer any reason to camp out in the wilderness, so Kirichenko, who despite Semyon's death still intended to negotiate a ransom, sent his younger brother to Komissarenko's home with instructions for the men to meet at five p.m. the next day in a freight yard behind the railway station. The brother was arrested, however, and, having intercepted the messages, the police and Chambon's men made plans for an ambush.

Sunset occurred at about four p.m. in Harbin at that time of year, so they planned to station four vehicles with sixteen Russian police and Japanese Kempeitai officers, Chambon's men, and Komissarenko in the immediate area. The police were to shine their headlights on the kidnappers when they showed up to render them clearly visible, and then to shoot them.

Bezruchko and Zaitsev didn't make it to the rendezvous; that same day, they were arrested by Colonel Oi's Railway Police. The pair were seized just as they were about to board a train.[4]

Early on November 29, Chambon got into a heated argument with the Moderne managers about the 50,000 yen reward the latter had offered to anyone who found Semyon. Chambon's investigators were counting on that money if they solved the case, but now the hotel managers were insisting it would be paid only if Semyon were found alive. Frustrated, Chambon agreed that the Consulate would pay the reward itself if Semyon were found dead, but the delay meant that neither he nor Golubev, his chief detective, arrived in time for the showdown. Only his two other detectives, Peters and Andreevich, were on the scene with the authorities when the kidnappers arrived behind the railway station.

Like every other time Chambon's detectives had sought the cooperation of the officials, their plans that afternoon were undermined. Kirichenko and Galushko quickly realized they had walked into a trap. They drew their pistols and opened fire. On Nakamura's orders, however, the police refused to shoot back and dropped to the ground instead. Only Peters and Andreevich attempted to return fire, but the guns they had been given by the police were defective and failed to discharge—surely no accident. During the melee, Konstantin Galushko was shot through the heart by one of his compatriots. Some said it was Komissarenko who did it, but by most accounts it was Kirichenko. The latter was wounded but managed to flee the scene alone.[5]

Once again Nakamura had disrupted a plan that might otherwise have been successful. It certainly seemed as if his aim was to protect, rather than subdue, the kidnappers.

Although Kirichenko got away, most of those involved in the kidnapping—directly or tangentially—had now been arrested. Shandar and Martinov were already in custody. They were now joined by Bezruchko and Zaitsev, courtesy of Colonel Oi, as well as the brothers of Kirichenko and Shandar and their wives, plus Martinov's wife. All were detained by the police.

By this time, Nakamura had officially notified the French Consulate that Semyon had been murdered by his kidnappers, feigning disappointment that there would be no good news for the young man's father. Once the prisoners told the authorities where the hideout was located, Chambon wanted to set out immediately for Xiaoling to recover the body of his friend. But Nakamura dragged his feet. Finally, Chambon and his investigators decided to go by themselves on what they had reason to believe might be a dangerous mission, since Kirichenko was still at large and thought to be heavily armed. At dawn on December 2, they set out for Xiaoling.[6]

When they arrived, they climbed to a mountaintop that commanded a panoramic view of the heavily wooded area. From there they followed footprints in the snow to a ravine that bore evidence of a recently extinguished campfire and other small clues that convinced them Kaspé had been held there. Continuing their search, they discovered the ruins of crude shelters made with tree branches, which they assumed had been temporary way stations for the kidnappers and their prisoner.

The next day, the gendarmes showed up at Xiaoling with Bezruchko in tow. He led the group to the campsite they had visited the day before, where, a few dozen feet away, they found the shallow grave that held the remains of Semyon Kaspé. They had unknowingly been standing on top of it. He had been buried just a foot and a half from the surface. His half-naked, emaciated body, covered with lice, dirt, and bruises and wrapped only in a canvas, was exhumed. Chambon recalled the horrible sight later, noting that "his face expressed suffering and his body had become skeletal from deprivation." The next day, December 4, it was carried to Xiaoling Station to be returned to Harbin by train for a proper Jewish funeral.[7]

14

Lies

When Nakamura notified the French Consulate of Semyon's death, Chambon had extracted a promise from him that he would not release the news to the press until his colleagues had had a chance to inform the Kaspé family. He was especially concerned that Marie Kaspé, who was shortly due to arrive in Shanghai on her way home, not learn of her son's death through the newspapers.

"I give you my word, Mr. Vice-Consul, that nothing will appear in the press," Chambon remembered Nakamura saying to him. The Frenchman was thus astonished when reporters from several Harbin newspapers accosted him at the Xiaoling Station asking about the circumstances of Semyon's death. Chambon initially lied and said that his trip had had nothing to do with the Kaspé case, but the reporters knew better. When they showed him clippings revealing the death that had already appeared in local papers, he realized that Nakamura, who was standing on the platform nearby with three of his officers, had engaged in one final act of treachery.

Chambon was beyond furious. Grabbing the clippings, he approached the Japanese and said to him in a loud voice, "Colonel, I already knew how the Japanese army achieved victory in Manchuria, but I did not know that a colonel of your army could break his word as you did." And with that, in a calculated insult, and in full view of many Russian and Chinese travelers who were also waiting for the train, Chambon slapped him on each cheek with the papers. Nakamura turned beet red and reached for his sword, but one of his officers said something to him in Japanese and restrained him. However grievous the insult, it would not do to strike a European diplomat.[1]

For her part, Marie Kaspé arrived in Shanghai on December 4, 1933, and stopped overnight at the Palace Hotel on the Bund. At the telegraphed request of her husband, local friends did all they could to shield her from the news of her son's murder, but she learned of it from a local paper. She was unable to make it to Harbin in time for her elder son's funeral.[2]

Perhaps it was just as well. Amleto Vespa recounted that Josef Kaspé had insisted on viewing his son's body, which was in the custody of the *chevra kadisha*, before burial. When the wooden coffin was opened and he was confronted with the mutilated, gangrenous, and emaciated corpse of his elder son, he let out a loud wail. Josef suffered a nervous breakdown that day and never recovered from the shock.[3]

Vespa was present at the viewing. "Ninety-five days of captivity had almost reduced him to a skeleton," the Italian wrote of poor Semyon. "The frightful cold of North Manchuria, which reaches 25° and 30° below zero in November, had frozen his cheeks, his nose and hands so that pieces of flesh had fallen off and gangrene had set in." The sight of him, he added, "made me feel glad he could suffer no more."[4]

Harbin's townspeople were indignant about the crime. All of Semyon's father's businesses closed their doors on the day of the funeral, as did most establishments on the city's main streets. Thousands lined the streets on December 5 to pay their respects as the cortege passed by; Chambon, who was present, recalled "practically the entire Russian population" turning out and shouting, "Death to the Japanese militarists! Death to the savage brutes! Death to the damned monkeys!" What was most shocking, apart from the condition of Semyon's body, was the involvement of Martinov, a police officer, in the plot. This engendered a good deal of resentment against the authorities, and so out of an abundance of caution, the Japanese Army sent in 250 gendarmes and an entire regiment of the infantry to keep order during the procession and the funeral.[5]

Dr. Abraham Kaufman delivered a eulogy at one of the synagogues before Semyon was laid to rest in the Jewish cemetery on Bolshoi Avenue. He said, in part: "The Jews were the first people in the world to declare the commandment 'Thou shalt not kill'. We do not pursue revenge, but we seek legal protection of our lives and property. The state authorities have an obligation to establish peace. The authorities must fight against and sweep out the bandits who foment the hatred of citizens against Jews and sow seeds of discord among citizens."[6] But other portions of his speech were more strident, including an assertion that "a country that allows bandits and assassins to harm innocents has no right to exist." The Tokyo-funded *Manchuria Daily News* reported that he had accused the city authorities of bearing partial responsibility for Semyon Kaspé's death.[7]

Although the Russian-language *Zarya* initially reported positively on Kaufman's remarks, the *Manchuria Daily* castigated him for "a fierce, anti-Manchukuo speech." The next day, he was called in and dressed down by the Japanese military mission. *Nash Put*, the Fascist paper, plowed in right behind the mission, denouncing his "nonsense talk" two days later. It portrayed him as "strongly against the Russian and the local authority," called for his expulsion from Manchuria, and asserted that Jews were welcome to leave if they did not like it there.[8]

"Moses took the Jews out of Egypt, so why doesn't Kaufman take the Jews out of Manchukuo?" the newspaper demanded, rhetorically.[9]

Apparently all the criticism alarmed Kaufman, because on December 9, *Zarya* reported that he had called on Nikolai Yagi to clarify that he had not intended an attack on the Manchurian authorities or their representatives.[10]

Kaufman wasn't the only target of what was shaping up to be a major hatchet job, however. Forces also began to mobilize against Albert Chambon. His dogged pursuit of the kidnappers had been the driving force behind their capture, which would never have occurred apart from his efforts, and both the Japanese police and the Russian Fascist Party knew it all too well. The police felt he had made them look, at best, incompetent, and at worst corrupt. Nor did it help when he made a statement to the newspapers on December 5 that the local police authorities were "powerless." Within a few days, he was skewered in the local press, a false story of how the case had actually been solved was fabricated, and pressure began to mount for his ouster from Manchukuo.[11]

Konstantin Rodzaevsky denounced the Catholic Chambon as a "dirty communist Jew" in the pages of *Nash Put*, and went so far as to challenge him to a duel. On December 7, *Harbinskoe Vremya* (Harbin Times), the most widely read local newspaper, which had a circulation of twenty-five thousand and was published in Russian but controlled by the Japanese Consulate, reported on "authoritative conversations" with unnamed officials who were ostensibly knowledgeable about the French diplomat's activities. Chambon was accused of having counseled Josef Kaspé not to negotiate in good faith with his son's kidnappers, and the paper asserted that if the diplomat had worked with the authorities, the young man would have been saved. He was further reported to have told a local journalist to "go to hell" and to have sought undue credit—at the expense of the Municipal Police—for solving the crime.[12]

Needless to say, there was little truth in this version of events. Although it was widely believed, and widely reported after the fact, that Josef Kaspé had played for time and been coy about negotiations with the kidnappers, the fact remained that he had always been unable to pay for his son's release. And there is no indication at all that Chambon had coached him to prolong the negotiations, or to bargain in bad faith; the Frenchman himself denied it. Nor could the accusations that Chambon had not worked with the authorities, or that Semyon's life could have been saved if he had, have been further from reality. In fact, at every turn it was the authorities who had impeded progress in the search.

The following day, the same newspaper carried an even more inflammatory item. It alleged that during a search of a Harbin print shop, police had discovered documents in French, English, and Russian purportedly written by Chambon and "ready for distribution." They allegedly expressed "violent criticism" of the local police. The pamphlets were said to accuse the police of putting obstacles in the way of the private detectives hired by the French Consulate, which, of course, they had.

Reynaud had reported to his superiors that he had provided the Japanese Consulate with an impartial statement of the facts of the case. Such a document, penned by Chambon, survives in the archives of the French Foreign Ministry; it may have been one of the those cited by *Harbinskoe Vremya*, if indeed there was any truth to its report. Later reporting suggesting the print shop documents had been found together with a cache of anti-Manchukuo literature suggests that the entire story is untrue. If these materials existed at all, the paper did not publish them. It reported further, however, that there was talk in local government circles "of either expelling Mr. Chambon from the country, or of making a serious protest against his more than strange actions."[13]

It turned out it was more than talk. Shortly after Chambon slapped Nakamura, Consul Reynaud received an official letter declaring his deputy persona non grata and ordering him to leave Harbin within twenty-four hours. As a matter of fact, even before the discovery of Semyon Kaspé's body, Chambon was already slated by the French Foreign Ministry for reassignment to its Tianjin consulate. After learning of the letter, however, the Ministry deliberately delayed his departure for a few weeks, lest anyone conclude that it was bending to the Japanese order.[14]

Reynaud did order Chambon to stop talking to the press, however, and for his own safety he was no longer able to move about town freely. But when the consul sent the clippings to Beijing and to the Foreign Ministry in Paris, he made sure to let his colleagues know what he thought of the disparagements of his deputy:

> On the whole, the criticisms leveled against Mr. Chambon are not based on any serious foundation and are absolutely undeserved; they can only have been formulated as dictated by the resentment of the competent authorities at the failure of the research carried out by their agents. It is indeed thanks to the urgent steps and the insistence of this Consulate, and to the sagacity of the special agents that he had hired in his service, that the trail of the kidnappers could be found, the arrests made, and a gang of dangerous recidivist criminals and kidnapping specialists locked up.[15]

By the middle of December, Chambon had left Harbin for the safety of Tianjin, which, of course, was not yet under Japanese jurisdiction.[16]

Reynaud was quite concerned about the campaign against local Jews being carried out in *Nash Put*, Konstantin Rodzaevsky's daily, which was rumored to be subsidized by the Japanese military mission. On December 8, it carried an article deeply critical of community leader Abraham Kaufman for his opposition to "the Russian and the local authority." It distorted his words and urged the Japanese authorities to expel him. For good measure, it also urged all Jews to leave Manchuria. Reynaud informed his ministry that several consulates had teamed up to press the

Japanese authorities to put an end to the smear campaign, and that they had agreed to do so.[17]

But the Japanese-controlled newspaper was not the only place where Chambon and the French Consulate generally came in for a drubbing. The police were angry, too. Chambon's version of the story, which highlighted their incompetence and corruption, constituted an unbearable loss of face for them. They got busy crafting their own narrative in which they would play the starring role in apprehending the kidnappers.

On December 15, Osamu Eguchi, head of the Criminal Police, released a statement about how Kaspé was killed and how his body had been found. It gave no credit at all to the French Consulate or to the detectives it had retained. He refuted the French version of the story in some detail. Much of his response appeared in the Shanghai-based *China Weekly Review*. Among his comments:

> On the accusation that the police did not make arrests, even after Chambon provided them with a list of the kidnappers: "The French detectives knew nothing of the crime. . . . They were entirely on the wrong trail, and consequently there was no exigency for arresting the fascist leaders, who had nothing to do with the crime."
>
> On the assertion that the police should not have freed Komissarenko after his arrest: "Komissarenko . . . was freed on purpose in pursuance of the *oyogashi* method of investigating, which consists in the release of the criminal and continued shadowing of him after it, so as to discover with whom he comes in contact after having been released."
>
> On the allegation that Nakamura's gendarmes had behaved in cowardly fashion, dropped to the ground and refused to return fire during the November 29 ambush behind the railway station: "All the agents acted bravely, killing a dangerous bandit."

Eguchi also categorically denied the story that the lone Kempeitai officer sent by Nakamura to Komissarenko's house on November 21 had failed to shoot Kirichenko because he didn't think he was being paid enough to risk his life. And he wrote the rest of the Chambon report off as having been penned by the vice-consul "with a view to glorifying himself and receiving a favorable comment from his seniors."[18]

But Eguchi was just getting started. This was only the beginning of the big lie.

On December 18, in a small town outside of Hailar, a station on the Chinese Eastern Railway not far from the Russian border, officers from Colonel Oi's Railway Police captured Nikifor Kirichenko, the last of Semyon Kaspé's known captors who remained at large. That meant all save Galushko, who had been shot and killed near Harbin Station, were now behind bars.[19]

In a December 11 dispatch to his superiors, Reynaud expressed the hope that now that the abductors had been arrested, the courts would deal with them ruthlessly. But if he had learned anything during his time in Manchukuo, it was surely that one's highest hopes for anything resembling justice had a perverse way of being dashed.

15

Not Criminals but Heroes

The Japanese inherited a balkanized legal system when they invaded in 1931. The railway zone still operated largely along Russian legal lines, and the rest of Manchuria worked according to the Chinese penal code when it worked at all. Japan immediately went about imposing its own system on its new colony, and it did this the same way it handled the Manchurian civil service: it assigned at least one Japanese judge to each court to call the shots while initially leaving many local jurists in place. The idea was, on the one hand, to maintain strict control over the local population and, on the other, to create a system that, on its surface, at least, might appear to be locally managed and pass international muster. All the better to secure legitimacy and recognition for Manchukuo.[1]

Most of the Japanese judges were recruited from Japan both to advise on the law and to try cases, but there were never enough of them for Manchuria's needs. In 1932, twenty of them arrived, followed by an additional thirty in 1934. That same year, there was a mass ousting of judges and prosecutors inherited from the earlier Chinese system. Some were replaced with hand-picked, local Chinese who, it was thought, could be controlled, but not all of these newcomers were well trained. Courts and prosecutors' offices were now administered by a combination of Japanese and Chinese, with the former, naturally, in charge.[2]

Among those imported from Japan was Saiji Maru, who was named the new procurator of the High Courts of Manchuria. In July of 1934, he received some Russian reporters who questioned him about why the Kaspé defendants had not yet been tried. The accused kidnappers had languished in jail for nearly a year before Osamu Eguchi had announced the charges arrayed against them. Since so much time had passed and there was still no action, it was reasonable to ask why.

"Shortly after taking up the post and duties of the Procurator," Maru told the journalists, "I looked into the case. According to the laws of the Manchurian Empire, there is a definite time during which such criminals should be handed over to the Procurator with a definite charge." Maru continued:

During the term of one year, the authorities concerned have more than once requested more time to investigate the whole affair, from which it may be concluded that the case is far from finished and that they hope to arrest other participants who have so far not gotten into their hands. Thus the murderers of Kaspé will remain in prison until all those who participated in the case are brought to justice. . . .

Unfortunately, this affair began before I took up my position, but if it had commenced *after* that date I should simply have given an order to hand everything over to the Procurator. Because the authorities have the right to get extensions of time for new investigation, this case may be continued forever. It is possible that this is not logical, but it is so.

Possibilities aside, however, Maru predicted that eternal postponement would not be the case with Kaspé's accused kidnappers. "As soon as the authorities have discovered all the participants, all the documents will be immediately handed over to the courts," he asserted. "The present situation may be explained by the fact that the authorities are not quite certain that they have all the participants in this crime in their hands."[3]

In fact, that wasn't the issue at all. Eguchi had actually concluded his investigation the previous fall. It was the sentencing recommendations that had been holding him up. His entire report, which he finally turned over on November 29, 1934, took the form of a trilingual document that ran eight hundred pages in its Russian version, sixteen hundred in Japanese, and fourteen hundred in Manchu. Of those totals, his recommendations as head of the criminal department—which he described as his "personal opinion" but was certainly anything but—occupied only thirty-two pages of the Russian document and sixty of the Japanese version.[4]

The delay was surely due to the fact that Eguchi was not a free agent. His higher-ups were hardly likely to leave the disposition of a case that had garnered so much international opprobrium to the discretion of a local police official. What had appeared as a crime motivated by avarice would now certainly be handled as the political hot potato it had become. For political reasons, the powers-that-be had concluded that it was in their interest, on the one hand, to go through the motions of a trial, but on the other, to treat the prisoners leniently. To do otherwise could jeopardize the valuable alliance the Japanese military had struck with the Russian Fascists.

What Eguchi did produce was scandalous and surely came as a severe shock to all foreigners in Manchuria who were paying attention when it was summarized in the local press. This is how it began:

> After personally examining all the details pertaining to the [Semyon] Kaspé kidnapping affair, I came to the conclusion that all of the accused . . . acted from motives of ardent patriotism. The act they committed was essentially criminal in character, but the rationale behind it was not ordinary. The criminals' motives had a political character, stemming from their nationalistic desire to fight for their country.
>
> The accused were convinced that the communists and the leaders of the communist movement, *i.e.*, the Jews, were responsible for the downfall of the Russian monarchy, and of the Tsar and his family. That was the reason for their desire to avenge their country, and for their anti-Soviet feeling and virulent anti-Semitism.[5]

He went on to explain that the men had been planning an anti-Soviet revolt on Russian soil, but lacked the necessary resources to pull it off. They had turned to kidnapping and ransom as a "non-conventional means" to raise funds, and selected Semyon Kaspé because of who his father was. Eguchi repeated accusations from the Russian Fascist press that the elder Kaspé was dealing in Russian national treasures—"holy articles" obtained illegally from churches, museums, and private individuals in Russia. He even repeated the absurdity that they had included the crown jewels of the Romanovs. "They conceived of themselves," he wrote of the kidnappers, "as passionate defenders of their country, for whom all means of achieving their goal were permissible."

Eguchi conceded—he could hardly have done otherwise—that the men had, indeed, broken the law and deserved to be punished. But then he went on to detail all the mitigating factors he could possibly dredge up to justify leniency:

Nikolai Andreevich Martinov. "As a police officer and a civil servant, Martinov's duty was to uphold law and order, and his responsibility in the affair is therefore particularly grave." But Martinov "realized his grave responsibility" after his arrest and eventually confessed his crimes to Eguchi. Accordingly, "his behavior should be considered a mitigating circumstance."

Alexei Yelievich Shandar. Shandar declared that he was not guilty and refused to confess, but "after hearing the statements by the other defendants, however, and in view of Shandar's behavior during his interrogation and his repeated requests for time to think, I am convinced that he took part in the affair." Eguchi believed he organized the kidnapping and considered him "the principal accused." But taking into account his motives, he recommended that his sentence be "reduced somewhat."

Nikifor Pavlovich Kirichenko. Eguchi described the man who led the team as a "good and sincere person." He refused to accept that Kirichenko organized the kidnapping, insisting that because of his character he could only have played a secondary role. "He certainly deserves punishment," Eguchi wrote, "but I suggest that he be punished in the spirit of mercy."

Yakov Kirillovich Zaitsev. Although he was "unsociable and stubborn," and had led a hard life as a homeless orphan, he did play a role in the abduction, though he was not its organizer, Eguchi wrote. He deserved "the legally prescribed sentence for his part in the kidnapping."

Dionisy Grigoryevich Komissarenko. Because he came from a family of "extremely simple peasants," was a man of limited ability, and had played only a secondary role in the kidnapping, "I therefore suggest that he be treated with mercy," Eguchi wrote.

Panteleimon Ignatievich Bezruchko. Eguchi noted that he was a mere *muzhik*—a peasant—who became involved in the crime only after the kidnapping had already occurred, and had been forced to guard Semyon Kaspé, "probably under threat." Citing his "more insignificant role in the affair," Eguchi recommended that he be treated "more mercifully than the others."[6]

In conclusion, Eguchi asked for sentences of fifteen years at hard labor for Martinov, thirteen for Shandar, and five to twelve years for the rest.

Reynaud was outraged by Eguchi's report. "These conclusions are quite disconcerting," he wrote his superiors. "They depict the members of this group as Russian patriots who wanted to provoke an anti-Soviet uprising in Russia and who, in order to obtain the necessary propaganda funds, decided to kidnap a well-known and wealthy Jewish personality under the pretext that the Jews were the founders and beneficiaries of the Soviet regime." He was particularly incensed at the headline atop the *Harbinskoe Vremya* article that contained the summary and reproduced photographs of the gang members. It proclaimed the men "not criminals, but heroes."[7]

Eguchi, of course, already had a record of lying about the investigation to protect the image of the police, so the fact that his indictment was studded with falsehoods might have been expected. In his version of Semyon's murder, for example, it was Kirichenko who had proposed releasing the prisoner and it was Galushko who fired the shot that killed him. That was totally at odds not only with a report to the Foreign Ministry written by Morito Morishima, the Japanese consul, which named Kirichenko as the trigger man, but also with an earlier statement by Eguchi himself back in December, publicly pronouncing Kirichenko the main murder suspect.

Since Galushko was dead, there was no harm in hanging the actual act on him, rather than on a man Eguchi had decided was a "good and sincere person" who deserved mercy. This meant that no one would be tried for Semyon Kaspé's murder, only his kidnapping.[8]

The Eguchi report dealt only with the Russians accused of carrying out the operation. Notably absent from it was any mention of who had actually conceived of the idea of kidnapping Semyon Kaspé in the first place. Eguchi's silence on that question was deafening.

16

No Longer Safe

Eguchi's cloyingly sympathetic indictment triggered a furious reaction around the world.

In the section devoted to his so-called personal opinion, he parroted the antisemitic tropes of the Russian Fascists by implicating Jews in the murder of the czar—a falsehood repeated in some quarters to this day—and blaming them for the October Revolution. It aroused the ire of Jews everywhere.

Shanghai's Jewish community took the lead in criticizing it. Several members of the Shanghai Ashkenazi Jewish Communal Association, including Boris Topas, the president of the Shanghai Jewish community; Meir Ashkenazi, its chief rabbi; and Nissim Elias Benjamin Ezra, editor of the Zionist *Israel's Messenger*, were so incensed that they sought a protest meeting with Japan's senior envoy to China, Akira Ariyoshi. They used it to denounce the "persistent anti-Semitic campaign against the treatment of the Jews in Harbin at the hands of the Japanese judicial officials employed by the Manchukuo government, who encourage anti-Semitism on the part of the White Russians in Harbin."[1]

"We cannot be without concern about the present unwholesome display of activities in Harbin insofar as the Jewish community as a whole is concerned," Ezra said. "For the past 20 months there has been persistent agitation in the press to slander them and accuse them of all crimes. That this criminal agitation by a group of White Russians should be tolerated by the police is hard to understand. The motive behind it should be investigated and we hope the Manchukuo government will not overlook this vital question."[2]

Ariyoshi promised to take the matter up with the Foreign Office. After-ward, in the monthly *Israel's Messenger*, Ezra focused specifically on Eguchi:

> What is most astounding is the attitude taken by Mr. Eguchi, chief
> of the Harbin detectives whose duty it ought to have been to bring
> the foul murderers to justice, in openly siding with and lauding
> the criminals. As if inspired by the most violent anti-Semite known
> in history, Mr. Eguchi delivered himself of anti-Semitic outbursts,
> repeating the oft-refuted allegations of Jewish sympathy with com-
> munism and even went so far as to accuse the Jews of the murder of
> the late Russian emperor. . . . No wonder a Russian daily in Harbin
> has published the photos of the accused and referred to them as
> martyrs to their country! No wonder we have news from Harbin that
> the whole Jewish population has become panicky![3]

Ezra also brought the matter to the attention of Edwin S. Cunningham, the American consul in Shanghai, and to Sir Alexander Cadogan, the British minister to China, asking both to intervene with the Manchukuo authorities. Thanks to the Jewish Telegraphic Agency, an international wire service, news of the meetings was picked up in Jewish publications around the world. New York's *Jewish Daily Bulletin*, for example, quoted Ezra's statement that "the exoneration of the culprits has thrown the Jewish community in Harbin into a state of panic and terror. It implies that Jewish lives are no longer safe when criminals are shielded and even lauded."[4]

The Japanese authorities in Manchuria were not about to allow the Shanghai Jews' allegations to go unchallenged; Japan still sought rec-ognition and foreign investment for its puppet state and had no desire for bad relations with Western powers. The authorities quickly issued a statement that "Jews in Harbin are treated with the same impartiality as are White Russians of other religious and racial affiliation, and there is no truth in the claims of ill-treatment."

But N. E. B. Ezra, as he was known, wasn't having any of it. "We are entitled to ask why," he wrote, "the *Nash Put* is allowed freedom to slander and vilify the Jews with impunity. To permit one section of the community to incite against another is not an indication of 'impartiality'.

On the contrary, it opens the way to ferment and uneasiness, which will not spell peace but strife and feud."[5]

Nor was this the end of the protest. Soon the American Jewish community got involved. Reform rabbi Stephen S. Wise and noted philosopher Horace M. Kallen paid a call on Japanese ambassador Hiroshi Saito in Washington in early February 1935 as representatives of the American Jewish Congress. They reminded Saito of earlier statements by Japanese officials that their government would not tolerate persecution of Jews in its dominions, and asked him to relay their concerns to the Foreign Office. The ambassador appeared sympathetic and agreed, and the meeting was reported in Jewish publications in France, Poland, and elsewhere in the world.[6]

If Tokyo had not gotten the message before, it certainly had now. On February 21, likely acting on instructions from the Foreign Ministry, the Harbin consul, Morito Morishima, invited Abraham Kaufman, president of the local Jewish community organization, and Josef Berkovich, a member of its board, to a two-hour meeting. He said he was willing to listen to their problems and do what he could to ameliorate their hardships.

Kaufman pointed out that Jews had lived in the city peacefully for thirty years and only recently had some "misguided groups" begun to poison the atmosphere with antisemitic agitation. And he made it clear that the problem was not the majority of White Russians in Harbin, with whom the community had no quarrel, but rather a small minority of extremists. At the end of the meeting, which was reported by at least one local Russian-language newspaper under the headline "Japan Consul General Morishima Criticizes Attack on Jews," Morishima pledged to "take steps to nullify the force from which Jews had suffered" and "suppress all lawless and iniquitous agitation."[7]

In the months that followed, however, there was zero evidence of those steps. *Nash Put* struck back on February 26, reserving special venom for Ezra, whom it saw as the instigator of the whole protest:[8]

It was in autumn of last year when the *Nash Put* reported the campaign which was undertaken against us by the well-known millionaire, Ezra. This Ezra has declared that all the White Russians in Harbin are persecuting the poor Jews, and this campaign is conducted by the *Nash Put*, which the Manchukuo authorities have promised Ezra to suppress. . . .

Not being satisfied with the campaign they are making outside of Manchukuo, the Jews are trying to delude the Japanese [Consul] General Morishima and annoy him with groundless complaints which need investigations. Before starting them, we would like to ask the Harbin Jews: what kind of persecution are the Jews in Harbin undergoing? What good has Kaspé done to Manchukuo? . . . What kind of slander is there in articles published by the *Nash Put*, which always reveal the Judo-Masonic works [designed] against Russia, Manchukuo, Germany and against everything which is not Jewish? By revealing the provocations, intrigues and lies, the *Nash Put* is only fulfilling its duty.[9]

The paper continued to publish antisemitic speeches from Nazi Germany and it called for Russians to boycott Jewish shops in Harbin just as the new school term was beginning and the local Jewish tailors were doing a brisk business in student uniforms.

And then, in late 1935, local police made a sudden raid on the main synagogue. The entire compound was encircled and for a full hour every corner of the building, including the *Aron HaKodesh*, the Holy Ark where the Torah scrolls were kept, was searched for arms and banned literature. Then, on Yom Kippur, police burst into the home of Rabbi Lev Levin, the principal of the Talmud Torah, or religious school, and rifled through his private papers to see what they could find. Following that, they conducted a similar search of Dr. Kaufman's home.

Clearly Consul Morishima, if indeed he was sincere in the concern he expressed for local Jews, had little or no sway over the police, who warned the local papers not to publish anything about the raids, lest another hue and cry arise from outside Manchuria. But their activities were clear signals to local Jews, in case they needed any reminding, that they still had enemies on the police force whose mischief had not been checked.[10]

Nor did the abductions cease.

17

The First Trial

By the time the accused were called before Procurator Maru, who was preparing the case against them, all had confessed save Zaitsev and Shandar. Shandar believed the others intended to pin the blame on him and said as much to Maru. This enraged Kirichenko, who physically attacked him in the police transport on the way back to jail, bloodying his mouth. For this, Kirichenko was placed in handcuffs and leg irons and chained so tightly that he was unable to lift his arms.[1]

Although there was a popular impression that the prisoners were treated quite leniently in prison, Martinov, in his memoir, insisted they had in fact been dealt with quite severely. He recalled that the daily prison fare, cooked by a fellow inmate, included tea with two lumps of sugar and two "funts" (about twenty-eight ounces) of rye bread for breakfast; borscht, cabbage soup, and soup with salted cucumber, noodles, and barley or millet gruel for lunch; and soup or gruel and tea for dinner. Inmates were also allowed groceries from shops outside the prison and from their relatives every Sunday that they could cook themselves. The men were given work to do; the prison had its own bookbindery, printing press, woodshop, and machine shop. Smoking was officially prohibited, but cigarettes could be procured from the outside by inmates who worked in the prison greenhouse, where contact with outsiders was possible.[2]

Although many believed the men would never actually be tried, tremendous international pressure was being brought to bear on Japan for justice in the Kaspé case, and not to deliver it—or at least something that *passed* for it—would confirm the view of many that Manchukuo was little more than a lawless dictatorship, a pawn of Japan undeserving of world respect or recognition. Under pressure from Tokyo, therefore, the District Court of Harbin finally convened on June 7, 1935, nearly two years after the crime, to hear the case.[3]

The accused kidnappers were to be tried by three Chinese judges working under Japanese "advisers" for violation of the Provisional Law for Punishment of Banditry. Although in its early years Manchukuo retained most of the laws it had inherited from Russia and China, this was a draconian piece of legislation adopted in 1932 after the Japanese invasion, aimed primarily at eradicating Chinese *honghuzi*. The penalty for those convicted of banditry was death and, by edict of Pu Yi, whom the Japanese had by now installed as the emperor of Manchukuo, punishment was to be administered within ten days of a verdict. The law allowed no possibility of appeal by the defendants, but for a verdict to be valid it had to be approved by the supreme court in the capital city of Xinjing.

The men were the first ever to be tried under the new law.[4]

No transcript of their actual trial survives, but press coverage provides a serviceable summary of events. In Harbin, *Zarya*, a relatively unbiased Russian-language newspaper read by White Russian exiles and Jews alike, reported on the proceedings, as, of course, did *Nash Put*, Konstantin Rodzaevsky's Fascist Party organ. In China, Shanghai's *North China Herald* and *Israel's Messenger* carried the story, although not on a daily basis, as did Hong Kong's *South China Morning Post*.

The defendants were represented by different attorneys; in the case of Shandar and Zaitsev, these were public defenders. All were Russian. The proceedings had to be postponed almost as soon as they began when some of the accused refused to enter pleas. But by fall things were back on track and the trial was reconvened. It continued, on and off, for the balance of 1935.[5]

On October 11, there was drama in the courtroom. On that day, both Bezruchko and Zaitsev were scheduled to be cross-examined. The latter, who had left school in St. Petersburg as a very young man, had fought in World War I, and was a member of the Brotherhood of Russian Truth, was greatly agitated, and he asked for ten minutes to make some notes. When he was finished, he announced to the court, "I have kept quiet, but now I shall tell all."

FIG. 18. Aisin-Gioro Pu Yi following his investiture as the Emperor of Manchukuo. Wikimedia Commons.

"The Procurator has stated that the leader of the gang was Martinov, but he was not the head. . . . The head of the gang that killed Kaspé is a free man and is not among the six men now in prison. The affair of kidnapping Kaspé was arranged by five men, none of whom are amongst us. Do not be surprised at the names I shall mention. Here there are only adjutants and their assistants."

Zaitsev went on to name several men who had committed *other* crimes, including murders and the kidnapping of Sherel de Florence, until the judge instructed him to stick to the Kaspé case. At that point, he gave several names, including one of "a well-known detective police officer." Then, as Shanghai's *North China Herald* reported it, he "made various statements incriminating various people in high positions." The paper did not report the names, but it did note that Zaitsev had fingered both Russian *and* Japanese participants. It is therefore nearly certain that he implicated Kostya Nakamura.[6]

That Nakamura had played a starring role in the kidnapping plot made a great deal of sense. First, he had been behind previous abductions of Jews. And second, at every opportunity, he had commanded his men to pull their punches and foil efforts to apprehend the kidnappers.

It had been Nakamura who had ordered the Criminal Police *not* to arrest the men fingered by Komissarenko in his confession to the French Consulate, but rather to take Chambon's detectives—who had been making progress on locating the kidnappers—into custody instead. It had been Nakamura who had limited the Kempeitai's participation in the November 20 ambush at Komissarenko's house to one officer with a single pistol, and apparently ordered him not to fire it. And it had been Nakamura who had given the orders to the police to hit the ground and hold their fire when they confronted the kidnappers behind the railway station on November 29. It had no doubt also been Nakamura who had seen to it that the arms his men provided to Chambon's detectives were defective and would fail to discharge.

Implicating Nakamura would also explain the odd phone call Nikiforov of the Criminal Police had received from one of the kidnappers while he was in charge of the investigation. The man, somewhat surprisingly, had assured Nikiforov that the caller's gang was not at all worried about the Kempeitai. Now it was clear why. At every turn, Nakamura had protected the men and sabotaged all efforts to capture them, for one simple reason: *they were working for him.*

Evidently, Nakamura had planned the entire operation with Martinov and been involved in every decision made during Semyon Kaspé's three months of captivity. And not only did he direct the operation and protect the kidnappers from arrest; he had demanded bribes for the participation of his officers in the efforts to apprehend them, and then made sure they would be of little or no help.

Nakamura had been playing both sides against the middle.

Needless to say, none of this was reported in Manchukuo, where the Japanese controlled the press. It was embarrassing enough that Martinov, a former police officer, albeit a Russian, had been one of the abductors; it simply would not do for a Japanese, still less a high-profile one, to be implicated as well. And whether or not Zaitsev mentioned Nakamura by name, his accusations meant that the trial had to be halted, ostensibly so the police could conduct further investigations. But it's a safe bet that they weren't about to launch an investigation of an adviser to the Kempeitai, or if by some chance they did, they weren't about to make it public.

Since the court's judges were Chinese and not Japanese, they could not be completely controlled, and they seemed intent on ferreting out the facts of the case, refusing to accept at face value either the arguments in Eguchi's outrageous indictment or his purported facts. Amleto Vespa recalled an important piece of the trial's backstory. Efforts by the judges to gather evidence outside of courtroom procedures worried the Japanese Intelligence Service for which Vespa worked, and his chief wanted it stopped because he had a vested interest in hiding the facts. And so he ordered Vespa to watch the homes of the three judges and arrest anyone who visited them. "I don't want another Chambon affair," Vespa quoted his chief as telling him.

Vespa, who loathed his Japanese handlers and worked for them only under duress, resolved to do just the *opposite* of what he was ordered. He sought an introduction to one of the Chinese judges and pledged to give him whatever information about the accused men they might want. He turned over materials proving that Martinov, under orders from the chief of the Kempeitai, had earlier committed several murders; that Shandar and Kirichenko were brothel owners who had trafficked in white slaves; that it had been Shandar who had severed Semyon Kaspé's ear; and that it had been Kirichenko, and not Galushko, who had murdered the young man.[7]

But most importantly, he turned over documents found in the pockets of the men who had been arrested by Colonel Oi's Railway Police and hence were not in the possession of the Municipal Police. Among them were "laissez-passer" certificates advising anyone the men came in contact with that they were working as agents of the Kempeitai and were not to be detained. This was *documentary* evidence of the organization's involvement.

In December, someone in authority dissatisfied with the proceedings decided summarily to transfer Chang Ping, the chief judge, to another court. This could well have been a consequence of the judges' attempts to seek information about the defendants outside of court proceedings. This meant not only that the trial had to be halted on December 25, but also that the entire process would have to begin anew under new judges in the new year.[8]

Since very little undercover activity went unnoticed in Harbin, Russian Fascist Party head Konstantin Rodzaevsky got wind of Vespa's visits to the judges. In an ominous letter to the Italian in March, he wrote: "Our party considers that your work is in opposition to our principles and in favor of the Jews. You who occupy such a high position should know what you are doing. We hereby warn you to stop working against people whom we consider brothers and patriots."[9]

Vespa immediately brought Rodzaevsky's threats to the attention of his boss, the head of the Tokumu Kikan, who trusted Vespa and did not suspect his perfidy. The boss, whose name Vespa never revealed, also knew that Rodzaevsky was a loose cannon who often had to be reined in. He made a call to the chief of the Kempeitai demanding that Rodzaevsky be ordered to back off.

Soon Vespa discovered who it was who had informed on him. It was none other than Fotopulo, the Greek spy who worked the lobby of the Hotel Moderne for Nakamura and who had provided key information on Semyon Kaspé's comings and goings before the latter's abduction. Fotopulo denied being the source, but he did reveal to Vespa that Nakamura was after him and planned to seek his arrest.[10]

18

The Second Trial

On March 23, 1936, the tribunal was reconvened under new Chinese judges and the six defendants, under heavy guard, were marched into the packed courtroom shackled to one another. Each bore two tags on his chest: one showing his prison number and the second his court number. *Nash Put* reported that they looked the worse for their long months in prison; Zaitsev had lost a good deal of weight and Martinov appeared particularly unhealthy, as he was suffering from a toothache that day. The rest just seemed depressed and frightened.[1]

When Chief Judge Liu asked the defendants how many people had been involved in the kidnapping and what its purpose was, Martinov spoke up. "All six of us in court, plus two others who are currently hiding in Soviet territory," he said. "The purpose was to obtain funds for the struggle against the Comintern, which I have been fighting for eighteen years now." He added, "I believe the crime was political, because Kaspé himself was an agent of the Bolsheviks, and he was selling jewelry that had been stolen from the czar's palace. The gold was not his; it belonged to the Russian people, who were weeping and begging him to return it to them. I wanted to get the money back and fight with the people."

Martinov's beliefs appear to have been sincere, but that didn't mean his so-called facts could be trusted. In his later testimony, he elaborated further that he had received information from an agent in the Soviet Union that the source of funding for underground Soviet activities in the Far East was none other than Josef Kaspé. But he presented no evidence for this, nor has any ever surfaced in the years since. And Kaspé's precarious financial position makes it even less likely that this was true.[2]

Kirichenko testified next, but when he insisted on going off-topic and detailing his background as a partisan rather than dealing with the kidnapping, the judge admonished him. After that, complaining of a headache, he sulked and refused to answer questions. The next day, March 28, he recounted that the kidnappers had disagreed about the ransom demands. He said he and Zaitsev had been willing to pare down the sum and accept Kaspé's offer of 35,000 yen, but that the others had opposed this. Galushko, who had been negotiating with the Moderne managers, had refused to budge and no progress was made. Kirichenko also implicated Shandar, who had declined to confess his role.[3]

The next day, Kirichenko received the shocking news that his six-year-old son had died. When the judge learned of the boy's death, he expressed his condolences to the defendant, but also pointed out the obvious parallel: that as a grieving father, he should understand the suffering of Josef Kaspé. Kirichenko was having none of it. He retorted that Kaspé may have been heartbroken over the loss of his son, but that he had not felt pain when he had received jewelry from the Bolsheviks with full knowledge that it had been obtained at the expense of the Russian people.[4]

When Komissarenko took the stand, he confirmed that the defendants had followed Semyon Kaspé for five days to determine his habits. The moment Kaspé's car arrived at Shapiro's house, it had been Shandar, Kirichenko, and Zaitsev who jumped out of the gate of a nearby Japanese bathhouse and hijacked the vehicle. Komissarenko insisted he was merely acting as a lookout.

Bezruchko testified that while in custody, Semyon Kaspé had assured Galushko that his father would pay the ransom immediately, and asked to let him negotiate with his father on the phone. He also stated that Semyon had told him that his father was dealing in old Russian jewelry and gold received from Soviet agents, and that he was donating the proceeds to the Soviet Union. But again, Bezruchko provided no evidence to back up this hearsay testimony.

Years later, Martinov elaborated on that story. He asserted that Josef Kaspé had often boasted about his wealth and his success—something Amleto Vespa confirmed—and that before Semyon had grasped the gravity of his situation, he had told his captors that his father had recently earned $200,000 from the sale of some Russian jewelry and would easily be able to afford the 300,000 yen demanded.

According to Martinov, Semyon had also told them Josef was obligated to deposit the proceeds in an account at the Far Eastern Bank, or Dalbank, in the name of the trade representative of the Soviet Union, and that once that was done he could not withdraw the money without Soviet permission. Semyon, Martinov wrote, believed the deposit had not yet been made. If this is accurate, it was Semyon who led his kidnappers to believe his father would have no trouble coming up with the money, and persuaded them further of Josef's alleged Communist sympathies. It seems unlikely, however, because no evidence that the elder Kaspé *was* pro-Soviet or in any way tied to the Soviet Union was ever produced, nor, apparently, was anyone from Dalbank called to testify at the trial.[5]

Bezruchko had provided a vivid account of the circumstances of Semyon's murder during his initial interrogation, and this was read in court. He had placed the blame for the shooting on the dead Galushko rather than Kirichenko, who had almost certainly fired the shot; both had been present and both had had guns. It cost nothing to accuse a dead man.

Zaitsev and Shandar, who took the stand next, both denied any involvement in the kidnapping. Zaitsev insisted he had been on an undercover mission in the Soviet Union at the time, even though Kirichenko, Komissarenko, and Bezruchko had all implicated him. And Shandar maintained he had been in church the day and night of the murder, mourning the death of his brother in the United States. Kirichenko, however, had made it clear that Shandar, too, had participated.[6]

Photographs of the scene of the murder and the weapons used, including an image of Galushko's dead body after he had been shot by police, were introduced. And one other grisly piece of evidence was produced: the severed piece of Semyon Kaspé's ear, which had been preserved under glass for all to see.[7]

On April 15, Lydia Shapiro was called to testify. Other than the defendants and the chauffeur, she was the only witness to the kidnapping. She seemed overwhelmed by the attention, and when asked if she could identify any of the kidnappers, admitted she could not. At this, Kirichenko broke into an uncharacteristic smile. He later confirmed that it had been he who had made her lie down in the back seat of the car and that he had covered her face with a piano score.[8]

Lydia estimated that it had been around eleven p.m. when the car arrived at her house, where the abduction took place. Semyon, she recounted, had asked the kidnappers to do as they wished with him, but to leave her alone. Somewhere in Novy Gorod, Semyon was transferred to another car and she and Semyon's driver were released. They were instructed not to move from the spot for a period of time, and Lydia was told to tell Josef Kaspé to prepare a 300,000 yen ransom and to warn him not to report the incident to the police. After waiting the requisite amount of time, they returned to the Moderne to deliver the bad news.

Nash Put made sure to include one more detail in its report of Lydia's testimony. It was an exchange between her and the judge that can only have been intended to suggest that she was a woman of low morals:

"Are you married?" the judge inquired.
"Yes, I am."
"Was your husband in Harbin in 1933?"
"No, he was not. My husband was in Japan."
"Who else have you been with other than Kaspé?"
"I had *many* acquaintances," the witness replied coldly.[9]

The trial went on for twenty-eight sessions before it was over. While it was going on, to bolster the defense's argument that the crime had been political, the Russian Fascist Party issued an unusual statement in which it claimed responsibility for the kidnapping. "We openly declare to the whole world, including the Russian emigration, that the kidnapping of S. I. Kaspé was carried out under our orders and that this crime was purely of a politico-nationalist nature."[10]

In his summation, the procurator made just this argument. He asserted that the act "was not done with the purpose of personal enrichment. They did not want to get money for themselves, but desired to use it for opposing communism." To this end, he made a point of discussing the suffering Kirichenko, Zaitsev, Komissarenko, and Bezruchko had experienced under the Bolsheviks after the Revolution when their relatives had been killed and they had barely escaped with their lives.

"They had not the slightest intention to kill the kidnapped youth," the procurator continued, "but only to deprive him for a while of his liberty.

They are guilty of kidnapping, but not of murder," he argued. That, of course, was only because the police had conveniently decided that the deceased Galushko had fired the shot that killed Semyon Kaspé.

Oddly, however, Procurator Maru argued *against* trying the case as a violation of the banditry law, with death as its highest penalty, even though the decision to do so had been specified in the indictment. This was highly unusual, but the explanation lay in the fact that that document had been prepared under the supervision of his predecessor, and he clearly did not agree with its approach. Maru suggested that the men ought to have been tried instead under the criminal code, which did not provide for capital punishment. He went on to recommend sentences of fifteen years' penal servitude for Martinov and Shandar, eleven for Kirichenko, Komissarenko, and Zaitsev, and two-and-a-half for Bezruchko.[11]

The *China Weekly Review* smelled a rat. "Such juggling with 'laws' is possible only in Manchukuo," it suggested, "for it is not the practice of prosecuting attorneys in other countries to demand, as if by a second thought, a punishment at variance with the bill of indictment."[12]

In the summations of the various defense attorneys, the patriotism card was played for all it was worth, even though the subject was Russian patriotism rather than Manchurian patriotism. The men had not sought personal enrichment, they insisted, only funds necessary to help them reclaim Holy Mother Russia from the Bolsheviks. And the appeal to patriotism was combined with an imported but now familiar xenophobia: "Adopting [the] latest Nazi tactics, the defending counsel caused to be inserted into the record extracts from certain authors alleging that members of the Jewish race should be removed from the earth," the *China Weekly Review's* correspondent reported. The conclusion: the blackmailing and murder of Jews was justified, and extortion of money from Jews like the Kaspé family was no crime, because their money actually belonged to the Russian people.[13]

Other arguments were presented as well. Martinov's attorney pointed out that no ransom had actually been obtained—as if that negated the act of kidnapping—and also insisted that his client was not an antisemite. Zaitsev's and Shandar's lawyers observed that there was no evidence against their clients other than the testimony of other defendants. Kirichenko's counsel dwelled on the difficult life his client had led—his mother and brother had been murdered by Bolsheviks, and he had been detained in a remote prison camp. But the attorney veered off course with a denunciation of Josef Kaspé, which was ruled out of order by the judge. And finally, the lawyer who represented both Komissarenko and Bezruchko pointed to the former's willingness to surrender himself and the latter's having been "forced" to act as a guard, and having played no role in the kidnapping per se.[14]

"Never has such a crowd been seen outside the Harbin courts," the *South China Morning Post* reported of the scene early in the morning of June 15, 1936. There was much pushing and shoving among potential spectators that morning, since word had leaked out that verdicts were forthcoming. Well before the opening hour, the courtroom was packed. Komissarenko's two sisters, one of whom was married to Bezruchko, were in the front row; so were Martinov's wife and Kirichenko's wife and daughter. In addition, the press was there in force, as were representatives of local civic organizations and several foreign diplomats.

Manacled at the wrists and ankles, the prisoners arrived at the courthouse under heavy police escort at half past ten. All looked pale and unhappy. At eleven a.m., the judges took their places.[15]

Chief Judge Liu asserted that Martinov, Shandar, Kirichenko, Zaitsev, and Komissarenko had formed a gang to kidnap wealthy merchants for ransom, that they planned and carried out the kidnapping of Semyon Kaspé, that all of the defendants knew exactly what they were going to do, and that Bezruchko, who joined the gang later, clearly understood his role as well. The kidnapping was carried out with weapons the defendants intended to use if necessary. When the ransom negotiations stalled, Galushko had fired his revolver and killed the hostage.

"There seems no doubt but that the accused are guilty on what they said during the trial and also on other proof. Participation in the crime by Shandar and Zaitsev has been proved during the questioning of the rest of the defendants, though they have not confessed to the crime," he added.

"Under the laws concerning banditry, Martinov, Shandar, Kirichenko, and Zaitsev are sentenced to death," he went on, while Komissarenko and Bezruchko, who had played no role in planning the abduction, were condemned to penal servitude for life. The verdicts, he said, "will be passed on to the high court for confirmation."

Despite the pressure they had undoubtedly received from their Japanese advisers, and despite the recommendations of the procurator, the Chinese jurists had shown a degree of independence and courage that was rare in occupied Manchuria.

The words of the chief judge hit like a bombshell, given that the procurator had recommended punishments substantially less severe. The defendants initially maintained their composure, but when the interpreter began to translate the sentences into Russian, their faces showed confusion, agitation, and indignation. Martinov's wife avoided eye contact with her husband. One of Komissarenko's sisters fell to the floor sobbing. Bezruchko's wife seemed dazed. Kirichenko's wife clutched their daughter and let out a loud wail as copies of the sentences were passed to the defendants, who were asked to sign them. Shandar and Martinov complied; the others refused.

By one account, Martinov, on hearing the verdict, cried out, "It's a swindle! You promised that I should not get more than ten years." It's unclear to whom he directed that remark.[16]

Alexander Ivanovich Churkin, Kirichenko's lawyer, asked to speak, but the judge shut him down. Komissarenko asked if he could appeal the sentence and was told that under the banditry law he had no right of appeal. Shandar then asked to address the court. He was also refused, but as he was escorted out of the courtroom, he called out, "There is still an Emperor! I request all those who are present to petition His Imperial Majesty. I protest the sentence, and from this moment will not eat a morsel of bread and will not drink a drop of water till the verdict is revised."[17]

The verdict took Harbin by surprise. After the judge permitted the defendants to plead that they had acted out of Russian patriotism and allowed antisemitic screeds to be read into the record, the Russian newspapers in town had naturally expected light sentences for the "martyrs" and prepared their readers for them.

There was strong opposition not only on the part of Russians but also of Japanese, though for different reasons. *Nash Put* ran a scathing piece referring to the defendants as "a group of sacrificial men." While the

Japanese authorities confiscated the paper and called Rodzaevsky, its editor, onto the carpet because he had run it without permission of their censors, the *Harbinskoe Vremya*, controlled by the Japanese Consulate, opined that the case ought to have been decided "from the point of view of higher justice and fairness" rather than according to the letter of the law. It maintained that the crime had been purely political and had had nothing to do with banditry, but rather had stemmed from "the ardent patriotism of the Russians, who were pursuing only the best goals." It demanded a retrial.[18]

For local Jews, of course, the sentences came as a relief, and there was much drinking and celebration at the Hotel Moderne that night. Jews took the verdicts as a sign that the judicial system, under its new Japanese overlords, could perhaps be counted on after all for protection and a measure of justice. "We congratulate the Harbin Court for the courageous stand it has taken in vindicating law and order and redeeming the good name of the Manchukuo government," wrote N. E. B. Ezra in Shanghai's *Israel's Messenger*. "The result should inspire confidence in the Harbin administration," he asserted hopefully, "and put a stop to Jewish exodus from the country, where the law will hereafter be administered more fairly and impartially."[19]

Two days after the verdict was rendered, Reynaud informed his superiors that as soon as it was confirmed by the Supreme Court, the execution of the four who had received death sentences would likely take place within twenty-four hours, and probably by hanging. He predicted there would be "little chance that the decision of the tribunal will be changed or that the appeal to the Emperor's right of mercy will be used."[20]

He could not, alas, have been more wrong.

19

Powerful Influences

Their Japanese "advisers" had certainly made sure that the Chinese judges knew how they were expected to rule in the case, so the latter showed a good deal of courage in straying from the script. Four death sentences and two life sentences were not the verdicts the Japanese expected or wanted, and two days after they were announced, the judges were arrested.[1]

There is no evidence that Shandar went through with his threatened hunger strike, but as he had requested while being hurried out of the courtroom, the Russian Fascist Party began to collect signatures on a petition to Emperor Pu Yi to annul the verdict. By early July *Nash Put* reported that nearly three thousand people had signed; *Israel's Messenger* later revised that figure upward to ten thousand.

Osamu Eguchi, who had since been promoted and now headed the police department of the Ministry of Internal Affairs in the capital city of Xinjing, was quite dismayed by the severity of the verdicts and determined to do something about them. He ordered the sentences postponed for a week and approached Grigory Mikhailovich Semyonov, the former head of the White Army in Siberia, who now worked for Pu Yi. No friend of Jews, Semyonov had distributed copies of the *Protocols of the Elders of Zion* to the Japanese troops under his command in Siberia before his defeat. Eguchi asked Semyonov to request intervention by the Guandong Army, and Semyonov arranged for the chief of the army's headquarters staff to receive Lydia Mikhailovna, Martinov's wife, and Alexander Churkin, Kirichenko's lawyer. The man assured them the executions would be postponed indefinitely.[2]

By one account, Emperor Pu Yi declined to issue the requested pardon. But it's more likely that he was never forced to act on it one way or the other, as the Supreme Court handily relieved him of the burden.[3]

Although the sentences were not technically appealable, the law did require that the Supreme Court approve the verdicts for them to be valid, and they had been submitted for review immediately after they were issued. Because the court's role was seen as merely a rubber stamp, the decision it announced on June 18 came as a total surprise. Under what Reynaud described as "pressure from several high Japanese officials in the Manchu government," its three Japanese justices declined to ratify the verdicts. They gave no reason for their refusal; they merely remanded the cases to the Harbin High Court for a new trial.[4]

The *China Weekly Review* found the decision ominous. "Powerful influences seem to be at work behind the curtain for the complete exoneration of the culprits," it warned, presciently. If it had not been apparent before, it was now abundantly clear that the Japanese authorities did not want the kidnappers to die or to serve life sentences.

On September 6, Tamizi Yamaguchi, the chief judge of the foreign department of the Harbin High Court, announced that the case would shortly be retried in his courtroom. He would preside together with two other Japanese judges. The procurator, Saiji Maru, would once again prosecute the case for the government.[5]

The proceedings—and the outcome of the case—would now be safely, and exclusively, in Japanese hands. No more Chinese judges would be involved.

The third trial was set to begin in mid-October but was postponed twice. It finally began on January 11, 1937. News coverage of it was spotty. It was reported that Martinov took the stand to insist that he was not an antisemite. It had never been important to him whether those he kidnapped were Jewish or not, he insisted, and the reason for the abduction and ransom demand was Josef Kaspé's alleged membership in the Communist Party and the substantial fortune he had made selling Russian jewelry. If indeed Martinov did not hate Jews, which is doubtful, he certainly had no problem associating with many who did.

Some of Maru's January 18 summation survives. Noting that the crime of the men was evident, and that most of them had already confessed to it, he added:

We cannot apply to their case the laws concerning banditry, on which the first verdict was passed, since these laws deal with organization of a gang for committing crimes for personal enrichment. But these persons attempted to raise funds for their fight with communism by means of temporary captivity. This aim is evident from the trial.

Furthermore, Mr. Josef Kaspé, father of the kidnapped man, was a member of the Comintern himself.[6] I sympathize with the convicts, who, being ardent patriots, decided to start a fight with the communists and usurpers of their country. However, we cannot excuse their act, since peace and order in this country should be placed first. Therefore, I request only to lessen the sentence.[7]

In other words, positioning the kidnapping as a political act rather than one motivated by financial gain had provided the excuse the government needed to justify trying the case under a less draconian law. Never mind the fact that the prosecution accepted the allegation of Kaspé's party membership as truth without presenting any supporting documentary evidence.

In fact, such membership is unlikely. Kaspé was a successful capitalist who had never lived under Soviet rule, and no one has ever presented any evidence that he even applied for Soviet citizenship. But even if he *had* had Communist sympathies, it would in no way have justified the torturing and the taking of the life of his son, about whom no such allegation was made. Additionally, the assertion that the men had done what they had done entirely for Mother Russia and not for personal gain was, at best, highly questionable.

Since there was no denying that an illegal kidnapping had taken place, Maru ended by recommending that Shandar be sentenced to fifteen years penal servitude; Martinov thirteen years; Kirichenko and Zaitsev, ten years each; Komissarenko eight years; and Bezruchko two-and-a-half years. But it hardly mattered what Maru recommended, because the fix was in. The judges had no intention of subjecting the men to further incarceration.

The head of the panel announced their final verdict in a January 29, 1937, statement:

In order to obtain resources for the counterrevolutionary movement, counterrevolutionary Russian immigrants kidnapped [Semyon] Kaspé, the son of Josef Kaspé, one of the wealthiest men in Harbin, and demanded a large ransom for his release. The regional special court handled this affair as a violation of the gang law, and four of the accused were consequently sentenced to death, while two were sentenced to life at hard labor. Nevertheless, the president of the panel of judges thought that doubts could arise regarding the enforcement of the law, and realized the need to reconsider the affair.

This was the first suggestion that the judges who had initially presided over the case had had any doubts about the application of the banditry law, and it very possibly was not true. The verdict had been submitted to the Supreme Court for approval because the law required it; if the chief Chinese judge had expressed any misgivings about the law, there is no record of it.

The presiding judge continued: "The first court termed the affair an act of criminals; the second verdict, handed down today, described it as a kidnapping, with a demand for ransom. These crimes are included in Section 371 of the criminal code. The punishment can consist of either life imprisonment at hard labor, or seven years in prison." Next, he allowed— as he *had* to in order to preserve a modicum of credibility—that a crime had, indeed, been committed and that it justified punishment:

> There is no doubt that these criminal acts, even if stemming from a deep feeling of patriotism towards the old Imperial Russia, as the accused explained, contravene the basic policy of Manchukuo . . . We cannot forgive these acts, neither in the name of divine laws, nor in the name of human laws. The motives and purposes of the crimes . . . cannot completely justify the means that were used. If the means employed contravened the law of the land, they can be neither justified nor forgiven, even if the goals and circumstances did affect the sentence.

But then came the clincher. Thanks to a dazzling display of legal sleight-of-hand, there was to be *no punishment* after all:

His Majesty, the Emperor of Manchukuo, in order to lift the people's spirits, consented in the first year of his rule to publish an edict of amnesty pardoning crimes previously committed. . . . The accused are fortunate that their crimes came under Section 371 of the criminal code, and were included in the category of crimes committed before March 1933, and consequently were eligible for the amnesty granted by the Emperor.[8]

It should be emphasized again that the court does not regard the deeds of the accused as legal acts, since they violated the law of the land. The accused deserve severe punishment. According to His Majesty's order of amnesty, however, they are entitled to a pardon, and we have therefore decided to allow them to benefit from the amnesty.[9]

The court ruled that although the accused were guilty *even* under the criminal law, convicting them under that law came conveniently prepackaged with amnesty. They were not officially exonerated, but who cared? The important thing was that, presuming the prosecutor did not appeal the decision within ten days, they would not need to serve any further jail time.

Needless to say, since it had been Maru himself who had first raised the issue of which law the men had been tried under, the decision was not appealed. And so ten days later, on February 9, after more than three years in prison, Semyon Kaspé's kidnappers—and his murderer—were set free.

The Russian Fascists were jubilant, of course; this was the verdict they had wanted and expected from the beginning. But now the Japanese had to deal with the opprobrium they knew would be coming from foreign sources. In a feeble attempt to contain the damage, the local Japanese authorities confiscated the American and British newspapers on the day after the outcome was announced. But this did not stop the press outside of Manchuria from reporting on it. Using a flimsy legal justification to free men who had committed unspeakable crimes appeared to be the act of a brutal dictatorship, and it must certainly have helped to tarnish further the image of Manchukuo in the eyes of the world.[10]

Reynaud saw the decision as regrettable, but also unsurprising and inevitable; once the fate of the defendants had been placed in the hands of Japanese judges, it was sealed. As for the Harbin Jews, the *Chicago Tribune* noted that "a wave of resentment" had flared up among them. World Jewry was incensed. Even the Soviets spoke out against the verdict. *Pravda*, their official mouthpiece, which published a detailed account of the trial, claimed that the proceedings had furnished proof of the intimate connection between the White Russians and the Japanese.[11]

The encouragement experienced briefly by the Jewish community when Kaspé's abductors were sentenced to death and life imprisonment was dashed to pieces when the men were let off scot-free. The fortunes of the Jews of Harbin had not been the same since the arrival of the Japanese, and now that their new masters had demonstrably found common cause with the Jew-hating Russian Fascists and decided to work in tandem with them, life became increasingly intolerable. The final verdict in the trial of Semyon Kaspé's kidnappers and murderer was thus a watershed in many lives.

It convinced many that Russian antisemitism, from which they had enjoyed safe harbor for the first decades of the twentieth century, had finally caught up with them, and that it was now receiving an unexpected and unwelcome assist from the Japanese conquerors. "The worst of stepmothers that have ever nursed the Children of Israel," as Lev Levin, Harbin's first rabbi, had once referred to the two countries, had joined forces to make their lives miserable. For many—and, over the next few years, for most—it was a signal to do what Jews have done since time immemorial when others made their lives intolerable: emigrate.[12]

20

What Really Happened

Even if it had not been rigged, the trial of the kidnappers would have left many questions unanswered. The most important, of course, was *who* had ordered the kidnapping of Semyon Kaspé, and *why*? And what was going on behind the scenes during his captivity?

Definitive answers to these questions did not come out during the trial or its immediate aftermath. But four participants in the drama left memoirs or sat for interviews later in their lives, giving their own recollections and views of the events, and a fifth left behind an archive of letters. Their accounts do not agree in all respects, in part because certain aspects of them are likely fabricated, or at best self-serving, and in part because memory is sometimes unreliable. But there are certain conclusions on which they are more or less in accord.

Amleto Vespa's recounting in *Secret Agent of Japan*, which was published in 1938, was the first memoir to appear. Although his own role in the case was relatively minor, as a secret agent he knew a great deal about the activities of others. Vespa wrote the book, which excoriated his former Japanese handlers, in Shanghai, where he had landed after escaping Manchuria. He was hopeful the attention it got would raise his profile and that it would serve as his family's ticket out of China, and he pulled relatively few punches in it. But because Japan had already occupied Shanghai while he was writing, he left certain things out, and not everything in it can be taken as gospel.

Alexandre Pernikoff's *Bushido*, which appeared in 1943, is ostensibly the personal story of a former Kempeitai functionary who played a peripheral role in the events. In this as-told-to memoir, the author masked the man's identity with the pseudonym Oleg Volgin. And Petr Balakshin, in the Russian-language *Final v Kitae* in 1958, drew on the unpublished memoirs and diaries of police inspector Nikolai Martinov, who, of course, played a central role in the kidnapping and knew a great deal of the story.

We also have a treasure trove discovered in the archives of the French Foreign Ministry at the Quai d'Orsay in Paris by French scholar Sabine Breuillard. The files of the French Consulate in Harbin have been lost, but thanks to her efforts, a dossier of dispatches written by Louis Reynaud, the French consul in Harbin, to his superiors in Beijing and Paris was declassified and released in 2004. It consists primarily of reports about Deputy Consul Albert Chambon's investigation, his observations about the lack of cooperation from the Japanese authorities, and suspicions about their involvement in the abduction. The file also includes letters exchanged between Semyon Kaspé and his father while the former was in captivity, as well as articles that appeared in the local newspapers as the search progressed.

And finally, we have Chambon's own recollections in the form of an unpublished manuscript, *Tribulations d'un jeune diplomate dans la vielle Chine*, which details his own participation in the drama and his candid assessments of several of the other actors.

More recently, we have important contributions from Japan by one journalist and two scholars. *The Harbin Church Garden*, a 2009 work by the late Tetsuya Sunamura, a reporter for the *Yomiuri Shimbun*, was the first study of the Kaspé case in Japanese. Scholar Takeshi Nakashima of Tokyo Metropolitan University drew on surviving records from the Ministry of Foreign Affairs in his 2013 article, "The Kaspé Incident in Harbin, Russian Society and Japan, 1933–1937," and shed light on how the local Japanese Consulate dealt with the events. The Foreign Ministry and Consulate papers appear to be the only surviving Japanese government documents about the case, the records of the Harbin Kempeitai having been destroyed in 1945. And Osaka University's Noriko Uchiyama Valuev, in articles written in 2015 and 2017 in the journal *Sever*, has drawn some valuable conclusions from Martinov's papers, now on deposit at Columbia University, and from the contemporary Russian press coverage of the events.

Is there any consensus in these materials? It seems certain there was high-level Japanese involvement in the Kaspé kidnapping; almost all the sources point to this, many in considerable detail, though two do not. That there is no mention of any Japanese role in the archives of the Japanese Foreign Ministry is fairly easily explained; the Kaspé affair was a project of the Guandong Army, and one it had every reason to keep secret. It is entirely plausible that the military would have deliberately kept the Foreign Ministry in the dark about it. Even the Kempeitai's records, if they still existed, might not have been dispositive, since it would not have been prudent to leave behind written evidence of misdeeds.

A thornier question is why Nikolai Martinov mentioned no Japanese role in his memoirs. He insisted the crime had been planned entirely by White Russian partisans as a means to amass funds for their anti-Soviet struggle. Why he did not implicate at least Kostya Nakamura in the planning of the kidnapping, as others did, is a puzzle. When he recorded his memories in the 1950s, he was living in Belgium and had no reason to fear Japanese retaliation. But Martinov had always been intent on portraying the campaign against Josef Kaspé as a political act intended to advance the struggle against Bolshevism, and allowing a role for the Kempeitai, which was in it only for the money, would undermine that interpretation.[1]

Most of the sources attribute responsibility for *planning*—though not *ordering*—the kidnapping to Nakamura, who worked with Rodzaevsky and Martinov to recruit the team and execute the plan. He "had a gang of about 15 criminals at his disposal, picked with the help of Rodzaevsky," Amleto Vespa wrote of Nakamura, "from the membership of which the Japanese authorities recruited the hoodlums they needed. The kidnapping plot had been hatched at the Fascist Club quarters." Chambon, too, recalled that under interrogation, Komissarenko had confirmed Nakamura's oversight in the recruitment of the team.

Nakamura was the perfect choice to organize the abduction, because he was experienced in this gruesome line of work. It was he who had supervised the kidnapping of Meir Koffman in March of 1932, and Kirichenko and Galushko had been among those he had recruited for that crime. In many ways the Koffman abduction was a dress rehearsal for the Kaspé kidnapping that followed. Koffman was also attacked at night in Pristan, pushed into a waiting automobile, and taken to Novy Gorod before being moved further out of town. There had even been a threat to cut off his ears. When the ransom was not raised quickly, Koffman had been murdered.

What is more, Rodzaevsky had been deeply involved in the Koffman affair, and had given in to his sadistic urges in the process. According to Vespa, he had personally torched the man's hands, feet, and face, and choked and killed him. "This damned pig of a Jew loved his money more than his skin," he had told Vespa, adding, "This is the way all the dirty Jews, enemies of Russia, should die."[2]

Although Nakamura saw the Semyon Kaspé abduction as a means to pressure the latter's father to give up his valuable properties, Rodzaevsky viewed it quite differently. He saw it as a golden opportunity to make a political statement, and a viciously antisemitic one at that: he wanted to paint Semyon Kaspé as the son of a Jewish Communist agent who had profiteered from the misfortunes of the White Russians—a portrayal that the kidnappers' attorneys eventually more or less *did* adopt in their trial—and he wanted Semyon killed as an example.

Nakamura, however, had balked at this. He didn't want the affair to be seen as political or to be public; for him it was all about the ransom, and the more quietly it could be obtained, the better. He also had serious reservations about Rodzaevsky's ability to keep the plans secret. Because of this difference of opinion, the latter withdrew, or was forced out, and Martinov took complete responsibility for the actual operation, working under Nakamura's supervision.[3]

Martinov commanded the kidnappers, several of whom, like him, had extensive experience in abductions and murder. He assigned them their roles. He knew Shandar, a military man, from their time in Vladivostok before it fell to the Red Army. Kirichenko, too, had been in that city; he had been a bodyguard of one of the leaders of the White movement, and together with Zaitsev, had fled to Manchuria after escaping a Soviet prison. Like Kirichenko, Galushko was a veteran of the Koffman case. Only Komissarenko and Bezruchko were first-timers, and they were given only scut work to do.[4]

Martinov divided his men into two groups. The first, led by Shandar, included Kirichenko, Zaitsev, and Komissarenko. They were tasked with following Semyon, assisted by the Greek Fotopulo and Oleg Volgin, who were to spy on the young man to learn his habits and routines. This first group was also responsible for executing the kidnapping and transporting their quarry to the hideout. It had been Shandar who had subdued Semyon's chauffeur, Kirichenko who had slid into the back seat with Semyon and Lydia Shapiro, and Zaitsev who had driven Semyon to the Staryi Gorod hideout after Lydia and the chauffeur were released.[5]

Zaitsev had delivered Semyon to the custody of Galushko and Bez-ruchko, members of the second group, which also included Komissa-renko and a few others who apparently escaped justice. These men were charged with preparing a temporary shelter outside Harbin and guarding the prisoner. Martinov himself declined to appear that night or later at the encampment, as he did not want Semyon to know of his involvement and be able to identify him later.[6]

Martinov also recalled the meeting between himself and his boss, the chief of the Criminal Investigation Department of the Harbin Municipal Police, and Josef Kaspé, during which they reassured the man that his son's release was imminent. This had probably taken place in September 1933, around the time Reynaud met with the Japanese consul. It meant that even as Martinov was holding the son captive, he was pretending to the young man's father to be working to free him.[7]

Galushko had been in charge of the negotiations, Martinov wrote later, assisted by Shandar. And these were as difficult logistically as they were substantively. They communicated the kidnappers' demands by phone through four people: Lydia Shapiro; a friend of Semyon's named Ziskaliani; a woman named Lara who lived with Semyon's uncle, Abraham Pevsner; and Josef Kaspé himself. Knowing all the calls would be monitored and traced by the police, they made certain to telephone only from faraway places that could be vacated well before police arrived. Sometimes they placed more than one call at the same time to make it more difficult to trace them.[8]

Both Chambon and Vespa also revealed the circumstances of Galushko's death: he was discovered by his coconspirators to have hatched a plan to go it alone. Chambon explained that as the situation went from bad to worse for the kidnappers, they began to fear that they would be hung out to dry by their Japanese overlords if they were discovered.

According to both sources, Semyon had gotten to know his guards reasonably well during his long incarceration, and when the two were alone in Xiaoling, Galushko had told him a good deal about who was behind his abduction and seized the opportunity to strike his own deal for Semyon's freedom.

Galushko had told Semyon that if his father gave him 10,000 yen, he would set the young man free. The two agreed that Semyon would address a note to this effect and that Galushko would deliver it, or have it delivered, to Josef Kaspé.[9]

That afternoon, Galushko told Kirichenko he had to go to Harbin, which raised the latter's suspicions, since there was no obvious reason for the trip. Before Galushko left, Kirichenko went to the railway station and phoned Nakamura, who told him to instruct Galushko to meet him near the freight depot at the Harbin station when he arrived at five p.m. Nakamura was waiting there for him with Komissarenko and some gendarmes, who seized and searched him and found Semyon's letter. Although it was written in French, which neither understood, it was clear enough what had transpired. Accordingly, it was Nakamura, and not Komissarenko or Kirichenko, who drew his pistol and shot Galushko, a traitor to the cause, through the head.

Then, according to Vespa, Nakamura, who had concluded that Semyon knew too much about who was really behind his abduction to be permitted to live, told Kirichenko to kill the prisoner. Vespa knew of all this because the following day, Rodzaevsky, who had become involved in the plot once again, had sought his help in translating Galushko's letter. Vespa confirmed that it was indeed a promise to free Semyon for 10,000 yen.

On this point, Oleg Volgin more or less agreed. In his account, when Colonel Oi's railway police seized Bezruchko and Zaitsev just as they were boarding a train for Xiaoling to relieve Kirichenko and Galushko on November 28, 1933, Nakamura found out about it and hurried there by car. Seeing that everything was closing in on the entire operation, he ordered Kirichenko to finish Semyon off.[10]

Perhaps the most discomfiting revelation in Vespa's *Secret Agent of Japan* was the suggestion that Semyon's death was inevitable. Vespa believed Semyon had spoken directly to Nakamura at least once during his three months of captivity, and if Oleg Volgin's account is accurate, that conversation may have occurred shortly before his death. But even if Semyon had *not* met Nakamura, he had learned too much about his kidnappers' activities and affiliations. Chambon explained that Semyon's captors had told him stories of other abductions with which they had been involved in the past couple of years, as well as an attempted kidnapping of George C. Hanson, the longtime United States consul in Harbin. Historian John Stephan revealed that Zaitsev had told Semyon about his connection to the Brotherhood of Russian Truth and, in the process, mentioned Martinov, which meant that the police had been involved. Kirichenko knew about this. If Nakamura's name had been brought up as well, it would also have implicated the Kempeitai. Ransom or no ransom, they could not have risked letting Semyon live, given how much he knew of his captors.[11]

All sources agreed that had Chambon not pursued the matter, the crime would never have been solved and the kidnappers would never have been arrested. That is why the Russian Fascist newspapers ran such a vicious smear campaign against him, and why the Japanese, in a desperate and ultimately futile attempt to hide their involvement, had insisted on his ouster from Manchukuo.

Japanese participation is also strongly indicated by the herculean efforts expended by the Japanese authorities to protect, exonerate, and free the kidnappers. Given the international pressure on Japan for justice for Semyon Kaspé, why risk international opprobrium and pull out all the stops to save an essentially expendable group of White Russian criminals on whom the Guandong Army surely looked down?

On the one hand, as Takeshi Nakashima has pointed out, the execution of the criminals might have caused a rift in the cooperative working relationship the Kempeitai had forged with the Russian Fascists, and have lost them a useful collaborator. But a more compelling reason might be that the men knew too much, and that failure to protect them posed a significant risk that the Kempeitai's own role in the abduction and murder would be revealed. Indeed, Nakamura's name and his role apparently *were* mentioned at the trial, though not—no accident—in the press coverage that followed it.[12]

Of all the memoirs, only Vespa's fingers a particular individual as the man who gave the order to abduct Semyon Kaspé. It was his boss, a man described by the Italian only as the "chief of the Japanese Intelligence Service."

Who was this man? Even though he reported to him, Vespa either never knew his name, as he claimed, or, more likely, chose not to reveal it in his memoir. But he left enough clues that it's possible to identify that chief, or at least a likely candidate, today.

We learn from Vespa that the man had been in Siberia in 1918 as a member of the Japanese military mission, that he spoke fluent Russian, and that he arrived in Harbin to take up his post at around the same time the League of Nations' Lytton Commission issued its final report, which was in September 1932. He reportedly revealed to Vespa that acquiring money was one of his chief missions and, as early as May 1933, told him that he wanted Josef Kaspé abducted and held for ransom. Because the elder Kaspé was so well guarded and because he so seldom left the Moderne, however, in mid-August of that year he changed his mind and gave orders to the Kempeitai to kidnap the hotelier's son instead. We are also told by Vespa that his boss was about fifty years old at the time and that he had a "bristling mustache."[13]

Most of this points to one man: General Michitarō Komatsubara, an Imperial Japanese Army career man. Komatsubara was a "Russia hand" who had served as a military attaché in Russia from 1909 to 1910 and was fluent in the language. In 1918, he was assigned to the Soviet branch of army general staff, so it is no stretch to believe he was in Siberia on business in that year. He was forty-eight years old at the time of the kidnapping, and he sported a short, stiff mustache. According to several sources, from April 1932 to August 1934 he headed the Tokumu Kikan. That organization was responsible for Japanese military intelligence, and was surely the same bureau Vespa referred to as the "Japanese Intelligence Service."[14]

This was the man Vespa recalled telling him that the rich Chinese and Russians—and especially the rich Jews—of Manchuria would be made to foot the bill for the occupation and that the money had to be extracted in such a way that no one could accuse Japan of extorting it. The Japanese wanted the Hotel Moderne; using the White Russians was a way to wrest control of it from Josef Kaspé without fingerprints, and without creating an international incident.[15]

Komatsubara's tenure in Harbin coincides with all the activities Vespa ascribes to his chief in *Secret Agent of Japan* save one. Vespa reported receiving an order from his chief during the kidnappers' trial to stop the Chinese judges of the Harbin District Court from reaching out for factual information about Kaspé's abduction to counter the lies in Eguchi's indictment. That did not occur until late 1935 or early 1936, when Komatsubara had already returned to Japan. But in his memoir, Vespa was occasionally unreliable as far as facts and dates are concerned. And it is possible that the order came from Komatsubara in Tokyo. Then, too, Vespa reported that the man spoke English. Whether Komatsubara was an English speaker is unclear.

Various records and articles give different titles for Komatsubara during his time in Harbin. He is referred to, variously, as chief of the Harbin Special Services Agency, head of the Military Intelligence Service, Japanese Amy resident officer, and chief of the Japanese military mission. In any of those capacities he would have been empowered to give the orders Vespa ascribed to him.[16]

We also learn from Vespa that fully ten days before Semyon's abduction his chief had inquired whether Josef Kaspé had close relations with Reynaud, adding that "the French flag is not going to stop us from doing what we please." He had initially thought of assigning the kidnapping to hired Chinese thugs to prevent anyone from suspecting Japanese participation, but had decided instead to give the mission to Russians who sometimes worked with the Kempeitai. The chief had little regard for Jewish people, a prejudice he may have picked up during his years in Russia. He blamed Jews for the League of Nations' decision on Manchukuo and told Vespa that those under his jurisdiction were—"indirectly"—to be "persecuted, tortured, humiliated [and] reviled without respite."[17]

By "indirectly," he meant that Japanese fingerprints must not be on any actions taken against the Jews. For example, he assigned Russian thugs under his command to break the windows repeatedly of the two synagogues in town. But Vespa insisted that, his deep antisemitism notwithstanding, his key motivation for the attacks he ordered on local Jews

FIG. 19. Michitarō Komatsubara, chief of the Special Services Agency in Harbin from 1932 to 1934. Wikimedia Commons.

was not politics or Jew hatred but money. Part of Komatsubara's role, if indeed he was the man to whom Vespa referred, was to help fulfill the Japanese plan to make Manchuria underwrite its own colonization. And if, in the process, some local Japanese officials managed to siphon some "squeeze" out of the local Jews to fill their own pockets, that was fine with him too, as long as it was done quietly.

Why Vespa declined to name Komatsubara is unclear. It seems unlikely he was telling the truth when he asserted that he had never learned his boss's name. Komatsubara's name and his title were no secret; they appeared in the local newspapers from time to time. Most likely, because the Japanese occupied Shanghai in late 1937 when Vespa was working on the manuscript, withholding the name was a prudent move. Komatsubara was still very much alive at the time. And Vespa still feared Japanese retaliation, with—as it turned out—good reason, for the Kempeitai would eventually catch up with him.

What is perhaps most shocking about Komatsubara as the ultimate authority who had ordered the abduction of Semyon Kaspé is the degree of his deceit. On November 13, 1933, he had personally paid a call on French consul Reynaud and for two full hours, with full knowledge of Semyon's condition and whereabouts, promised the complete cooperation of the Kempeitai and the police in the young man's rescue and the capture of his abductors.[18]

That meeting took place just eleven days before those very men— who had tortured Semyon Kaspé for three months—shot him to death.

21

The Fugu Plan

Although the kidnapping of Semyon Kaspé and the subsequent trial of his kidnappers placed Harbin under international scrutiny, the spotlight did not stop persecution of its Jews. The ill-treatment not only continued unabated; it got worse.

Harbinskoe Vremya kept up its daily slander, and the *Manchuria Daily News* published a list of Jewish shops and an appeal to Japanese people not to patronize them because they were "Reds" and "Bolsheviks." But it was *Nash Put* that played all the angles. It accused local Jews of hating Manchukuo and Japan and portrayed them as Soviet spies. In late 1933, in an effort to arouse Japanese indignation, it asserted that the members of the Harbin Jewish community were disloyal to Japan, citing their alleged failure to display Japanese flags to celebrate the birth of Japanese Crown Prince Akihito to Emperor Hirohito and Empress Nagako. It was actually a lie; the community had, in fact, sent its congratulations via the Japanese consul.[1]

According to a letter-writer to *Israel's Messenger*, *Nash Put* also placed posters on the city's main thoroughfares with slanderous headlines like, "The Jew Mazin Declares He Is Going to Wipe Out All Russian Bakers by Use of His Capital," "The Jew Akershtein Slaps Russians at the Cinema," and "Dr. Kaufman, You Have Murdered My Daughter." And it called for Russians to "settle accounts" with those responsible for such acts—"an open invitation," the author wrote, "for a pogrom." It ran a front-page story with a faked image of a telegram from Afghanistan alleging that local Jews had slaughtered a Moslem child there to use his blood for ritual purposes. And on November 17, 1935, two Harbin Jews named Vitenson and Kassovsky disappeared entirely, presumably the victims of foul play.[2]

But it wasn't only the Russian Fascists who persecuted the Jews. After Japan took over, the police did their share. Raids on the synagogue compound, on the home of the Talmud Torah principal, and another on Dr. Abraham Kaufman's house were ultimately driven by the Japanese authorities, not *Nash Put*. And when the Emperor Pu Yi paid a visit to Harbin, a dozen of the most respected Jews in town were detained for a week in the cellar of the Kempeitai, together with common criminals. No non-Jews received comparable treatment.

"It is impossible to describe the terrible condition in which the Jews of Harbin are living," *Israel's Messenger* wrote. "The latter are encircled by a horde of bloodthirsty beasts who are after Jewish blood." If *Nash Put* could call openly for the annihilation of the Jews of Harbin and the world, and if the authorities, from Tokyo on down, would do nothing about it, it seemed time to head for the exits.[3]

Even before the Japanese invasion, Harbin had become a troubled place for Jews. But when their new Japanese masters found common cause with the extremists among the Russians, the local Jews quickly realized that things had changed for the worse. During the first ten months of 1932, the year the Japanese took control of the city, some six hundred Jews left for points south. More than half settled in Shanghai. The following year, Hong Kong, then a British crown colony, received five hundred Jewish refugees from the north, mostly Russians from Harbin, Tianjin, and Shanghai.[4]

When the Soviet government sold Russia's Chinese Eastern Railway holdings to the Japanese in 1935, the line's nearly five hundred Jewish employees were dismissed and they lost Soviet protection. Many were in central management or in the railroad's repair and construction shops; others were members of the faculties of the primary, secondary, and high schools or the medical staff of the hospitals owned by the railroad. This decision impacted a few thousand Jewish Harbin residents, taking into account their relatives and the owners and employees of the shops that did business with them. Many faced the unappealing prospect of having to move back to Russia. Indeed, more than eight hundred of the railroad's employees and members of their families departed for Russia the next year and another two hundred went elsewhere.[5]

During 1935, the Far Eastern Jewish Central Information Bureau, a Harbin-based organization founded in 1917 to address the problems of Jewish refugees, reported that even as it had received some five hundred inquiries from desperate German Jews seeking to emigrate *to* the Far East (a handful of whom ultimately settled in Harbin), it had helped 1,071 Jews emigrate *from* Manchukuo. About half went to the Soviet Union, from whence many had come after the 1917 Revolution. The rest fanned out to South China and Japan (260); Poland, Lithuania, Latvia, and Romania (91); the United States (53); Palestine (22); the Philippine Islands, the Straits Settlements, and the British and Dutch East Indies (13); Argentina (9); South Africa (6); Chile (5); Mexico (5); Canada (4); Uruguay (4); Brazil (3); Australia (3); and Colombia (2).[6]

Of course, there were factors other than the disposition of the Kaspé case that caused the Jews of Harbin—and the rest of Manchuria—to pack up. Japan and Russia were blaming each other for border skirmishes, and war once again seemed possible. And the Depression had hit some very hard. Although many Jews had prospered in Manchuria, there were also throngs living in poverty who could see no way out of it.

And then there were the harassment and the kidnappings, which never stopped. In January 1935, a young Jewish man named Weizman was attacked and beaten at a skating rink by four young Russians. In June, twenty-one-year-old Leib Mali was abducted by White Russians in the vicinity of one of the Harbin synagogues. He was kept in a field behind the Jewish cemetery for twenty-six days until his father, Jacob, a former contractor for the Chinese Eastern Railway, came up with $3,000—a discount from the original demand of $15,000. After Leib's release, father and son left immediately for Russia. Nor were they the only Jews to conclude that Harbin no longer offered them safe harbor.[7]

Other victims were not so fortunate. Merchant Mendel Leonson disappeared within a month of Leib Mali. It took two years, but his body was eventually discovered at the bottom of a well. Mark Abramovich, a student whose father was a well-known figure in Harbin, was held for ransom and killed in 1936. Isaac Klurman, also a businessman, was abducted in 1938. And the execution the year before of Jacob W. Hammer, a thirty-three-year-old Polish Jewish merchant who was accused of spying for

Soviet Russia, arrested, held incommunicado, and convicted in a secret trial, also sent a chill through the community. Hammer's corpse, when interred in the Jewish cemetery, showed signs of torture and starvation. And he had been in *police* custody.[8]

In the mid-1930s, however, a possible counterpoint to what appeared an unstoppable Jewish exodus emerged. Just as Russia had suddenly decided at the turn of the century that its Jews might be useful in cementing its economic position in Manchuria, some Japanese, on the lookout for assistance in their planned conquest of East Asia, began to envision a potential use for Jews beyond merely fleecing them of their accumulated wealth. The bold idea came in the form of a proposal not only to stanch the exodus of Jews from Japanese-occupied territory, but also to resettle tens of thousands *more* of them who were desperate to flee the Nazis.

Under development for several years, the plan first saw daylight in 1934 when Yoshisuke Aikawa, the industrialist who founded the Nissan conglomerate, published an article detailing a plan to invite fifty thousand German Jews to live in Manchuria. His scheme was reported in the Western press in early October of that year, though the Japanese Foreign Ministry initially denied its existence.[9]

The plan, which *was*, in fact, under discussion, was based on the assumption that Jews played a major role in world economic affairs and were influential in world capitals, especially Washington, which Japan feared might impose sanctions on it for its incursion into Manchuria or future adventures in Asia. It envisioned attracting and putting the financial resources of international Jewry to use and taking advantage of Jewish political power and technical skills. It labored under the misguided notion that wealthy Jews, especially in America, could be persuaded—during the worst of the Great Depression—to park their capital in Manchurian industry if there were local Jews in the picture.

The plan was the brainchild of Aikawa, a colonel in the Imperial Japanese Army named Norihiro Yasue, and a Navy captain named Koreshige Inuzuka. The latter two had served between 1918 and 1922 in the Japanese Siberian Intervention and been introduced to the *Protocols of the Elders of Zion* forgery by the anti-Jewish General Semyonov. Yasue had gone on to translate it, under a pseudonym, into Japanese. For better or worse, these men, who knew relatively little about Jews, became the chief "Jewish hands" in a country that knew even less. The Japanese Foreign Ministry had arranged for Yasue to travel to Germany and Palestine in 1926–27 to gather information about the Jewish people; in the latter, he had met both Chaim Weizmann and David Ben-Gurion.

Shaped by the *Protocols*, by Nazi antisemitism, and by Japan's own experience with Jacob Schiff, the Jewish-American financier who had helped the country obtain credit during the Russo-Japanese War, the proposal was dubbed the Fugu Plan by Captain Inuzuka. It was named for the Japanese word for a blowfish—an expensive and tasty dish that could be fatal to a diner if not prepared with the utmost delicacy. The metaphor suggested that Jews had much to contribute to fulfilling Japan's aspirations, but had to be handled and managed with great care, lest Japan itself suffer a "Jewish problem" of the kind alleged by its allies, the Nazis.

Although the plan envisioned putting out a welcome mat to many stateless Jews, it was, of course, no philosemitic endeavor. Yasue and his associates had digested much of the bile that appeared in the *Protocols*. They believed Jews already controlled most of America's capital and its media, that they were the power behind the U.S. government, and that they were intent on taking over the world economy. Their plan set out a cynical but pragmatic strategy to avoid offending this apparently influential minority on the one hand, and to harness their perceived power and wealth in the service of the emperor on the other. It was not cost-free to Japan, as it risked endangering its nascent alliance with Nazi Germany and its cooperation with local White Russian extremists, who would be important if Japan ever did battle with the Soviet Union. Nevertheless, as Inuzuka remarked at the time: "if we can remain ever-alert to the sly nature of the Jews, if we can continue to devote our constant attention to this enterprise lest the Jews, in their inherently clever manner, manage to turn the tables on us and begin to use us for their own ends, if we succeed in our undertaking, we will create for our nation and our beloved Emperor the tastiest and most nutritious dish imaginable. But if we make the slightest mistake, it will destroy us in the most horrible manner."[10]

The Fugu Plan continued to be fleshed out throughout the 1930s. After Japan invaded the rest of China in 1937, it envisioned not only

Jewish settlement in Manchuria, but also in Shanghai. Remarkably detailed, it set out the organization, boundaries, and target populations for various planned Jewish settlements, specifying how much autonomy they would be accorded, how they would be controlled, and how world Jewry would fund them. It also anticipated sending Japanese delegations to America to make contact with American rabbis, suggest similarities between Japanese religious beliefs and their own, and persuade them of Japan's benign intentions toward Jews. After extensive internal debate, Japan finally formalized the policy in 1938, and shortly after that, several thousand Jews were indeed granted asylum in the Japanese quarter of the city of Shanghai.[11]

Naturally, the Jews already in Manchuria would be called upon to play a part in the scheme. But that community's view of Japan had soured considerably since the invasion. In the aftermath of the Kaspé affair and similar kidnappings and murders, Harbin's Jewish population had already halved in size to about ten thousand souls. In an effort to build their confidence, stem the tide of further departures of Jews and their capital, and improve Japan's image among world Jewry, Colonel Yasue embarked on a charm offensive. He suppressed *Nash Put*, the Russian Fascist newspaper that had for years been the bane of Harbin Jewry, and ousted Osamu Eguchi, the hated former prosecutor. And, together with Lieutenant General Kiichirō Higuchi, who took over the Harbin Tokumu Kikan in 1937, he reached out to Abraham Kaufman, the much-slandered head of the community.[12]

On the initiative of Yasue and Higuchi, Kaufman organized and chaired a Far Eastern Jewish Council that mounted three conferences, the first of which was convened at the Hotel Moderne in December of 1937. It brought together twenty-one Jewish delegations from Harbin, Tianjin, Dalian, Mukden, Hailar, Qiqihar, and Kobe—seven hundred people in all—and was ostensibly about Zionism.

Although the effort was carried out only under careful Japanese supervision—all meetings were required to have Japanese observers present—the benefit to the Jewish community of the new organization was that it conferred on them recognition as a community and gave them a direct line to the authorities and a modicum of protection against White Russian

FIG. 20. The first meeting of the Far Eastern Jewish Council, held at the Hotel Moderne in December 1937. Courtesy of Dan Ben-Canaan.

reactionaries. It also enabled them to lobby successfully for transit visas for thousands of Jewish refugees who had traveled through Siberia and needed to pass through Manchuria on their way to Shanghai and other points. To the Japanese, however, it was a vehicle to promote the idea of Jewish colonies in their occupied lands, and a first step toward winning over the hearts and minds of world Jewry.

Yasue and Higuchi pulled out all the stops in romancing Dr. Kaufman. They arranged for him to receive a medal from the Manchukuo government and to make an official visit to Tokyo, where he was honored with an imperial award. He visited the Ministry of War and the Ministry of Foreign Affairs and toured Osaka, Kyoto, Nagoya, Tokyo, Kamakura, and Nikko. Kaufman discussed the needs of the Manchurian Jews and received assurances that Japan did not, and would not, discriminate against them.[13]

Kaufman called Yasue—the very man who had translated the *Protocols of the Elders of Zion* and other works of antisemitic literature into

Japanese—a "true friend of the Jew." He became an intermediary between Japan and Jewish communities around the world and a willing messenger, if not a strong advocate, for their plans for Jewish colonies in Asia. His readiness to work with Japan, given the experience of the Harbin Jewish community with the Japanese Army, remains the subject of some debate. Was he manipulated by the Japanese and used for their own ends? Or was cooperation a strategic move on his part, during very desperate and dangerous times, to improve conditions for suffering Far Eastern Jews, to whom he bore responsibility as a leader? Kaufman defended himself years later, claiming he had viewed working with Japan as nothing less than a survival strategy for the Jews of Manchuria. That is, he asserted that it had been an offer he had dared not refuse.[14]

The Japanese charm offensive didn't go nearly as well in America, where Japan was already unpopular. Luminaries like Cyrus Adler, president of the American Jewish Committee, and Rabbi Stephen S. Wise, head of the American Jewish Congress, were both approached by representatives of the Far Eastern Council and the Japanese government. Rabbi Wise, who had been publicly critical of the Eguchi indictment a few years earlier and was no friend of Japan, made his opposition to the Fugu Plan known in late 1938, when he declared in a letter to the council that "it is wholly vicious for Jews to give support to Japan, as truly Fascist a nation as Germany or Italy," and pledged to "do everything I can to thwart your plans."[15]

Wise eventually softened his stance a bit, but it didn't matter. Although some Jewish emigration from Europe to Asia did occur—some eighteen thousand German, Austrian, and Polish Jews were permitted to land in Japanese-occupied Shanghai between 1938 and 1940, and approximately six thousand more from Nazi-occupied lands were sheltered in the Japanese port of Kobe—relocation became more and more difficult. In 1939, after the Soviet Union signed a nonaggression pact with Nazi Germany, travel to the Far East from Europe became more difficult for Jews. And it became even *less* feasible in 1940 when the Soviets annexed the Baltic states, cutting off more escape routes, and when Nazi Germany began to pressure Japan to withdraw its support for Jews. Thanks to German pressure, the fourth conference of the Far Eastern Jewish Council, slated to take place in 1940, never happened; the Japanese government did not permit it.[16]

The Fugu plan, never fully developed, was dead. Nor had it ever come close to stopping the departure of Manchuria's Jews, who continued to suffer from persecution, and who had lost any confidence that their rights would be protected. Who could trust a government that allowed a promising young Jewish man, in the prime of his life, to be brutally murdered and then gave his kidnappers and killers a free pass?

Japanese actions had belied their words.

The exodus continued throughout the 1930s — mostly to Shanghai, Tianjin, and Hong Kong, though others opted for the United States, Australia, Russia, and Palestine — wherever Jews were welcomed, or at least tolerated. The Jewish population of Harbin declined from thirteen thousand in 1931 to five thousand in 1935, and then to three thousand in 1938, meaning that only a small fraction of the once-proud community of twenty thousand endured World War II there.

Manchuria's Jews, although cut off from funding from Jewish organizations in the West during the war, were not ill-treated by the Japanese during the war years. The Japanese Army did assign "advisers" to oversee the activities of each local Jewish organization, but the relationships were mostly benign. The few Jews who had remained were able to live unmolested until the arrival of the Soviet Army in 1945.[17]

As far as they were concerned, the Soviet Union's "liberation" of Manchuria was anything but liberating. After the war, another thousand of Harbin's Jews left for Palestine, leaving about two thousand. Some, like Abraham Kaufman, were charged as Japanese collaborators, accused of spying, and transferred to Russian gulags.

Nor were Jews the only foreigners who departed. From its peak of 120,000 in 1922, Harbin's Russian population shrank to fifty-five thousand after the Japanese invasion. When the Red Army thrashed Japan's Guandong Army and took control in 1945, about half of those left were repatriated, many to Kazakhstan, and Harbin ceased to be a significant Russian settlement. The rest of the Russians trickled out in the years that followed, after Harbin reverted to Chinese sovereignty.[18]

When the Chinese Communists consolidated their control of the China mainland in 1949, the new People's Republic of China they established had little use for the foreigners who remained, Harbin's Jews, who now numbered fewer than a thousand, included. They didn't specifically single out Jews when they confiscated property and took over private enterprises, but for those few who remained, the handwriting was on the wall. By 1955, only a little over 300 Jews were left in Harbin, and by 1962 the city's Jewish community institutions were officially closed down.[19]

After the last Jewish family departed in 1962, only one Jewish woman remained. Her name was Hannah Agre, and she lived longer than she wished. She had been born in Harbin in 1908 to a father who had fled Ukrainian pogroms and taken a Siberian wife. He had worked for a time for the Chinese Eastern Railway. Hannah herself had worked as a domestic for a wealthy Jewish family and married a Russian sailor from whom she later separated. After the Communists took over, she continued to live in a one-room apartment at the Old Synagogue on Artilleriyskaya Street, which was also where the surviving records of the Harbin Jewish community were stored.

Even after enduring persecution from Red Guards during the Cultural Revolution, Agre adamantly refused to leave, though she had been offered opportunities to move to Russia, Israel, and Denmark. She never learned to speak Chinese and communicated only in Russian and Yiddish until her death in 1985, closing the chapter on the Russian Jewish experience in Harbin.[20]

Epilogue

Because they headed east and not west at the turn of the twentieth century, the Jews of Harbin were, in the main, *less* fortunate than many of their brethren who left Russian lands entirely, but better off than those who stayed and perished at the hands of the Nazis. Most had already moved on by the time the Second World War broke out, but those few who waited out the war in Manchuria found their Japanese hosts far more obliging than their Nazi counterparts.

The story of the Kaspés is more or less the story of what Harbin was to the Jews: a momentary refuge from persecution, disrupted all too soon by unassailable geopolitical forces allied against them. In the short span of a few decades, Jews lived there under various degrees of protection—or lack of it—from *five* regimes: Russia (which controlled the Chinese Eastern Railway corridor), the Republic of China (but really a powerful local warlord), "Manchukuo" (but really Japan), the Soviet Union (after "liberation" in 1945), and, by the end of the 1940s, Communist China. And their fortunes rose and fell accordingly. The upshot for them was, ultimately, the same as for that of Jews in foreign lands since time immemorial. When they felt they could no longer count on the protection of the authorities, they fled.

Lured to northeastern China by promises of freedom from harassment, many prospered. But what had begun on a hopeful note—an unprecedented opportunity to live unmolested in a version of Russia without pogroms, punitive laws, and arbitrary restrictions—ended with a mass exodus when Russia and its problems pursued them, and Japan enabled their persecution.

Harbin had never been a paradise for Jews, but it had offered a relatively secure life until then. The unholy alliance struck by Russians and

Japanese—"the worst of stepmothers"—changed the course of their lives, and eventually made Manchuria intolerable for them.

If there is a positive note to their story, it is that unlike those who died at Auschwitz and Treblinka—and unlike poor Semyon Kaspé—most of these Jews survived and went on to rebuild their lives elsewhere in Asia, in Australia, in North America, and in the Holy Land.

After the Second World War, the individuals in the Kaspé story went their separate ways, some on to better lives, others in chains. Among them:

Aisin-Gioro Pu Yi left Xinjing by train as the Soviet Army advanced into Manchuria; a few days later, he decreed Manchuria once again a part of China and abdicated his position as emperor of Manchukuo. Captured by the Red Army, he was brought to the Soviet Union, which rebuffed the Republic of China's demands that he be repatriated and tried for high treason. In 1950, however, after the establishment of the People's Republic of China, he was sent back to China. Though he feared he would be executed, the Chinese Communists saw great propaganda value in his rehabilitation as a Communist and granted him an opportunity to "reform." He was eventually given a government sinecure and he died in Beijing in 1967.

Albert Henri Chambon remained in Tianjin, where he was posted after his assignment in Harbin, for only three months. Fearful that he had been targeted for assassination by Japanese agents, the Foreign Ministry recalled him. He went on to a distinguished career in the French foreign service, holding high-ranking positions in Monaco, Tangier, Boston, Naples, and Rio de Janeiro and ambassadorships in Costa Rica, Panama, Peru, Sri Lanka, and the Maldives. During World War II, he headed an important network within the Conseil National de la Résistance (CNR), the French Resistance, and was apprehended and deported to Buchenwald, where he remained for one year. He wrote a book about his experience at that camp entitled 81490. He later held offices within the French Foreign Ministry and represented France at several diplomatic conferences and international organizations. A decorated civil servant and a prolific author, Chambon died in 2002 in Le Chesnay, in north central France.

Kenji Doihara was arrested by the Allies after Japan's defeat in World War II and tried in Tokyo before the International Military Tribunal for the Far East as a "Class A war criminal," that is, one who had committed "crimes against peace." The judges, representing eleven countries, found him guilty and sentenced him to death. He was hanged in 1948 at Sugamo Prison in Tokyo.

Nissim Elias Benjamin Ezra remained editor-in-chief of *Israel's Messenger* until his death in Shanghai in 1936.

Josef Alexandrovich Kaspé departed Manchuria a broken man shortly after the death of his son Semyon. He and his wife joined their son Vladimir in France. The Japanese authorities took over his hotel and theater, retaining an émigré to manage them, and his jewelry store was liquidated in 1935. He died in France in October 1938.[1]

Marie Semyonova Zaitchik Kaspé returned to Paris with her husband after Semyon's death. She returned to Harbin twice more, in 1935 and 1939, but died in Digne-les-Bains, France, in 1941. In 1944, she was stripped of her French citizenship by the Vichy government, which was apparently unaware of her death.

Semyon Kaspé was interred on December 5, 1933, in the Jewish cemetery on Bolshoi Avenue, which no longer exists at the site. But Semyon's wish that a memorial be established in his memory, expressed in a letter to his mother and brother written from captivity shortly before his murder, was honored. Between 1958 and 1962, the Chinese authorities, eager to redevelop the property (which today is the site of the Harbin Fair and the Harbin Ice Palace), supervised the removal of a few hundred of the approximately twelve hundred gravestones in the cemetery to the new Huangshan Public Cemetery outside of the city, though not the graves themselves. Semyon's tombstone, a horizonal grave marker, was among those relocated, and though badly worn, it rests there today.[2]

Vladimir Kaspé was stripped of his French citizenship by the Vichy government in 1943, but he had already left the country with his wife, Marie Schapiro Kaspé. He emigrated to Mexico by way of Casablanca and embarked on a successful career as an architect and academic. He died in 1996.

Abraham Josevich Kaufman was arrested by the Red Army after it invaded Manchuria in 1945 and taken to Russia. For his cooperation with the Japanese he was imprisoned in a gulag for eleven years. After his release in 1956, he moved to Kazakhstan and in 1961 emigrated to Israel, where he resumed his career as a physician. He died in Tel Aviv in 1971.

Nikifor Pavlovich Kirichenko, after being freed from prison, was exiled from Harbin by the Japanese authorities and sent to Pogranichny, fifteen kilometers east of the Chinese border in Russia.[3]

Michitarō Komatsubara returned to Japan in 1934; he took command of the Eighth Infantry Brigade, the Second Independent Garrison Unit, and, in 1936, the new 23rd Division of the Army, the primary Japanese division involved in the 1939 battle of Khalkhin Gol, a border conflict among the Soviet Union, Mongolia, Japan, and Manchukuo. After Japan was defeated, Komatsubara was called back home in disgrace. He retired from military service in early 1940 and took his own life eight months later, at the age of fifty-four.[4]

Dionisy Grigoryevich Komissarenko, like Kirichenko, was exiled from Harbin by the Japanese authorities and sent to Pogranichny, fifteen kilometers east of the Chinese border in Russia, after being freed from prison.[5]

Nikolai Andreevich Martinov was exiled to Dalian with his wife by the Japanese authorities after his release from prison. Because of his notoriety, he was instructed to change his name and sent to work as a guard in a coal mine. Eventually, however, he was called back to Harbin and given a job in the Tokumu Kikan. After the Soviet invasion of Manchuria, he fled to Tianjin, where he allegedly barely escaped lynching by local Jews. After World War II, like many other Russian refugees, he left Communist China with his family for Tubabao Island in the Philippines, a former U.S. Navy base, but eventually found asylum in Belgium, where he is presumed to have died.[6]

Konstantin Ivanovich "Kostya" Nakamura became, by one account, an interpreter for SMERSH, the Red Army's counterintelligence unit after the Soviet invasion in August 1945. But he was eventually taken to the Soviet Union and interned in a detainee camp in Siberia, where he informed on his former Kempeitai colleagues. After two years he was transferred to a Moscow prison as a suspected war criminal, but in 1948 he was repatriated to Japan. After his return, he found work in Tokyo as a building manager and an advertising salesman and claimed to be a professor of Russian.[7]

Louis Osmond Ferdinand Reynaud was appointed French consul in Hong Kong in 1940. The following year the government he served fell to the Nazis, and Hong Kong came under Japanese control. He refused to swear loyalty to the Vichy government and spoke out against it, living on his own savings when funds from Paris dried up. Under Japanese pressure, he eventually closed the consulate and retired, but he did not quit Hong Kong. He died in the French Hospital there in 1943 after a long illness.[8]

Konstantin Vladimirovich Rodzaevsky gave himself up to the Soviet authorities in Harbin to avoid capture by the Red Army. He was promised freedom and a job in Russia, but once back in the country of his birth he was arrested and sentenced to death in a show trial. He was shot to death that same day in the basement of Moscow's Lubyanka Prison.

Alexei Yelievich Shandar was exiled from Harbin to Dalian by the Japanese authorities after his release from prison. Because of his notoriety, he was instructed to change his name and sent to work as a guard in a coal mine. He eventually emigrated to the United States, where he died in 1994. He is buried in Gresham, Oregon.[9]

Lydia Abramovna Chernetskaya Shapiro left Harbin with her four boys after she testified at the trial of Semyon Kaspé's kidnappers and rejoined her husband in Japan. She bore a fifth son, taught piano, and continued to perform. The family lived in Japan throughout World War II and was not ill-treated. Although their sons went their separate ways, Lydia and her husband remained in Japan until 1952, when they emigrated to America with their youngest child. They settled in California and became American citizens, and Lydia resumed her musical career, teaching and playing chamber music. She died of heart disease in 1983 at the age of 78.

Amleto Vintorino De Chellis Vespa had run into serious trouble with his Japanese keepers by the beginning of 1936; they had ceased to pay him, and even after selling off assets, he began to run out of money. With both Nakamura and Rodzaevsky plotting against him, he escaped Manchuria by boat to China, eventually landing in Shanghai, but his family was held hostage and not permitted to join him. This led him to threaten to publish all he knew of Japanese misdeeds in Manchuria if his family were not released, and he set about composing his memoir, *Secret Agent of Japan*.

His wife and daughter were released in early 1937, but later that year the Japanese took Shanghai and he was again in peril. Believing that publication of his manuscript might raise his profile and shield him from Japanese reprisals, he delivered it to an Australian journalist friend who brought it to London. The book was published in London in 1938 and New York in 1939, but in 1940, accused of spying for the United States, Vespa was imprisoned by the Kempeitai. His family lost contact with him after the Japanese attacked Pearl Harbor, and he is presumed to have been executed by the Japanese military in Taiwan or the Philippines in 1945.

Oleg Volgin, Alexandre Pernikoff's alias for the young Russian who worked for the Kempeitai, fell out of favor with Kostya Nakamura, who believed he had been disloyal. He was arrested on trumped-up charges, bound and gagged, and taken from his home in a waiting automobile to the second floor of the Gendarmerie building, where all forms of torture occurred. For two weeks he was kicked and beaten, placed in a cage, and dehumanized. But his tormentors' goal was not his death; it was his unquestioning obedience. Upon his release, he was offered a new job. Instead he managed to escape Manchuria by stowing away on a ship bound for Tianjin.[10]

Norihiro Yasue did not flee when Japan surrendered to the Red Army in 1945. He was taken to the Soviet Union and died in a labor camp in Khabarovsk in 1950.

Yakov Kirillovich Zaitsev was exiled from Harbin to Dalian by the Japanese authorities after his release from prison. He was instructed to change his name and sent to work as a guard in a coal mine.[11]

The Hotel Moderne was placed by the Japanese in the care of a Russian named Korosh after the departure of Josef Kaspé, but the local Jewish community negotiated for it to be transferred to one of its officials, Moisei G. Zimin. After the Red Army marched in, arrested Zimin, and took him to the Soviet Union in 1945, management was taken over by the Chinese government. In 1949, the Chinese Communist Party designated it the Harbin City Government Guesthouse. Four years later, it was given the name of the Harbin Hotel, but at the onset of the Cultural Revolution in 1966 it was renamed the Harbin City Revolutionary Committee Second Guesthouse. In 1983, the property reverted to the name Harbin Hotel and a decade later it once again assumed the venerable moniker of Moderne Hotel. It remains in business to this day.[12]

Acknowledgments

No one's works have been more helpful to me in the research and writing of this book than those of Dan Ben-Canaan, Professor Emeritus of Heilongjiang University's School of Western Studies and Chair of the Sino-Israel Research and Study Center in Harbin, who has written extensively on the Kaspé case and the history of Harbin Jewry. A generous Israeli-born scholar who may well be the *only* Jew living in Harbin at this writing, Dan has made much of his work freely accessible on the internet and has always been at the ready with the answer to a question or a hard-to-find image or document. I am deeply indebted to him.

I was fortunate to be able to piggyback not only on his research, but on that of Noriko Uchiyama Valuev, an instructor at Osaka University and a freelance historian whose inquiry into the life and times of one of Semyon Kaspé's kidnappers, exhaustive search of Russian-language media of the period, and willingness to correspond with me and answer my innumerable queries opened a window I would otherwise have been unable to open for myself. I thank her for her scholarship and her generosity.

I am equally indebted to Steven I. Levine, a retired professor of Chinese politics and history at the University of Montana with a side interest in Russia. Fortunately for me, his somewhat peculiar hobby is editing history manuscripts. He was of immeasurable help in cheerfully and tirelessly reviewing multiple drafts of the manuscript and whipping it into shape.

And special thanks go to my good friend Marsha Cohan, another "China hand," who, throughout the research and writing stages of this book, was a willing, frank, and reliable sounding board. Her candid comments and suggestions were exceptionally useful in shaping the final work.

My gratitude also goes to scholars who generously shared their own work with me, including Zvia Bowman, Mark Gamsa, Ming Hui Pan, and Chizuko Takao.

Others who reviewed all or part the manuscript or offered suggestions include Chris Billing, Beatrice Camp, Nicholas Chen, John Colletta, Roy Delbyck, John Donaldson, Paul French, Rita Gotfried, Lester Lau, Susan Levine, Stephen Markscheid, Stephen Mink, Madelyn Ross, Harvey Solomon, Deborah Strauss, Glenn Sugameli, the late Roger Sullivan, David Summers, Anne Thurston, Wang Yukui, David Warner, Xu Xin, and Suzanne Zunzer. All deserve my heartfelt thanks, as do Toru Matsubayashi, Martine Schultz, Yoshiko Nagano, and Galina Spivak for invaluable translation help.

And a special word of appreciation to the family of Lydia Shapiro for sharing stories and photographs: her sons Isaac, Jacob, and Michael Shapiro as well as John McDonald, Daniel McDonald, and Kayomi Shapiro McDonald. Also to Bernard and Isabel Chambon for sharing an unpublished memoir by their father, Albert, about his time in China and his role in the Kaspé case.

Many other people helped me gather materials or pointed me in useful directions, including Wendy Abraham, Manja Altenburg, Melvyn Arshan, Ira Belkin, Arnold Berke, Beverly Bossler, Charlotte Brooks, Mark Cohen, Thomas David DuBois, Jules Feldman, Paul French, Mark Gamsa, Madeleine Herren, Gulnara Klebche, Lester Lau, Jeremy Lichtman, Craig Michael, Alain Peyrot, Jeffrey Schultz, Martine Schultz, Daniel Seligman, Howard Spendelow, Robert Steinbaum, Diana Sykes, and Steve Temkin.

Finally, thanks to my indefatigable literary agent, Peter W. Bernstein, to Amy Pattullo, for an excellent job of copyediting, to Vicki Low, for her meticulous work on the index, and to Tom Swanson, Taylor Rothgeb, and Kayla Moslander and their colleagues at Potomac Books and the University of Nebraska Press, for their confidence in me, and for affording me the very pleasant opportunity of working with them once again.

Chronology

1894–95

The First Sino-Japanese War is fought in Korea and Manchuria. China is forced to open several ports to Japanese trade, pay a large indemnity to Japan, and cede control over lands including Manchuria's Liaodong Peninsula. Pressured by Russia, Germany, and France, Japan reluctantly gives up the latter.

1896

China's Qing (Manchu) Dynasty grants czarist Russia a concession to allow it to complete the Trans-Siberian line to Vladivostok by building a railway across Manchuria. Russia is granted extraterritorial rights in the zone along the route.

1897

Construction begins on the Chinese Eastern Railway. The location at which the tracks cross the Sungari River is selected as its headquarters, heralding the growth of the city of Harbin.

1899

The czar offers Jews who settle in Manchuria freedom from restrictions they are forced to endure in Russia. As a result, Jews begin to settle in Manchuria.

1902

The railway begins operation. Though most of Manchuria remains under Chinese sovereignty, Russia becomes the dominant power there.

1903

A census of Harbin counts forty-five thousand people, about 63 percent Chinese and 33 percent Russian, with small populations of Japanese and other nationalities. Among them is a smattering of Jews, most of whom live in the Pristan waterfront district.

1904–5

The Japanese stage a surprise attack on the Russian Navy at Port Arthur, launching the Russo-Japanese War, which is fought mostly in Manchuria. Japan prevails and comes into possession of much of southern Manchuria, including the South Manchuria Railway.

Josef Kaspé, a Russian-Jewish soldier in the Russo-Japanese War, settles in Harbin after he is decommissioned.

1909

Semyon Kaspé is born in Harbin.

1912

The Qing Dynasty is overthrown and the new Republic of China is established. Although it has nominal sovereignty over Manchuria, the real law there resides in warlord Zhang Zuolin.

1914

Josef Kaspé's Hotel Moderne opens in Harbin.

1917–23

The Russian Civil War, in which the czar and his family are murdered and the Bolsheviks seize power, results in the establishment of the Soviet Union and a mass exodus from Russia. Manchuria receives about 250,000 Russian refugees.

1924

The Republic of China recognizes the Soviet government and agrees to joint Soviet-Chinese administration of the Chinese Eastern Railway.

1926

Marie Kaspé takes her sons Semyon and Vladimir to France to study.

1931

In what became known as the Mukden incident, Japan's Guandong Army stages an explosion on the South Manchuria Railway and uses it as a pretext for an invasion of Manchuria.

The Russian Fascist Party, dedicated to overthrowing the Soviet regime and establishing a fascist system in Russia, is founded in Manchuria. It is suspected of setting fire to Harbin's main synagogue.

Marie, Vladimir, and Semyon Kaspé become naturalized French citizens.

1932

JANUARY 25–FEBRUARY 4
Japan's Guandong Army seizes control of Harbin.

MARCH 1
A puppet government created by Japan proclaims Manchukuo an independent state and Aisin-Gioro Pu Yi, former emperor of China, is installed as its president.

MARCH 10
Michael V. Koffman, a Jewish pharmacist, is kidnapped in Harbin and held for a $30,000 ransom his family cannot pay. Koffman is tortured to death, and his body is never found.

MAY 9
A commission of the League of Nations headed by Lord Victor Bulwer-Lytton arrives in Harbin on a fact-finding mission to Manchuria. Japanese officials attempt to shield its members from all contact with locals who oppose Japan's plans for Manchuria.

JUNE–JULY
Semyon Kaspé graduates from the French Music Conservatory.

AUTUMN
Semyon Kaspé returns to Harbin. Josef Kaspé transfers ownership of his properties to his sons.

SEPTEMBER
The Lytton Commission rejects Japan's justification for its invasion of Manchuria and finds no popular support for the State of Manchukuo.

OCTOBER
I. Sherel de Florence, son of a local Jewish merchant, is kidnapped and held for ransom. He is released after 105 days when a ransom of $25,000 is paid.

1933

FEBRUARY 24
The League of Nations adopts the Lytton Commission report and declines to recognize Manchukuo.

MARCH
Japan denounces the Lytton Commission report and withdraws from the League of Nations in protest.

AUGUST 24
Semyon Kaspé and Lydia Shapiro are abducted in front of her home

after a party at the Moderne Hotel. Lydia and the driver are released, but Semyon is taken to a secret hideout. A ransom demand of 300,000 yen, or about $1.4 million, is made.

AUGUST 25

The Kaspé case is assigned to Nikolai Nikiforov, head of the Criminal Police.

Josef Kaspé, distraught, meets with French Consul Louis Reynaud to seek assistance in freeing his son, who holds French citizenship.

AUGUST 26

Kidnappers phone Nikiforov and promise him a share of the ransom if he does not pursue them. They tell him they do not fear the Japanese Gendarmerie. Whether due to incompetence or corruption, Nikiforov proves ineffective in pursuing the investigation.

AUGUST 29

Marie Kaspé is informed in Paris of her son's abduction and the ransom demand by the Ministry of Foreign Affairs.

SEPTEMBER 25

Josef Kaspé agrees to pay 35,000 yen, but only *after* his son is freed. The offer is rejected.

SEPTEMBER 27

Lydia Shapiro receives a package containing a piece of one of Semyon's ears, with instructions to deliver it to Josef Kaspé.

SEPTEMBER 28

Because of Nikiforov's lack of progress, French consul Louis Reynaud and Albert Chambon, his deputy, hire their own investigators to find Semyon Kaspé. They also secure permission from Paris for the French embassy in Tokyo to press the Japanese government to intervene with the military and police authorities in Harbin.

The Kaspé case is reassigned to Chief of the Criminal Affairs Division Osamu Eguchi, who collaborates with the Japanese Gendarmerie, represented by Kostya Nakamura.

SEPTEMBER 30

Marie Kaspé informs the French Foreign Ministry that her family is unable to pay the ransom and asks that the French government guarantee the funds. She is told this is counter to regulations.

EARLY OCTOBER

A driver informs Hotel Moderne manager Gurevitch that before the kidnapping, two people named Komissarenko and Bezruchko offered him a million yuan to lend them his car for a kidnapping. Gurevitch fails to ask his name or get his car number, but these names are passed on to the police.

OCTOBER 9
Alexei Shandar and Nikolai Martinov, suspects in an earlier kidnapping, are arrested, as is Dionisy Komissarenko.

OCTOBER 22
Semyon Kaspé writes his father a plaintive letter from captivity urging him to meet the kidnappers' demands. Additional letters follow.

OCTOBER 30
Josef Kaspé responds to his son's letter in the only way he can: by releasing his answer to the local Russian newspapers. He explains that he is deeply in debt and cannot meet the kidnappers' demands.

NOVEMBER 2
Chambon writes his superiors that he believes the kidnappers are in bed with the Japanese officials in charge of the case.

NOVEMBER 13
Komissarenko is released by the police for lack of evidence, but Chambon's detectives pick him up for interrogation.

Reynaud meets with Colonel Michitarō Komatsubara, chief of the Tokumu Kikan, or Special Service Agency in Harbin, responsible for military intelligence. He promises Reynaud the assistance of the Kempeitai and the police in the search.

NOVEMBER 15
Chambon's men question Komissarenko. He names the band of kidnappers, who are all Russians. He also confirms that these same men had been responsible for earlier kidnappings of Jews. He reveals that Semyon has been taken to Ashihe, twenty-five miles from the city.

NOVEMBER 16
Chambon's agents travel to Ashihe with Komissarenko and eight members of the Japanese Gendarmerie, or Kempeitai. But the kidnappers have already left, together with Semyon Kaspé. In the debris left behind, they find a bloody bandage.

NOVEMBER 17–18
Komissarenko and two of Chambon's agents proceed to Xiaoling, a hiding place forty-six miles from Harbin on which the kidnappers had previously agreed in the event one of them was captured. There they find an abandoned hideout,

but they believe the kidnappers are still in the area.

Expecting to be murdered, Semyon writes what he believes will be his final letters to his father, mother, and brother.

NOVEMBER 21

Kostya Nakamura agrees to cooperate with Chambon's men in the arrest of some of the kidnappers during their trip to Harbin to collect supplies, but secretly sabotages the operation.

NOVEMBER 22

Negotiations continue between Josef Kaspé and the kidnappers, who lower their demands several times. Kaspé's insistence that the ransom be paid at the same time as his son's release continues to be a sticking point.

NOVEMBER 23

Konstantin Galushko allegedly offers to release Semyon for a payment of 10,000 yuan and returns to Harbin with a secret letter from Semyon to his father. The letter is discovered by Nakamura, who orders Nikifor Kirichenko to kill Semyon.

NOVEMBER 24

After telling Semyon Kaspé he will be freed that night, Kirichenko shoots him to death at the hideout.

He is buried nearby in a shallow grave.

NOVEMBER 29

Chambon's detectives work with police to ambush the kidnappers during a planned rendezvous near the Harbin railroad station. At the last minute, the operation is botched by the Kempeitai. Galushko is shot to death, but Kirichenko escapes.

Separately, two of the kidnappers, Panteleimon Bezruchko and Yakov Zaitsev, are arrested by the Railroad Police.

DECEMBER 2

Chambon and his three investigators travel to Xiaoling. They question locals and follow footprints in the snow.

DECEMBER 3

Kempeitai representatives show up at Xiaoling with Bezruchko in tow. He leads them to the campsite, where they find Semyon Kaspé's shallow grave. They recover his emaciated, mutilated, and decomposed body.

DECEMBER 4

Semyon's body is returned to Harbin for burial.

DECEMBER 5

The streets of Harbin are filled for Semyon Kaspé's funeral cortege, as 250 gendarmes and a regiment of the Japanese infantry are dispatched to keep the peace. Dr. Abraham Kaufman delivers a fiery eulogy critical of local authorities. Semyon is buried in the Harbin Jewish cemetery.

Chambon tells press that the local police authorities are "powerless."

DECEMBER 8

In an antisemitic rant, the Russian Fascist newspaper *Nash Put* denounces Kaufman's funeral speech and criticizes him for being "strongly against the Russian and the local authority." It recommends his expulsion from Manchuria and suggests the rest of the Jews go with him.

A press report alleges that police discovered documents in French, English, and Russian written by Chambon containing "violent criticism" of the local police. The paper reports talk in local government circles of expelling Chambon from Manchuria.

DECEMBER 9

Unnerved by the criticism of his funeral speech, Abraham Kaufman assures Nikolai Yagi of the Criminal Affairs Division of the Harbin Police that his speech did not constitute an attack on the Manchurian authorities or their representatives.

DECEMBER 18

Kirichenko, the last of the living kidnappers still at large, is arrested in Hailar by the Railroad Police.

LATE DECEMBER

Osamu Eguchi, head of the Criminal Police, who is charged with drafting the indictment against the kidnappers, publicly refutes Chambon's comments with a fabricated version of the events of the previous months.

1934

FEBRUARY

The prisoners, who have been thoroughly interrogated, are summoned to repeat their testimony to the procurator of the Harbin Court. Only Shandar and Zaitsev refuse to confess.

MARCH 9

Aisin-Gioro Pu Yi ascends the throne of Manchukuo.

NOVEMBER 29

Osamu Eguchi turns over an outrageous report to the Office of the

Procurator, in which he asserts that the kidnappers had acted out of patriotism. It blames the Russian Revolution on Jews and denounces Josef Kaspé as a Communist sympathizer. Eguchi asks for sentences of fifteen years at hard labor for Martinov, thirteen for Shandar, and five to twelve years for the rest. He blames the murder on the dead Galushko.

1935

JANUARY–FEBRUARY

Worldwide, the Jewish press denounces Eguchi's antisemitic screed. Jewish leaders protest official antisemitism in Manchukuo to Japanese diplomats in China, the United States, and elsewhere. A Japanese official pledges to muzzle *Nash Put*, but it continues its slanderous, antisemitic rants.

JUNE 7

The District Court of Harbin convenes to hear the case against the kidnappers. The accused, the first to be charged under the 1932 Provisional Law for Punishment of Banditry, are tried by three Chinese judges, working under Japanese "advisers."

SPRING–SUMMER

Amleto Vespa provides the judges with damning, ex parte information proving that the kidnappers were working for the Kempeitai.

OCTOBER 11

During his testimony, Zaitsev fingers Martinov and accuses several Japanese of responsibility for planning the kidnapping, though their names are not reported in the press.

DECEMBER 25

The trial comes to a halt, allegedly due to the sudden transfer of the chief judge.

1936

MARCH 23

A new trial begins before a second panel of Chinese judges.

JUNE 15

Police reinforcements are present on street corners on the day of the verdict. The defendants, shackled at the wrists and ankles, are brought into the packed courtroom.

Surprisingly, the court ignores the recommendations of the procurator and sentences Martinov, Shandar, Kirichenko, and Zaitsev to death by hanging and Komissarenko and Bezruchko to life imprisonment and deprivation of civil rights.

JUNE

Eguchi orders the sentences suspended and appeals for intervention by the Guandong Army. The chief of the headquarters staff receives Martinov's wife and Kirichenko's attorney and assures them the case will be reviewed and the executions postponed indefinitely.

JULY 9

Without citing a reason, the Supreme Court in Xinjing, the highest court in Manchukuo, refuses to approve the verdict and orders a new trial in the High Court of Harbin.

SEPTEMBER 6

The chief judge of the foreign department of the Harbin High Court, who is Japanese, announces that he will preside over the new trial.

1937

JANUARY 11

The new trial begins. The accused are charged under the criminal code, which does not provide for the death penalty, instead of the law against banditry, under which they had previously been charged.

JANUARY 29

The men are convicted, but although the procurator had recommended penal servitude for all, the men benefit from an amnesty earlier decreed by Emperor Pu Yi..

FEBRUARY

After more than three years in prison, the kidnappers are released.

SPRING

Sensitive to public reaction to the verdicts, the authorities banish the kidnappers from Harbin, sending Martinov, Shandar, and Zaitsev to Dalian and Kirichenko and Komissarenko to the Russian border. Some are later called back to Harbin to continue serving under the Japanese police and gendarmes.

JULY 7

Japan invades the rest of China and begins the Second Sino-Japanese War.

DECEMBER

The first of three conferences of the Far Eastern Jewish Council, which gathers delegates from Jewish communities in the Far East, is held in Harbin under Japanese supervision. The Fugu plan, a Japanese scheme that envisions resettling large numbers of European Jews in Japanese-occupied territories, is discussed.

1938

Due to steady emigration throughout the 1930s that accelerates after the murder of Semyon Kaspé, the Jewish population of Harbin has declined to three thousand.

A Japanese campaign to build support for the Fugu Plan in the American Jewish community is unsuccessful. Rabbi Stephen S. Wise, head of the American Jewish Congress, pledges to thwart the plan.

1945

The Soviet Union invades Manchuria and defeats the Guandong Army. This contributes to the surrender of Imperial Japan. It also engenders a mass exodus of Russians remaining in Manchuria.

After the war, another thousand Jews leave for Palestine, leaving about two thousand in Harbin.

Abraham Kaufman is charged as a Japanese collaborator by the Soviets and sent to a forced labor camp.

1955

Only a few more than three hundred Jews are left in Harbin.

1962

The last Jewish family departs Harbin.

1985

Harbin-born Hannah Agre, the last Jew left in Harbin, dies, closing the chapter on the Russian Jewish experience in Harbin.

Glossary and Gazetteer

Note: *Abbreviations designate the term's language of origin: Mandarin Chinese (CH), English (EN), French (FR), Hebrew (HB), Japanese (JP), Manchurian (MA), Mongolian (MO), Russian (RU).*

Amur River (RU): the river that forms the border between the Russian Far East and northeastern China. Known in Chinese as Heilongjiang.

Ashihe (CH): a station on the Chinese Eastern Railway twenty-five miles southeast of Harbin.

Artilleriyskaya Street (RU): today's Tongjiang Jie.

Banzai (JP): a Japanese exclamation meaning "ten thousand years" or "long life."

Bingtang hulu (CH): *see* Takhuli.

Bolshoi Avenue (RU): today's Xidazhi Jie.

Chabad (HB): a Hasidic movement founded in 1775.

Changchun (CH): *see* Xinjing.

Chevra kadisha (HB): an organization of Jewish men and women who prepare bodies for ritual burial.

Dairen (JP): *see* Dalian.

Dalian (CH): a provincial port on the southern tip of Manchuria's Liaodong Peninsula traditionally known in the West as Port Arthur.

Diagonalnaya Street (RU): today's Jingwei Jie.

Droshky (RU): a low, open, four-wheeled carriage formerly used in Russia.

Ercengdianzi (CH): a station on the Chinese Eastern Railway forty-three miles southeast of Harbin.

Evreiskaya Zhizn (RU): A Russian-language weekly ("Jewish Life") published by Abraham Kaufman in Harbin.

Excelsior (FR): an illustrated French daily published in Paris.

Fengtian (CH): *see* Shenyang.

Fugu Plan (JP): a Japanese scheme in the runup to WWII that envisioned resettling large numbers of European Jews in Japanese-occupied territories in Asia.

Funt (RU): a unit of weight equal to about fourteen ounces.

Gobi (MA): a unit of currency used in Manchukuo. Rendered as *guobi* in Mandarin.

Guandong (CH): traditional Chinese name for Manchuria, i.e., the lands beyond Shanhaiguan, the easternmost pass of the Great Wall of China.

Guandong Army (CH): the subdivision of the Imperial Japanese Army that operated in China, Manchuria, and Mongolia.

Gulag (RU): a Russian forced labor camp.

Gymnazia Generezova (RU): a secondary school in Harbin that educated young women.

Hailar (MO): a Mongolian city near the Russian border.

Harbin (CH): a Manchurian city on the Sungari River that became the headquarters of the Chinese Eastern Railway and was home, at one time, to the world's largest Russian diaspora community.

Harbinskoe Vremya (RU): ("Harbin Times"), the most widely circulated local newspaper in Harbin, published in Russian but controlled by the Japanese Consulate.

Heilongjiang (CH): one of the three northeastern Chinese provinces that make up Manchuria. *See also* Amur River.

Honghuzi (CH): Chinese bandits in the Russian-Chinese borderland. The name translates literally as "red beards."

Huangshan Cemetery (CH): a cemetery on the outskirts of Harbin that encompasses the largest extant Jewish graveyard in East Asia.

Jilin (CH): one of the three northeastern Chinese provinces that make up Manchuria.

Kempeitai (JP): the gendarmerie, or military police arm of the Imperial Japanese Army.

Kitaiskaya Street (RU): today's Zhongyang Dajie. Russian for "Chinese street."

Konnaya Street (RU): today's Dongfeng Jie.

Liaodong Peninsula (CH): a peninsula in southern Liaoning Province that is the site of the city of Dalian.

Liaoning (CH): one of the three northeastern Chinese provinces that make up Manchuria.

L'intransigeant (FR): a French newspaper published in Paris between 1880 and 1940.

Magazinnaya Street (RU): today's Huapu Jie.

Manchukuo (CH): the state of Manchuria, a puppet state created by the Empire of Japan that existed between 1932 and 1945.

Manzhouli (CH): a Manchurian city on the Russian border.

Maoershan (CH): a town in Heilongjiang Province sixty miles southeast of Harbin.

Mikveh (HB): a Jewish ritual bath.

Ming Dynasty (CH): the ruling Chinese dynasty from 1368 to 1644.

Minyan (HB): a quorum, traditionally of ten men, needed for formal Jewish worship.

Mohel (HB): traditionally, a Jewish man trained in ritual circumcision.

Moya-tvoya (RU): pidgin Russian sprinkled with Chinese words spoken in Manchuria. Literally, "my-yours."

Mukden (MA): *see* Shenyang.

Muzhik (RU): a Russian peasant.

Nash Put (RU): ("Our Way"), a daily newspaper that served as the official organ of the Russian Fascist Party.

Novy Gorod (RU): literally, "new town." Today's Nangang District.

Oyogashi (JP): an investigation method in which a criminal is released and shadowed. Literally, "let him swim."

Pekarnaya Street (RU): today's Hongzhuan Jie.

Pogrom (RU): a violent riot, particularly against Jews.

Polizeiskaya Street (RU): today's Youyi Lu.

Port Arthur (EN): *see* Dalian.

Pristan (RU): the wharf district of Harbin. Today's Daoli district.

Qing Dynasty (CH): the Manchu-led imperial dynasty in China that reigned from 1644 to 1912.

Qipao (CH): a high-necked, tight-fitting Chinese lady's garment with a slitted skirt.

Qiqihar (MA): a Manchurian city in western Heilongjiang Province.

Samannaya Street (RU): today's Xiaman Jie.

Shanhaiguan (CH): the easternmost pass of the Great Wall of China.

Shenyang (CH): a major city in Liaoning Province. Formerly known as Fengtian, or by its Manchu name, Mukden.

Shochet (HB): a Jewish ritual slaughterer of animals.

Songhuajiang (CH): *see* Sungari River.

Staryi Gorod (RU): literally, "old town." Today's Xiangfang district.

Strelkovaya Street (RU): today's Jianshe Jie.

Sungari River (RU): major Manchurian river that flows through Heilongjiang and Jilin provinces and is the longest tributary of the Amur River. Chinese: Songhuajiang.

Takhuli (RU): candied hawthorns or crabapples.

Talmud Torah (HB): a Jewish elementary school that emphasizes religious education.

Tokumu Kikan (JP): the Special Service Agency of the Japanese Army responsible for gathering military intelligence.

Weihaiwei (CH): a seaport on the northeastern shore of China's Shandong Province.

Xiaoling (CH): a town on the Chinese Eastern Railway forty-six miles southeast of Harbin.

Xinjing (CH): name given to the city of Changchun by the Japanese when it was designated as the capital of Manchukuo. Literally, "new capital."

Yen (JP): a unit of currency.

Yuan (CH): a unit of currency. Sometimes erroneously referred to as "yen."

Zarya (RU): a Russian-language newspaper ("Rays of Sunlight") published in Harbin.

Further Reading

On the Kaspé Case

"Affaire Kaspé." N.d., Archives du Quai d'Orsay, Affaire Kaspé, série Asie, sous-série Chine, 1940, no. 748bis.

Ben-Canaan, Dan. *The Kaspé File: A Case Study of Harbin as an Intersection of Cultural and Ethnical Communities in Conflict 1932–1945.* Harbin, China: Heilongjiang University School of Western Studies, 2008.

Breuillard, Sabine. "L'Affaire Kaspé revisitée." [In French.] *Revue des études slaves* 73, no. 2/3 (2001): 337–72.

——— . "A New Review of the Kaspé Affair." *Bulletin, Igud Yotzei Sin* 53, no. 385 (September–October 2005): 12–14.

Chambon, Albert. *Tribulations d'un jeune diplomate dans la vielle Chine.* [In French.] Unpublished manuscript, 1999.

Nakashima, Takeshi. "The Kaspé Incident in Harbin, Russian Society, and Japan, 1933–1937," [In Japanese.] *Humanities Bulletin* (Tokyo Metropolitan University): 490 (March 2014).

Pan, Ming Hui. "The Harbin Jewish Community and the Regional Conflicts of Northeast China, 1903–1963." PhD diss., Concordia University, 2020, 93–95.

Pernikoff, Alexandre. *Bushido: The Anatomy of Terror.* New York: Liveright, 1943.

Sunamura, Tetsuya. *The Harbin Church Garden.* [In Japanese.] Tokyo: PHP, 2009, 11–45.

Uchiyama Valuev, Noriko. "The Kaspé Affair Trial as Reported by Harbin Russian Newspapers." [In Japanese.] *Sever* 33 (March 2017): 46–47.

——— . "The Kaspé Case of Nikolai Martinov: The Full Story of the Case as Written by the Perpetrator Himself." [In Japanese.] *Sever* 31 (March 2015): 82–104.

Vespa, Amleto. *Secret Agent of Japan.* London: Victor Gollancz, 1938.

On Manchuria

Ben-Canaan, Dan, Frank Grüner, and Ines Prodöhl, eds. *Entangled Histories: The Transcultural Past of Northeast China*. Heidelberg: Springer International, 2014.

Dubois, Thomas David. "Rule of Law in a Brave New Empire: Legal Rhetoric and Practice in Manchukuo." *Law and History Review* 26, no. 2 (Summer 2008): 302.

Gamsa, Mark. *Manchuria: A Concise History*. London: I. B. Tauris, 2021.

Nish, Ian. *The History of Manchuria, 1840–1948: A Sino-Russo-Japanese Triangle*. Kent, UK: Renaissance Books, 2016.

Reardon-Anderson, James. *Reluctant Pioneers: China's Expansion Northward, 1644–1937*. Redwood City CA: Stanford University Press, 2005.

On Harbin

Gamsa, Mark. *Harbin: A Cross-Cultural Biography*. Toronto: University of Toronto Press, 2021.

Meyer, Kathryn. *Life and Death in the Garden: Sex, Drugs, Cops, and Robbers in Wartime China*. Lanham MD: Rowman & Littlefield, 2014.

Wolff, David. *To the Harbin Station: The Liberal Alternative in Russian Manchuria, 1898–1914*. Redwood City CA: Stanford University Press, 1999.

On the Harbin Jewish Community

Ben-Canaan, Dan. *Jewish Footprints in Harbin: Concise Historical Notes*. Jewishgen. https://kehilalinks.jewishgen.org/harbin/Jewish_Footprints_in_Harbin.htm.

Bowman, Zvia. "A People That Dwells Alone—The Russian, Chinese and Japanese Perceptions of Harbin Jewish Community, 1898–1945." *Points East* 36, no. 2 (July 2021).

Gamsa, Mark. "The Many Faces of Hotel Moderne in Harbin." *East Asian History* 37 (December 2011): 27–38.

Kaufman, Theodore. *The Jews of Harbin Live On in My Heart*. [In Hebrew.] Tel Aviv: Profil, 2004.

——— . "The Moderne Hotel as One of the Important Centers in the Life of Harbin." *Bulletin, Igud Yotzei Sin* 53, no. 389 (September–October 2006).

Klurman, Irene, and Dan Ben-Canaan. "A Brief History of the Jews of Harbin: How a Manchurian Fishing Village Became a Railroad Town and a

Haven for Jews." *Jewishgen*. https://kehilalinks.jewishgen.org/harbin/brief
_history.htm.

Moustafine, Mara. *Secrets and Spies: The Harbin Files*. Sydney: Random House Australia, 2002.

Takao, Chizuko. "Prewar Japan's Perception of Jews and the Harbin Jewish Community: The Harbin Jewish Community under Japanese Rule 1932– 1941." *Journal of the Interdisciplinary Study of Monotheistic Religions* 10 (2015): 32–49.

———— . "Russian-Jewish Harbin before World War II." *Japanese Slavic and East European Studies* 32 (2011): 39–53.

Vladimirsky, Irene. "The Jews of Harbin, China." *ANU Museum of the Jewish People*. https://www.anumuseum.org.il/jews-harbin.

On the Russian Fascists

Balakshin, Petr. *Final v Kitae*. [In Russian.] Munich: Sirius, 1958.

Nakashima, Takeshi. "Forming the Russian Fascist Party in Harbin, 1925–1933." *Journal of Social Sciences and Humanities* 505 (March 2015): 1–19.

Oberlander, Erwin. "The All-Russian Fascist Party." *Journal of Contemporary History* 1, no. 1 (1966): 158–73.

Stephan, John J. *The Russian Fascists: Tragedy and Farce in Exile, 1925–1945*. New York: Harper & Row, 1978.

On the Fugu Plan

Medzini, Meron. *Under the Shadow of the Rising Sun: Japan and the Jews during the Holocaust Era*. Brighton MA: Academic Studies Press, 2016.

Tokayer, Marvin, and Mary Swartz. *The Fugu Plan: The Untold Story of the Japanese and the Jews during World War II*. New York: Paddington Press, 1979.

Notes

Introduction

1. *WBGO Journal*, accessed July 30, 2021, https://www.wbgo.org/show/wbgo-journal/2017-07-10/newarks-jewish-community-pre-and-post-1967-rebellion.

Prologue

1. "Musique," *L'intransigeant*, April 24, 1932.
2. John J. Stephan, *The Russian Fascists: Tragedy and Farce in Exile, 1925–1945* (New York: Harper & Row, 1978), 81–82; "Kaspé Case Appealed to Japanese Judges in Harbin High Court," *China Weekly Review*, July 18, 1936.
3. "Anti-Jew Move in Harbin," *North China Herald and Supreme Court and Consular Gazette*, September 6, 1933.

1. Tug of War

1. Dan Ben-Canaan, Frank Grüner, and Ines Prodöhl, eds., *Entangled Histories: The Transcultural Past of Northeast China* (Heidelberg: Springer International, 2014), 5; Mark Gamsa, *Manchuria: A Concise History* (London: I. B. Tauris, 2021); James Reardon-Anderson, *Reluctant Pioneers: China's Expansion Northward, 1644–1937* (Redwood City CA: Stanford University Press, 2005).
2. "The Treaty of Portsmouth and the Russo-Japanese War, 1904–1905," Office of the Historian of the Department of State, accessed August 16, 2021, https://history.state.gov/milestones/1899-1913/portsmouth-treaty.
3. K. K. Kawakami, "The Russo-Chinese Conflict in Manchuria," *Foreign Affairs* 8, no. 1 (October 1929): 62.

2. Harbin—Cosmopolis in the North

1. Olga Bakich, "Origins of the Russian Community on the Chinese Eastern Railway," *Canadian Slavonic Papers/Revue Canadienne des Slavistes* 28, no. 2 (June 1986): 12.

2. Bakich, "Origins of the Russian Community on the Chinese Eastern Railway," 2; "Conditions in Manchuria," *Journal of the American Asiatic Association* 4, no. 2 (March 1904): 44.

3. "Conditions in Manchuria," 44.

4. Dan Ben-Canaan, Frank Grüner, and Ines Prodöhl, eds., *Entangled Histories: The Transcultural Past of Northeast China* (Heidelberg: Springer International, 2014), 5; Mark Gamsa, *Manchuria: A Concise History* (London: I. B. Tauris, 2021), 85–88; "Conditions in Manchuria," 44.

5. Tao Fan, "The Urban Structure of Harbin, China: An Urban Design Approach," (master's thesis, University of Calgary, 2002), 33, 39; Albert Chambon, *Tribulations d'un jeune diplomate dans la vielle Chine* [in French] (unpublished manuscript, 1999), 60, collection of the Chambon family.

6. "20 Daily Newspapers in Four Languages Are Published in Manchurian City of Harbin," *New York Times*, January 29, 1933.

7. Harry A. Franck, *Wandering in Northern China* (New York: Century, 1923), 82–108.

8. V. A. Chernov, "Peculiarities of the Formation of the Hospitality Industry in Russian Harbin," *Proceedings of the International Scientific Conference 'Far East Con'*, ISCFEC 2018, (Atlantis Press, 2019); Mina Muraoka, "Jews and the Russo-Japanese War: The Triangular Relationship between Jewish POWs, Japan, and Jacob H. Schiff," PhD dissertation, Brandeis University, 2014, 5, 55–62.

9. Irene Klurman and Dan Ben-Canaan, "A Brief History of the Jews of Harbin: How a Manchurian Fishing Village Became a Railroad Town and a Haven for Jews," *Jewishgen*, accessed June 20, 2021, https://kehilalinks.jewishgen .org/harbin/brief_history.htm.

10. Sabine Breuillard, "A New Review of the Kaspé Affair," *Bulletin, Igud Yotzei Sin* 53, no. 385 (September–October 2005): 12–14; Dan Ben-Canaan, *The Kaspé File: A Case Study of Harbin as an Intersection of Cultural and Ethnical Communities in Conflict 1932–1945* (Harbin, China: Heilongjiang University School of Western Studies, 2008), 13; Chernov, "Peculiarities of the Formation of the Hospitality Industry in Russian Harbin"; Amleto Vespa, *Secret Agent of Japan* (London: Victor Gollancz, 1938), 195–96.

11. "Dr. A. J. Kaufman," Jewish Communities of China, accessed August 24, 2021, http://www.jewsofchina.org/dr-a-j-kaufman; "Avraham Yosifovich Kaufman," Jewish Virtual Library, accessed August 24, 2021, https://www .jewishvirtuallibrary.org/kaufman-avraham-yosifovich.

12. Dan Ben-Canaan, "Jewish Footprints in Harbin: Concise Historical Notes," Jewishgen, accessed August 20, 2021, https://kehilalinks.jewishgen.org/harbin /Jewish_Footprints_in_Harbin.htm; Irene Clurman and Dan Ben-Canaan, "A Brief History of the Jews of Harbin: How a Manchurian Fishing Village Became a Railroad Town and a Haven for Jews," USC U.S.–China, accessed August 20, 2021, https://china.usc.edu/sites/default/files/forums/A %20Brief%20History%20of%20the%20Jews%20of%20Harbin%20Short %20version.docx; Abraham Kaufman, "The Little Hamlet Called Harbin," *Bulletin, Igud Yotzei Sin, Association of Former Residents of China* 52, no. 402: 54–55; "The Jewish Community of Harbin," ANU Museum of the Jewish People, accessed August 24, 2012, https://dbs.anumuseum .org.il/skn/en/c6/e204683/Place/Harbin?utm_source=google&utm _medium=cpc&utm_term=%2Bjewish%20%2Bharbin&utm_campaign = g & device = c & gclid = CjwKCAjwlrqHBhByEiwAnLmYUA1i3Rj _iKOO1ws5gpWEAhTwgRIaifxYlOrscvwNpfq2oVMugVFLCBoCL1IQAvD _BwE; "A Paradise in Russia," *Hebrew Standard*, October 15, 1909; Mara Moustafine, "Russians from China: Migrations and Identity," *Cosmopolitan Civil Societies Journal* 5 (2013), no. 2: 146.

13. Chizuko Takao, "Russian-Jewish Harbin before World War II," in *Japanese Slavic and East European Studies* 32 (2011), 41; Irene Klurman and Dan Ben-Canaan, "A Brief History of the Jews of Harbin: How a Manchurian Fishing Village Became a Railroad Town and a Haven for Jews," Jewishgen, accessed June 20, 2021, https://kehilalinks.jewishgen.org/harbin /brief_history.htm; "The Jewish Community of Harbin," ANU Museum of the Jewish People, accessed August 24, 2012, https://dbs.anumuseum .org.il/skn/en/c6/e204683/Place/Harbin?utm_source=google&utm _medium=cpc&utm_term=%2Bjewish%20%2Bharbin&utm_campaign = g & device = c & gclid = CjwKCAjwlrqHBhByEiwAnLmYUA1i3Rj _iKOO1ws5gpWEAhTwgRIaifxYlOrscvwNpfq2oVMugVFLCBoCL1IQAvD _BwE; "A Paradise in Russia," *Hebrew Standard*, October 15, 1909.

14. *Vestnik Azii* [Herald of Asia], May 9, 1911, in David Wolff, *To the Harbin Station—The Liberal Alternative in Russian Manchuria, 1898–1914* (Redwood City CA: Stanford University Press, 1999), 100–101.

15. Ming Hui Pan, "The Harbin Jewish Community and the Regional Conflicts of Northeast China, 1903–1963" (PhD diss., Concordia University, 2020), 93–95.

16. "Grant Legal Status to Harbin Kehillah," *Jewish Advocate*, June 30, 1927.

3. White Russians and Antisemitism

1. Mara Moustafine, "Russians from China: Migrations and Identity," *Cosmopolitan Civil Societies Journal*, Vol. 5 (2013), No. 2, 143; John J. Stephan, *The Russian Fascists: Tragedy and Farce in Exile, 1925–1945* (New York: Harper & Row, 1978), 1, 40; Erwin Oberlander, "The All-Russian Fascist Party," *Journal of Contemporary History*, Vol. 1, No. 1 (1966), 160.

2. Mara Moustafine, *Secrets and Spies: The Harbin Files* (Sydney: Random House Australia, 2002), 94–95.

3. Chizuko Takao, "Russian-Jewish Harbin before World War II," in *Japanese Slavic and East European Studies* 32 (2011): 48; Mara Moustafine, "The Harbin Connection: Russians from China," in Shen Yuanfang and Penny Edwards, eds., *Beyond China: Migrating Identities* (Canberra: Centre for the Study of the Southern Chinese Diaspora, Australian National University, 2002), 75–87.

4. Harry A. Franck, *Wandering in Northern China* (New York: Century, 1923), 82–108.

5. John J. Stephan, *The Russian Fascists: Tragedy and Farce in Exile, 1925–1945* (New York: Harper & Row, 1978), 51–56; Erwin Oberlander, "The All-Russian Fascist Party," *Journal of Contemporary History* 1, no. 1 (1966): 158–73.

6. Stephan, *Russian Fascists: Tragedy and Farce in Exile, 1925–1945*, 58.

4. The Kaspés

1. For the description and early history of the Moderne Hotel, I am indebted to Mark Gamsa, whose deeply researched "The Many Faces of Hotel Moderne in Harbin," in *East Asian History* 37 (December 2011), deftly sorts out fact from myth; "Teatr 'Modern'," *Zheleznodorozhnaia zhizn' na Dal'nem Vostoke* 36–37 (1914): 15; "Otkrytie gostinitsy 'Modern'" *Zheleznodorozhnaia zhizn' na Dal'nem Vostoke* 36–37 (1914), 14; Simon Karlinsky, "Memoirs of Harbin," *Slavic Review* 48, no. 2 (Summer 1989): 284–90.

2. "Our Manchurian Letter," *North China Herald and Supreme Court and Consular Gazette*, July 10, 1926; Gamsa, "Many Faces of Hotel Moderne in Harbin," 33; Julean Herbert Arnold, *China: A Commercial and Industrial Handbook* (Washington: Government Printing Office, 1926), 682.

3. Lilian Grosvenor Coville, "Here in Manchuria," *National Geographic*, February 1933, 233.

4. "M. S. Kaspé Dies in France," *Harbinskoe Vremya*, February 2, 1941.

5. "Kaspé to Play Tomorrow for Home Folks," *China Press*, April 18, 1933.

6. Mark Gamsa, *Harbin: A Cross-Cultural Biography* (Toronto: University of Toronto Press, 2021), 64; James H. Carter, *Creating a Chinese Harbin: Nationalism in an International City, 1916–1932* (Ithaca NY: Cornell University Press, 2002), 43; Yaacov Lieberman, *My China: Jewish Life in the Orient 1900–1950* (Jerusalem: Gefen, 1998), 18.

7. "École Alsacienne," *Le temps*, July 26, 1927.

8. "Paris Clubland," *New York Herald*, European edition, February 13, 1930; "The Social World," *Chicago Tribune*, European edition, February 16, 1930; Georg Predota, "Salle Pleyel," *Interlude*, accessed June 19, 2021, https://interlude.hk/salle-pleyel/; "Kaspé to Play Tomorrow for Home Folks."

9. "Récitals et concerts," *Comœdia*, June 14, 1930; Maxime Girard, "Concerts et récitals," *Le Figaro*, June 10, 1930.

10. "Musique," *L'intransigeant*, April 25, 1931; "Musique," La semaine à Paris, February 27, 1931; Pierre Leroi, "La Musique," *Excelsior*, April 25, 1931.

11. "Musique," *L'intransigeant*; "Concerts et récitals," *Comœdia*, May 28, 1932.

5. Lydia

1. For the description of Lydia Shapiro's early life, I have relied on memoirs written by two of her sons: Isaac Shapiro, *Edokko: Growing Up a Stateless Foreigner in Wartime Japan* (Bloomington IN: iUniverse, 2009), 7–13, and Michael Shapiro, *Palimpsest of Consciousness: Authorial Annotations of My Wife the Metaphysician, or Lady Murasaki's Revenge* (North Charleston SC: Booksurge, 2007); also Lydia Shapiro Petition for Naturalization, District Court of Los Angeles, California, December 23, 1957.

6. Invasion

1. "Doihara, Kenji," Records of the Office of Strategic Services, Nazi War Crimes and Japanese Imperial Government Records Interagency Working Group, Internet Archive, accessed October 1, 2021, https://archive.org/details /DoiharaKenji/DOIHARA%2C%20KENJI_0002/mode/2up.

2. Court Exhibit No. 730: Interrogation of Rodzaevsky Konstantin Vladimirovich, General Headquarters/Supreme Commander for Allied Powers, entry no. 327, court exhibits in English and Japanese, IPS, 1945–47, National Diet Library Digital Collections, accessed October 11, 2021, https://dl.ndl .go.jp/info:ndljp/pid/10274806.

3. "Flight of Ting," *Time*, February 15, 1932; Amleto Vespa, *Secret Agent of*

Japan (London: Victor Gollancz, 1938), 24–25, 37; "Harbin Memories from Charles (Ruvim) Isaac Clurman," Jewishgen: Kehilalinks, accessed November 21, 2021, https://kehilalinks.jewishgen.org/harbin/Charles_(Ruvim)_Isaac _Clurman.htm.

7. Two Toxic Elements

1. Amleto Vespa, *Secret Agent of Japan* (London: Victor Gollancz, 1938), 46–47, 96, 243–44.
2. *Manchukuo: The Founding of the New State in Manchuria* (New York: Japanese Chamber of Commerce, 1933), 1.
3. Vespa, *Secret Agent of Japan*, 29–30.
4. Vespa, *Secret Agent of Japan*, 32.
5. John J. Stephan, *The Russian Fascists: Tragedy and Farce in Exile, 1925–1945* (New York: Harper & Row, 1978), 70; Alexandre Pernikoff, *Bushido* (New York: Liveright, 1943), 24–25.
6. Kathryn Meyer, *Life and Death in the Garden: Sex, Drugs, Cops, and Robbers in Wartime China* (Lanham MD: Rowman & Littlefield, 2014), 123; Vespa, *Secret Agent of Japan*, 242; Stephan, *Russian Fascists: Tragedy and Farce in Exile, 1925–1945*, 65–66.
7. "Trying to Purge the Manchukuo Police from All 'Impurities'," *China Weekly Review*, February 24, 1934; Noriko Uchiyama Valuev, "The Kaspé Case of Nikolai Martinov: The Full Story of the Case as Written by the Perpetrator Himself" [in Japanese], *Sever* 31 (March 2015), 94–95.
8. C. F. Garstin, Letter to Sir Miles Lampson, December 7, 1933, Foreign Office files for China, 1919–1980, National Archives of the United Kingdom; Stephan, *Russian Fascists: Tragedy and Farce in Exile, 1925–1945*, 83; Vespa, *Secret Agent of Japan*, 213.
9. Franceso Totoro, *The Spying Game: Amleto Vespa's Chinese Affair, 1884–1944* (Italy: Youcanprint, 2019), 84–92.
10. Totoro, *Spying Game: Amleto Vespa's Chinese Affair, 1884–1944*, 5, 23, 26, 36, 43; "Italian Spy in China Tells Desperate Story: Life Saved by His Son," *Milwaukee Journal*, May 4, 1939.
11. Vespa, *Secret Agent of Japan*, 2.
12. "Harbin Murder Plot Uncovered," *China Press*, December 23, 1931; "Harbin Plot to Kill Agent Fails," *China Press*, January 31, 1932; Vespa, *Secret Agent of Japan*, 9.
13. Vespa, *Secret Agent of Japan*, 38–39.

14. Vespa, *Secret Agent of Japan*, 45–50.

15. Meron Medzini, *Under the Shadow of the Rising Sun: Japan and the Jews during the Holocaust Era* (Brighton MA: Academic Studies Press, 2016), 50.

8. An Unholy Alliance

1. Nava Blum and Elizabeth Fee, "The Sungari River Flood and the Jewish Community in Harbin, China," *American Journal of Public Health* 98, no. 5 (2008): 823, accessed October 13, 2021, U.S. National Library of Medicine, https://www.ncbi.nlm.nih.gov/pmc/articles/PMC2374809/.

2. Alexandre Pernikoff, *Bushido: The Anatomy of Terror* (New York: Liveright, 1943), 125–26.

3. Albert Chambon, *Tribulations d'un jeune diplomate dans la vielle Chine* [in French] (unpublished manuscript, 1999), 70–71, collection of the Chambon family.

4. Franceso Totoro, *The Spying Game: Amleto Vespa's Chinese Affair, 1884–1944* (Italy: Youcanprint, 2019), 175.

5. Lilian Grosvenor Coville, "Here in Manchuria," *National Geographic*, February 1933, 233.

6. Coville, "Here in Manchuria."

7. Amleto Vespa, *Secret Agent of Japan* (London: Victor Gollancz, 1938), 140–56; Pernikoff, *Bushido*, 127–29.

8. Chambon, *Tribulations d'un jeune diplomate dans la vielle Chine*, 76.

9. Vespa, *Secret Agent of Japan*, 225–26.

10. "Members of Manchuria Delegation," *American Jewish World*, June 10, 1932.

11. Vespa, *Secret Agent of Japan*, 226.

12. "Harbin Kidnapping Incident," *North China Herald and Supreme Court and Consular Gazette*, March 29, 1932; "Bandits Threaten to Cut Off Russian's Ears if No Ransom," *China Press*, April 8, 1932.

13. "White Russians Suspected of Murder of President of Jewish Community of Harbin," *Jewish Telegraphic Agency*, January 6, 1933; "Harbin Kidnapping," *North China Herald and Supreme Court and Consular Gazette*, May 3, 1932; Chizuko Takao, "Prewar Japan's Perception of Jews and the Harbin Jewish Community: The Harbin Jewish Community under Japanese Rule 1932–1941," *Journal of the Interdisciplinary Study of Monotheistic Religions* 10 (2015): 37; Vespa, *Secret Agent of Japan*, 188–94.

14. "White Russians Suspected of Murder of President of Jewish Community of Harbin"; Vespa, *Secret Agent of Japan*, 189; "Trace Harbin Bombing to White Russian Bandits," *Jewish Telegraphic Agency*, January 16, 1933.

15. "Harbin Jewish Merchant Murdered by White Guardists," *Sentinel*, August 5, 1932.
16. Theodore Kaufman, "The Moderne Hotel as One of the Important Centers in the Life of Harbin," *Bulletin, Igud Yotzei Sin* 53, no. 389 (September–October 2006): 21.
17. David Tucker, *Harbin to Hanoi: The Colonial Built Environment in Asia, 1840 to 1940* (Hong Kong: Hong Kong University Press, 2013), 63–64.
18. "Semyon Kaspé, Pianist, to Give Recital Here," *China Press*, April 13, 1933; "Kaspé to Give 2nd Concert Here Tuesday," *China Press*, April 29, 1933. "XCBL to Broadcast Kaspé Piano Recital," *China Press*, April 29, 1933; "Semyon Kaspé Scores in 2nd Concert Here: Enthusiastic Audience Applauds Virtuoso," *China Press*, May 3, 1933.
19. "Local News Brevities," *China Press*, June 2, 1933; "Radio Programmes," *Manchuria Daily News*, June 8, 1933.
20. "Kidnapping in Harbin," *Konkurent.ru*, May 3, 2011, accessed June 21, 2021, https://konkurent.ru/article/9309.

9. *Kidnapped*

1. Alexandre Pernikoff, *Bushido: The Anatomy of Terror* (New York: Liveright, 1943), 205.
2. The value of the Manchurian yuan in 1933 was 23.91 grams of pure silver, or about 24 U.S. cents. This meant the ransom demand was the equivalent of about $72,000 in 1933 dollars, which would be valued at about $1.5 million today: https://sdbullion.com/silver-price-by-year.
3. "£25,000 Ransom Demanded," *Hull Daily Mail*, August 25, 1933; title unknown, *Zarya*, August 25, 1933; "Young Polo Player Kidnapped," *Nottingham Evening Post*, August 25, 1933; "Des bandits, à Kharbine, enlèvent le fils d'un négociant français," *Le petit parisien*, August 26, 1933; "Enlèvement d'un Français à Kharbine," *Le matin*, August 26, 1933; "Frenchman Kidnapped by Harbin Bandits," *New York Herald*, European edition, August 26, 1933.
4. "Hotel Moderne Boy Kidnapped," *Manchuria Daily News*, August 26, 1933.
5. John J. Stephan, *The Russian Fascists: Tragedy and Farce in Exile, 1925–1945* (New York: Harper & Row, 1978), 81–82.
6. "Affaire Kaspé," undated, Archives du Quai d'Orsay, Affaire Kaspé, série Asie, sous-série Chine, 1940, no. 748bis.

7. Stephan, *Russian Fascists: Tragedy and Farce in Exile, 1925–1945*, 85.

8. "White Russians Suspected of Murder of President of Jewish Community of Harbin," *Jewish Telegraphic Agency*, January 6, 1933; Amleto Vespa, *Secret Agent of Japan* (London: Victor Gollancz, 1938), 189; "Trace Harbin Bombing to White Russian Bandits," *Jewish Telegraphic Agency*, January 16, 1933.

9. Louis Reynaud, letter to Auguste Wilden, August 26, 1933, Archives du Quai d'Orsay, Affaire Kaspé, série Asie, sous-série Chine, 1940, no. 748bis; "Affaire Kaspé," undated, Archives du Quai d'Orsay.

10. "Harbin Debates Revenge Theory," *Manchuria Daily News*, August 29, 1933.

11. George Deniker, letter to Marie Kaspé, August 29, 1933, Archives du Quai d'Orsay, Affaire Kaspé, série Asie, sous-série Chine, 1940, no. 748bis.

12. "No Trace Found of Simeon Kaspé," *Manchuria Daily News*, September 2, 1933; "Arrest Made in Kaspé Kidnapping," *Manchuria Daily News*, September 1, 1933; "Gunman Wanted for Kaspé Killing," *Manchuria Daily News*, September 4, 1933; "Suspects in Kidnapping of Pianist Nabbed," *China Press*, September 7, 1933; "Alleged Assassin of Romanoffs," *North China Herald and Supreme Court and Consular Gazette*, September 20, 1933.

13. "A Tragic Schism," *North China Herald and Supreme Court and Consular Gazette*, September 6, 1933.

14. "Jews in Harbin: A Report Discounted," *North China Herald and Supreme Court and Consular Gazette*, September 6, 1933.

15. C. F. Garstin, Despatch to His Majesty's Secretary of State for Foreign Affairs, September 16, 1933, Foreign Office files for China, 1919–1980, National Archives of the United Kingdom; unsigned letter from the French Foreign Ministry to Louis Reynaud, September 19, 1933, Archives du Quai d'Orsay, Affaire Kaspé, série Asie, sous-série Chine, 1940, no. 748bis; C. F. Garstin, Despatch to His Majesty's Secretary of State for Foreign Affairs; Louis Reynaud, letter to Auguste Wilden, September 25, 1933, Archives du Quai d'Orsay, Affaire Kaspé, série Asie, sous-série·Chine, 1940, no. 748bis.

16. C. F. Garstin, Despatch to His Majesty's Secretary of State for Foreign Affairs, September 16, 1933.

17. Amleto Vespa, *Secret Agent of Japan* (London: Victor Gollancz, 1938), 242.

18. Kathryn Meyer, "The Garden of Grand Vision: Slums, Deviance, and Control in Manchukuo, 1940–41," in Norman Smith, ed., *Empire and Environment in the Making of Manchuria* (Vancouver, Can.: University of British

Columbia Press, 2017), 186; Stephan, *Russian Fascists: Tragedy and Farce in Exile, 1925–1945*, 85–86.

19. Albert Chambon, "Summary Prepared at the Request of Louis Reynaud, December 11, 1933," translation in Dan Ben-Canaan, *The Kaspé File: A Case Study of Harbin as an Intersection of Cultural and Ethnical Communities in Conflict 1932–1945* (Harbin, China: Heilongjiang University School of Western Studies, 2008), 41.

20. "Biographie Albert Chambon," *Who's Who in France*, accessed August 13, 2021, https://whoswho.fr/decede/biographie-albert-chambon_9587; "Le consul de France à Boston," *Justice de Biddeford*, January 30, 1946; Albert Chambon, *Tribulations d'un jeune diplomate dans la vielle Chine* [in French] (unpublished manuscript, 1999), 86, collection of the Chambon family.

21. Albert Chambon, "Summary Prepared at the Request of Louis Reynaud, December 11, 1933," 40–45.

22. This was probably an error; the date intended was undoubtedly September 28.

23. Takeshi Nakashima "The Kaspé Incident in Harbin, Russian Society, and Japan, 1933–1937" [in Japanese], *Humanities Bulletin* (Tokyo Metropolitan University): 490 (March 2014), 36. Translation from the Russian courtesy of Galina Spivak.

24. Louis Reynaud, letter to Auguste Wilden, September 25, 1933; Chambon, *Tribulations d'un jeune diplomate dans la vielle Chine*, 87.

25. "Bandits Send Kaspé Portion of Son's Ear," *Manchuria Daily News*, October 2, 1933; "Unique 'Gift' of Ear Given," *Manchuria Daily News*, October 5, 1933; "Captive's Plight," *South China Morning Post*, September 30, 1933; "Text of Kaspé Note Sent to Sire Released," *China Press*, October 8, 1933.

26. Chambon, *Tribulations d'un jeune diplomate dans la vielle Chine*, 87.

27. Unsigned letter from French Foreign Ministry to French Embassy in Tokyo, September 30, 1933, Archives du Quai d'Orsay, Affaire Kaspé, série Asie, sous-série Chine, 1940, no. 748bis.

28. Louis Reynaud, telegram to French Foreign Ministry, September 28, 1933, Archives du Quai d'Orsay, Affaire Kaspé, série Asie, sous-série Chine, 1940, no. 748bis; unsigned letter from the French Foreign Ministry to Louis Reynaud, September 29, 1933, Archives du Quai d'Orsay, Affaire Kaspé, série Asie, sous-série Chine, 1940, no. 748bis; Albert Chambon, "Summary Prepared at the Request of Louis Reynaud, December 11, 1933," 40–45; "Murdered," *China Press*, December 5, 1933; Vespa, *Secret Agent of Japan*, 242.

29. Nakashima, "Kaspé Incident in Harbin, Russian Society, and Japan, 1933–1937," 33–63.

30. Louis Reynaud, letter to Auguste Wilden, September 30, 1933, Archives du Quai d'Orsay, Affaire Kaspé, série Asie, sous-série Chine, 1940, no. 748bis; Henry Cosmé, letter to Mme. Marie Kaspé, October 2, 1933, Archives du Quai d'Orsay, Affaire Kaspé, série Asie, sous-série Chine, 1940, no. 748bis; Petr Balakshin, *Final v Kitae* [in Russian] (Munich: Sirius, 1958), 215.

10. Search

1. Albert Chambon, *Tribulations d'un jeune diplomate dans la vielle Chine* [in French] (unpublished manuscript, 1999), 87–88, collection of the Chambon family.

2. "White Russians a Dying Breed," *Brownsville Herald*, September 30, 1984; emails to the author from Noriko Uchiyama Valuev, February 13 and 19, 2022.

3. "'White Bandits' of Manchuria," *China Weekly Review*, December 23, 1933.

4. Albert Chambon, "Summary Prepared at the Request of Louis Reynaud, December 11, 1933," translation in Dan Ben-Canaan, *The Kaspé File: A Case Study of Harbin as an Intersection of Cultural and Ethnical Communities in Conflict 1932–1945* (Harbin, China: Heilongjiang University School of Western Studies, 2008), 42; Louis Reynaud, letter to Auguste Wilden, November 18, 1933, Archives du Quai d'Orsay, Affaire Kaspé, série Asie, sous-série Chine, 1940, no. 748bis.

5. "Komissarenko Confirms His Testimony," *Nash Put*, March 31, 1936, as quoted in Noriko Uchiyama Valuev, "The Kaspé Affair Trial as Reported by Harbin Russian Newspapers" [in Japanese], *Sever* 33 (March, 2017), 46–47.

6. Chambon, *Tribulations d'un jeune diplomate dans la vielle Chine*, 88–90.

7. "'White Bandits' of Manchuria"; Charles F. Garstin, letter to Sir Miles Lampson, December 7, 1933; Sabine Breuillard, "L'affaire Kaspé revisitée," *Revue des études slaves* 73, no. 2–3 (2001): 358.

8. Albert Chambon, letter to Japanese author Tetsuya Sunamura, date unknown, as quoted in Uchiyama Valuev, "Kaspé Affair Trial as Reported by Harbin Russian Newspapers," 49; Chambon, *Tribulations d'un jeune diplomate dans la vielle Chine*, 88–90.

9. John J. Stephan, *The Russian Fascists: Tragedy and Farce in Exile, 1925–1945* (New York: Harper & Row, 1978), 87.

10. Stephan, *Russian Fascists: Tragedy and Farce in Exile, 1925–1945*, 88.

11. Louis Reynaud, letter to Auguste Wilden, October 10, 1933, Archives du Quai d'Orsay, Affaire Kaspé, série Asie, sous-série Chine, 1940, no. 748bis.

12. "Incident on the Amur," *North China Herald and Supreme Court and Consular Gazette*, October 18, 1933; Louis Reynaud, letter to Auguste Wilden, October 20, 1933, Archives du Quai d'Orsay.

11. Letters

1. About $233,000. Most sources give this sum as 35,000 yen.

2. Semyon Kaspé, letter to Josef Kaspé, October 22, 1933, translation in Dan Ben-Canaan, *The Kaspé File: A Case Study of Harbin as an Intersection of Cultural and Ethnical Communities in Conflict 1932–1945* (Harbin, China: Heilongjiang University School of Western Studies, 2008), 30–31.

3. Josef Kaspé, letter to Semyon Kaspé, October 30, 1933, translation in Ben-Canaan, *Kaspé File: A Case Study of Harbin as an Intersection of Cultural and Ethnical Communities in Conflict 1932–1945*, 30–31.

4. Louis Reynaud, letter to Auguste Wilden, November 2, 1933, Archives du Quai d'Orsay, Affaire Kaspé, série Asie, sous-série Chine, 1940, no. 748bis; unsigned letter from the French Foreign Ministry to Louis Reynaud, November 6, 1933, Archives du Quai d'Orsay, Affaire Kaspé, série Asie, sous-série Chine, 1940, no. 748bis.

5. Reynaud, letter to Auguste Wilden, November 2, 1933, Archives du Quai d'Orsay.

6. Reynaud, letter to Auguste Wilden, November 25, 1933, Archives du Quai d'Orsay; Albert Chambon, *Tribulations d'un jeune diplomate dans la vielle Chine* [in French] (unpublished manuscript, 1999), 90, collection of the Chambon family.

7. Semyon Kaspé, letter to Josef Kaspé, November 11, 1933, translation in Ben-Canaan, *Kaspé File: A Case Study of Harbin as an Intersection of Cultural and Ethnical Communities in Conflict 1932–1945*, 32–33.

12. Playing with Fire

1. Louis Reynaud, letter to Auguste Wilden, November 18, 1933, Archives du Quai d'Orsay, Affaire Kaspé, série Asie, sous-série Chine, 1940, no. 748bis.

2. Reynaud, letter to Auguste Wilden, November 18, 1933.

3. Albert Chambon, *Tribulations d'un jeune diplomate dans la vielle Chine* [in French] (unpublished manuscript, 1999), 91–92, collection of the Chambon family.

4. Semyon Kaspé, letter to Josef Kaspé, November 17 or 18, 1933, translation in Dan Ben-Canaan, *The Kaspé File: A Case Study of Harbin as an Intersection of Cultural and Ethnical Communities in Conflict 1932–1945* (Harbin, China: Heilongjiang University School of Western Studies, 2008), 33–35.

5. Semyon Kaspé, letter to Maria and Vladimir Kaspé, November 17 or 18, 1933, translation in Ben-Canaan, *Kaspé File: A Case Study of Harbin as an Intersection of Cultural and Ethnical Communities in Conflict 1932–1945*, 35–36.

13. Arrest

1. Albert Chambon, "Summary Prepared at the Request of Louis Reynaud, December 11, 1933," translation in Dan Ben-Canaan, *The Kaspé File: A Case Study of Harbin as an Intersection of Cultural and Ethnical Communities in Conflict 1932–1945* (Harbin, China: Heilongjiang University School of Western Studies, 2008), 44.

2. Chambon, "Summary Prepared at the Request of Louis Reynaud, December 11, 1933," 140.

3. Chambon, "Summary Prepared at the Request of Louis Reynaud, December 11, 1933," 44; Louis Reynaud, letter to Auguste Wilden, December 6, 1933, Archives du Quai d'Orsay, Affaire Kaspé, série Asie, sous-série Chine, 1940, no. 748bis.; "Kidnapper Tells about Kaspé's End," *China Press*, December 15, 1933.

4. Amleto Vespa, *Secret Agent of Japan* (London: Victor Gollancz, 1938), 202–5.

5. Chambon, "Summary Prepared at the Request of Louis Reynaud, December 11, 1933," 44–45.

6. Albert Chambon, *Tribulations d'un jeune diplomate dans la vielle Chine* [in French] (unpublished manuscript, 1999), 92, collection of the Chambon family; Reynaud, letter to Auguste Wilden, December 1, 1933, Archives du Quai d'Orsay.

7. Chambon, "Summary Prepared at the Request of Louis Reynaud, December 11, 1933"; "Kidnapper Tells about Kaspé's End," *China Press*; Chambon, *Tribulations d'un jeune diplomate dans la vielle Chine*, 92.

14. Lies

1. Albert Chambon, *Tribulations d'un jeune diplomate dans la vielle Chine* [in French] (unpublished manuscript, 1999), 92–93, collection of the Chambon family.

2. "Kaspé's Mother Not Told about Son's Murder," *China Press*, December 5, 1933; "Kaspé's Mother," *South China Morning Post*, December 6, 1933; "Police Resent Consul's Slam," *Manchuria Daily News*, December 9, 1933.

3. Alexandre Pernikoff, *Bushido: The Anatomy of Terror* (New York: Liveright, 1943), 214–15; Amleto Vespa, *Secret Agent of Japan* (London: Victor Gollancz, 1938), 207.

4. Vespa, *Secret Agent of Japan*, 207.

5. Chambon, *Tribulations d'un jeune diplomate dans la vielle Chine*, 95.

6. Chizuko Takao, "Prewar Japan's Perception of Jews and the Harbin Jewish Community: The Harbin Jewish Community under Japanese Rule 1932–1941," in *Journal of the Interdisciplinary Study of Monotheistic Religions* 10 (2014): 40.

7. Theodore Kaufman, *The Jews of Harbin Live On in My Heart* [in Hebrew] (Tel Aviv: Profil, 2004), 114; "Harbin Jews Start Tirade," *Manchuria Daily News*, December 8, 1933.

8. Vespa, *Secret Agent of Japan*, 209.

9. "Slain Frenchman Buried in Harbin," *Chicago Tribune*, December 6, 1933; "Harbin Jews Start Trade," *Manchuria Daily News*, December 8, 1933; "Body of Kaspé in Harbin," *North China Herald*, December 20, 1933; Vespa, *Secret Agent of Japan*, 207–8; Takao, "Prewar Japan's Perception of Jews and the Harbin Jewish Community: The Harbin Jewish Community under Japanese Rule 1932–1941," 40; Takeshi Nakashima "The Kaspé Incident in Harbin, Russian Society, and Japan, 1933–1937" [in Japanese], *Humanities Bulletin* (Tokyo Metropolitan University): 490 (March 2014): 33–63.

10. Title unknown, *Zarya*, December 6, 1933; title unknown, *Nash Put*, December 8, 1933, and title unknown, *Zarya*, December 9, 1933, all quoted in translation in Dan Ben-Canaan, *The Kaspé File: A Case Study of Harbin as an Intersection of Cultural and Ethnical Communities in Conflict 1932–1945,* (Harbin, China: Heilongjiang University School of Western Studies, 2008), 26.

11. "French Censure Arouses Ire of Harbin Police," *China Press*, December 9, 1933; "French Vice Consul Says Manchu Police Are Helpless," *China Weekly Review*, December 16, 1933.

12. Chambon, *Tribulations d'un jeune diplomate dans la vielle Chine*, 95; "L'affaire Kaspé et l'activité du vice-consul de France M. Chambon," December 8, 1933, Archives du Quai d'Orsay, Affaire Kaspé, série Asie, sous-série Chine,

1940, no. 748bis; John J. Stephan, *The Russian Fascists: Tragedy and Farce in Exile, 1925–1945* (New York: Harper & Row, 1978), 74.

13. "Étrange malveillance," *Harbinskoe Vremya*, December 7, 1933, "Étrange conduit de M. Chambon," *Harbinskoe Vremya*, December 7, 1933, "Les actes étranges de M. Chambon continuent," *Harbinskoe Vremya*, December 8, 1933, all translations in Archives du Quai d'Orsay, Affaire Kaspé, série Asie, sous-série Chine, 1940, no. 748bis; Louis Reynaud, letter to Auguste Wilden, December 9, 1933, Archives du Quai d'Orsay, Affaire Kaspé, série Asie, sous-série Chine, 1940, no. 748bis; "French Censure Arouses Ire of Harbin Police," *China Press*, December 9, 1933.

14. Chambon, *Tribulations d'un jeune diplomate dans la vielle Chine*, 93.

15. Reynaud, letter to Auguste Wilden, December 9, 1933.

16. "Mukden," *Manchuria Daily News*, December 14, 1933; Vespa, *Secret Agent of Japan*, 212.

17. Dan Ben-Canaan, *The Kaspé File: A Case Study of Harbin as an Intersection of Cultural and Ethnical Communities in Conflict 1932–1945* (Harbin, China: Heilongjiang University School of Western Studies, 2008), 26; Reynaud, letter to Auguste Wilden, December 9, 1933.

18. "French Consulate at Harbin Criticizes Laxness of Manchukuo Police," *China Weekly Review*, January 6, 1934.

19. "Alleged Kaspé Slayer Caught," *Manchuria Daily News*, December 19, 1933; "Body of Kaspé in Harbin," *North China Herald*, December 20, 1933; Vespa, *Secret Agent of Japan*, 203–4.

15. *Not Criminals but Heroes*

1. Dan Ben-Canaan, *The Kaspé File: A Case Study of Harbin as an Intersection of Cultural and Ethnical Communities in Conflict 1932–1945* (Harbin, China: Heilongjiang University School of Western Studies, 2008), 20–21.

2. Thomas David Dubois, "Rule of Law in a Brave New Empire: Legal Rhetoric and Practice in Manchukuo," *Law and History Review* 26, no. 2 (Summer 2008), 302.

3. "Japanese Lawyers for Harbin," *North China Herald*, August 15, 1934.

4. "The Case of Simon Kaspé Investigated," *North China Herald*, December 19, 1934.

5. "Conclusions of Mr. Ozma Egouchi [*sic*], Head of the Harbin Police Criminal Division," translation in Ben-Canaan, *Kaspé File: A Case Study of*

Harbin as an Intersection of Cultural and Ethnical Communities in Conflict 1932–1945, 45–47.

6. "Conclusions of Mr. Ozma Egouchi [*sic*], Head of the Harbin Police Criminal Division," translation in Ben-Canaan, *Kaspé File: A Case Study of Harbin as an Intersection of Cultural and Ethnical Communities in Conflict 1932–1945*, 45–47.

7. Louis Reynaud, letter to Auguste Wilden, November 29, 1934, Archives du Quai d'Orsay, Affaire Kaspé, série Asie, sous-série Chine, 1940, no. 748bis.

8. "The Case of Simon Kaspé Investigated"; Takeshi Nakashima, "The Kaspé Incident in Harbin, Russian Society, and Japan, 1933–1937," *Humanities Bulletin* (Tokyo Metropolitan University) 490 (March 2014): 33–63.

16. No Longer Safe

1. "Shanghai Jews Protest against Ill-Treatment," *China Press*, December 25, 1934; "The Status of Jews in Harbin," *North China Herald*, January 2, 1935.

2. "Trouble in Manchukuo," *Jewish Daily Bulletin*, February 4, 1935.

3. "Anti-Semitism in Harbin," *Israel's Messenger*, January 4, 1935.

4. "Jap Justifies Slaying of Jew in Manchukuo," *Jewish Daily Bulletin*, January 23, 1935.

5. "Manchukuo Denies Anti-Semitic Agitation," *Israel's Messenger*, February 1, 1935.

6. "Wise and Kallen Protest to Saito against Agitators in Manchukuo," *Jewish Daily Bulletin*, February 6, 1935.

7. "The *Nash Put*: A Case for Manchukuo," *Israel's Messenger*, April 5, 1935.

8. Chizuko Takao, "Russian-Jewish Harbin before World War II," in *Japanese Slavic and East European Studies* 32 (2011): 47–48.

9. *Nash Put*, February 26, 1935, as quoted in "The *Nash Put*: A Case for Manchukuo," *Israel's Messenger*, April 5, 1935.

10. "Outrage by the Harbin Police," October 1, 1935; "Harbin Police Search Synagogue," *Jewish Advocate*, September 6, 1935; "Reign of Terror for Jews in Harbin," *Israel's Messenger*, November 11, 1935.

17. The First Trial

1. Petr Balakshin, *Final v Kitae* [in Russian] (Munich: Sirius, 1958), 218.

2. Nikolai Andreevich Martynov [*sic*] Papers, 1930–1964, vol. 2, 178–90, Rare Book and Manuscript Library, Columbia University.

3. Amleto Vespa, *Secret Agent of Japan* (London: Victor Gollancz), 209.

4. "Kaspé Case Appealed to Japanese Judges in Harbin High Court," *China Weekly Review*, July 18, 1936.

5. "Postpone Murder Trial," *Sentinel*, July 18, 1935.

6. "Sensational Harbin Trial," *North China Herald*, October 30, 1935; "The Kaspé Murder Case," *North China Herald*, November 6, 1935.

7. Vespa, *Secret Agent of Japan*, 212–13.

8. Ryan Mitchell, "Manchukuo's Contested Sovereignty: Legal Activism, Rights Consciousness and Civil Resistance in a 'Puppet State'," *Asian Journal of Law and Society* 3 (2016): 364.

9. Vespa, *Secret Agent of Japan*, 214.

10. Vespa, *Secret Agent of Japan*, 218–19.

18. The Second Trial

1. Title unknown, *Nash Put*, March 24, 1936, as quoted in Noriko Uchiyama Valuev, "The Kaspé Affair Trial as Reported by Harbin Russian Newspapers" [in Japanese], *Sever* 33 (March 2017): 44.

2. Title unknown, *Zarya*, May 5, 1936, as quoted in Uchiyama Valuev, "Kaspé Affair Trial as Reported by Harbin Russian Newspapers," 45.

3. "Komisarenko's Testimony," *Nash Put*, March 31, 1936, as quoted in Uchiyama Valuev, "Kaspé Affair Trial as Reported by Harbin Russian Newspapers," 46.

4. Noriko Uchiyama Valuev, "The Kaspé Case of Nikolai Martinov: The Full Story of the Case as Written by the Perpetrator Himself" [in Japanese], *Sever* 31 (March 2015), 98.

5. Uchiyama Valuev, "Kaspé Affair Trial as Reported by Harbin Russian Newspapers," 46–47; Uchiyama Valuev, "The Kaspé Case of Nikolai Martinov: The Full Story of the Case as Written by the Perpetrator Himself," 86.

6. Title unknown, *Zarya*, April 10, 1936, as quoted in Uchiyama Valuev, "Kaspé Affair Trial as Reported by Harbin Russian Newspapers," 53; Uchiyama Valuev, "Kaspé Case of Nikolai Martinov: The Full Story of the Case as Written by the Perpetrator Himself," 97.

7. Valuev, "Kaspé Affair Trial as Reported by Harbin Russian Newspapers," 52.

8. Title unknown, *Zarya*, April 16, 1936, as quoted in Uchiyama Valuev, "The Kaspé Affair Trial as Reported by Harbin Russian Newspapers," 54.

9. Title unknown, *Nash Put*, April 16, 1936, as quoted in Uchiyama Valuev, "Kaspé Affair Trial as Reported by Harbin Russian Newspapers," 55.

10. Sabine Breuillard, "L'affaire Kaspé revisitée," *Revue des études slaves* 73, no. 2–3 (2001): 344.

11. "Protracted Trial of Kidnappers Nearing End: No Death Penalty Asked," *Manchuria Daily News*, May 6, 1936.

12. "Kaspé Case Appealed to Japanese Judges in Harbin High Court," *China Weekly Review*, July 18, 1936.

13. "The Kaspé Murder Case and the Abolition of Exterritoriality in Manchukuo," *China Weekly Review*, June 27, 1936; "Death Sentences for White Guardist Slayers of Jew Set Aside," *The Sentinel*, July 16, 1936.

14. Uchiyama Valuev, "Kaspé Affair Trial as Reported by Harbin Russian Newspapers," 57.

15. "Harbin Murderers," *South China Morning Post*, June 29, 1936; title unknown, *Zarya*, June 14, 1936, as quoted in Valuev, "Kaspé Affair Trial as Reported by Harbin Russian Newspapers," 59.

16. "Kaspé Murder Case Re-Opened," *North China Herald*, February 10, 1937; title unknown, *Zarya*, June 14, 1936, as quoted in Uchiyama Valuev, "Kaspé Affair Trial as Reported by Harbin Russian Newspapers," 48; title unknown, *Nash Put*, June 14, 1936, as quoted in Uchiyama Valuev, "Kaspé Affair Trial as Reported by Harbin Russian Newspapers," 48.

17. "Our Harbin Letter," *Manchuria Daily News*, June 15, 1936; "Slayers of Simon Kaspé, Harbin Pianist, Given Death Sentences," *China Press*, June 21, 1936; "Harbin Murderers."

18. Petr Balakshin, *Final v Kitae* [in Russian] (Munich: Sirius, 1958), 221–22; "La population attend la justice," *Harbinskoe Vremya*, June 15, 1936, translation in Archives du Quai d'Orsay, Affaire Kaspé, série Asie, sous-série Chine, 1940, no. 748bis; "Kaspé Murder Case and the Abolition of Exterritoriality in Manchukuo"; "Four Kaspé Murderers Will Pay Extreme Penalty," *North China Herald*, July 1, 1936.

19. "Harbin Gangsters to Die," *North China Herald*, July 1, 1936; "Antisemitism Collapses in Harbin: A Great Verdict," *Israel's Messenger*, July 3, 1936; Dan Ben-Canaan, *The Kaspé File: A Case Study of Harbin as an Intersection of Cultural and Ethnical Communities in Conflict 1932–1945* (Harbin, China: Heilongjiang University School of Western Studies, 2008), 118.

20. Louis Reynaud, letter to Henri Hoppenpot, June 15, 1936, Archives du Quai d'Orsay, Affaire Kaspé, série Asie, sous-série Chine, 1940, no. 748bis.

19. Powerful Influences

1. Amleto Vespa, *Secret Agent of Japan* (London: Victor Gollancz, 1938), 219; Alexandre Pernikoff, *Bushido: The Anatomy of Terror* (New York: Liveright, 1943), 216.

2. Noriko Uchiyama Valuev, "The Kaspé Case of Nikolai Martinov: The Full Story of the Case as Written by the Perpetrator Himself" [in Japanese], *Sever* 31 (March 2015), 99.

3. Dwight R. Rider, *Japan's Biological and Chemical Weapons Programs: War Crimes and Atrocities—Who's Who, What's What, Where's Where: 1928–1945*, Scribd, accessed July 28, 2021, https://www.scribd.com/document/466964787 /9-October-2018-Who-s-Who-Japanese-BW; Petr Balakshin, *Final v Kitae* [in Russian] (Munich: Sirius, 1958), 211–23. "Kaspé Case Appealed to Japanese Judges in Harbin High Court," *China Weekly Review*, July 18, 1936; "Anti-Semitism in Harbin," *Israel's Messenger*, August 1, 1936.

4. Louis Reynaud, letter to Paul-Emile Naggiar, July 9, 1936, Archives du Quai d'Orsay, Affaire Kaspé, série Asie, sous-série Chine, 1940, no. 748bis.

5. "Our Harbin Letter," *Manchuria Daily News*, September 6, 1936.

6. This is likely a mistranslation, as the Comintern was composed of political parties rather than individuals. The accusation sometimes leveled at Josef Kaspé (without evidence) was that he was a member of the Russian Communist Party.

7. "Our Harbin Letter," *Manchuria Daily News*, January 20, 1937.

8. The kidnapping did *not* occur before March 1933, but the actual date of the amnesty, which Pu Yi proclaimed upon his investiture as emperor, was March 1934, and the crime had, indeed, been committed before that date.

9. "The Reconsideration of the Trial of Simon Kaspé's Murderers," translation in Dan Ben-Canaan, *The Kaspé File: A Case Study of Harbin as an Intersection of Cultural and Ethnical Communities in Conflict 1932–1945* (Harbin, China: Heilongjiang University School of Western Studies, 2008), 48–50.

10. Balakshin, *Final v Kitae*, 223.

11. "Soviet Stiffening Attitude on Japan," *New York Times*, February 16, 1937; "Whites' Acquittal Stirs Soviet Ire," *Montreal Gazette*, February 16, 1937; Louis Reynaud, letter to Paul-Emile Naggiar, January 30, 1937, Archives du Quai d'Orsay; "Jews Stirred by Verdict Freeing Kidnap Killers," *Chicago Tribune*, March 6, 1937.

12. "The Jews in Manchuria," *Hebrew Standard*, November 2, 1906.

20. What Really Happened

1. Takeshi Nakashima, "The Kaspé Incident in Harbin, Russian Society, and Japan, 1933–1937" [in Japanese], *Humanities Bulletin* (Tokyo Metropolitan University) 490 (March 2014), 33–63.

2. John J. Stephan, *The Russian Fascists: Tragedy and Farce in Exile, 1925–1945* (New York: Harper & Row, 1978), 80; Amleto Vespa, *Secret Agent of Japan* (London: Victor Gollancz, 1938), 191–94.

3. Alexandre Pernikoff, *Bushido: The Anatomy of Terror* (New York: Liveright, 1943), 201–5.

4. Noriko Uchiyama Valuev, "The Kaspé Case of Nikolai Martinov: The Full Story of the Case as Written by the Perpetrator Himself" [in Japanese], *Sever* 31 (March 2015), 85–86.

5. Stephan, *Russian Fascists: Tragedy and Farce in Exile, 1925–1945*, 84.

6. Uchiyama Valuev, "Kaspé Case of Nikolai Martinov: The Full Story of the Case as Written by the Perpetrator Himself," 87; Stephan, *Russian Fascists: Tragedy and Farce in Exile, 1925–1945*, 84.

7. Petr Balakshin, *Final v Kitae* [in Russian] (Munich: Sirius, 1958), 215–16; Uchiyama Valuev, "Kaspé Case of Nikolai Martinov: The Full Story of the Case as Written by the Perpetrator Himself," 89.

8. Uchiyama Valuev, "The Kaspé Case of Nikolai Martinov: The Full Story of the Case as Written by the Perpetrator Himself," 90.

9. Albert Chambon, *Tribulations d'un jeune diplomate dans la vielle Chine* [in French] (unpublished manuscript, 1999), 92, collection of the Chambon family; Vespa, *Secret Agent of Japan*, 205.

10. Pernikoff, *Bushido: The Anatomy of Terror*, 206–8.

11. Pernikoff, *Bushido: The Anatomy of Terror*, 206–8; Balakshin, *Final v Kitae*, 215; Stephan, *Russian Fascists: Tragedy and Farce in Exile, 1925–1945*, 86; Chambon, *Tribulations d'un jeune diplomate dans la vielle Chine*, 92.

12. Nakashima, "Kaspé Incident in Harbin, Russian Society, and Japan, 1933–1937," 33–63.

13. Vespa, *Secret Agent of Japan*, 197–98.

14. *Biography of Lieutenant-General Michitarō Komatsubara*, Generals.dk, accessed July 31, 2021, https://generals.dk/general/Komatsubara/Michitar%C5%8D/Japan.html.

15. Vespa, *Secret Agent of Japan*, 45–50.

16. "Japanese Begin to Regret Talking of Fighting Russia," *Chicago Daily*

News, March 5, 1934; Nelson Trusler Johnson, telegram to the acting secretary of state, April 29, 1932, Office of the Historian of the Department of State, accessed August 3, 2021, https://history.state.gov/historicaldocuments /frus1932v03/d780; "League's Enquiry Commission," *Manchuria Daily News*, May 10, 1932; "Russia Ready to Start War with Japs or Anybody," *Waterloo Iowa Courier*, November 1, 1934.

17. Vespa, *Secret Agent of Japan*, 196–99.

18. Louis Reynaud, letter to Auguste Wilden, November 18, 1933, Archives du Quai d'Orsay, Affaire Kaspé, série Asie, sous-série Chine, 1940, no. 748bis.

21. The Fugu Plan

1. "Manchukuo Newest Scene of Tsarist Anti-Semitic Activities," *Sentinel*, January 2, 1934; "Violent Jew-Baiting in Manchukuo," *Israel's Messenger*, January 3, 1936.

2. "Antisemitism in Harbin," *Israel's Messenger*, February 2, 1934; "Reign of Terror for Jews in Harbin," *Israel's Messenger*, November 1, 1935.

3. "Reign of Terror for Jews in Harbin."

4. "Large Number of Jews Migrate from Harbin to Southern China," *Sentinel*, March 2, 1933; "Hong Kong Community Grows as Result of Far East Disturbances," *Sentinel*, March 17, 1933.

5. "Soviet Sells Railway to Japan," *Jewish Weekly News*, November 23, 1934; "Japs to Fire All Jews from Far Eastern Railway," *Sentinel*, April 18, 1935; "Thousand Jews Being Evacuated from Harbin," *Australian Jewish News*, October 4, 1935.

6. "Refugees from Germany Go to Far East," *Jewish Advocate*, April 7, 1936.

7. Ming Hui Pan, "The Harbin Jewish Community and the Regional Conflicts of Northeast China, 1903–1963" (PhD diss., Concordia University, 2020), n136; "Kidnapped Harbin Jewish Boy Ransomed by Father," *Sentinel*, July 18, 1935; "Editing the Cables," *Jewish Advocate*, April 17, 1936.

8. "Jewish Population of Harbin Cut by Terror Activities," *Jewish Press*, August 19, 1938; Chizuko Takao, "Prewar Japan's Perception of Jews and the Harbin Jewish Community: The Harbin Jewish Community under Japanese Rule 1932–1941," in *Journal of the Interdisciplinary Study of Monotheistic Religions* 10 (2014): 37; "In Manchuria," *Australian Jewish News*, May 29, 1936; "Polish Jew Executed in Manchukuo," *Sentinel*, October 21, 1937; "Japanese-Manchukuoan Police Execute Polish Jew," *Australian Jewish News*, November 19, 1937.

9. Kevin McGeary, "How Japan Tried to Save Thousands of Jews from the Holocaust," China Channel, March 28, 2019, accessed October 13, 2021, https://chinachannel.org/2019/03/28/japan-fugu/; "Tokyo Denies Report of Offer to German Jews to Settle in Manchukuo," *American Jewish World*, October 8, 1934.

10. Meron Medzini, *Under the Shadow of the Rising Sun: Japan and the Jews during the Holocaust Era* (Brighton MA: Academic Studies Press, 2016), 34–38; Marvin Tokayer and Mary Swartz, *The Fugu Plan: The Untold Story of the Japanese and the Jews during World War II* (New York: Paddington Press, 1979), 52–55; Gerald David Kearney, "Jews under Japanese Domination," *Shofar* 11, no. 3 (Spring 1993): 58–59.

11. "After the Jews Failed to Establish a Nation in Harbin, Where Did They Go?" [in Japanese], *Sina*, January 9, 2018, accessed October 15, 2021, http://k.sina.com.cn/article_6444738482_18022e7b20010037di.html.

12. "Hate Monger Sheet in Manchuria Is Suppressed," *American Jewish World*, March 18, 1938; Kearney, "Jews under Japanese Domination," 59–60; Zvia Bowman, "A People That Dwells Alone—The Russian, Chinese and Japanese Perceptions of Harbin Jewish Community, 1898–1945," *Points East* 36, no. 2 (July 2021).

13. Chizuko Takao, "Russian-Jewish Harbin before World War II," in *Japanese Slavic and East European Studies* 32 (2011): 41.

14. Kearney, "Jews under Japanese Domination," 60; Medzini, *Under the Shadow of the Rising Sun: Japan and the Jews during the Holocaust Era*, 58.

15. Kearney, "Jews under Japanese Domination," 61–62.

16. Steve Hochstadt, "Memories of Shanghai," *Jewish History* 10, no. 1 (Spring 1996): 113.

17. Medzini, *Under the Shadow of the Rising Sun: Japan and the Jews during the Holocaust Era*, 60–61.

18. John J. Stephan, *The Russian Fascists: Tragedy and Farce in Exile, 1925–1945* (New York: Harper & Row, 1978), 80; Amleto Vespa, *Secret Agent of Japan* (London: Victor Gollancz, 1938), 40.

19. Xu Xin, "Jews in Harbin: A Historical Perspective," paper delivered at the International Seminar on the History and Culture of Harbin Jews, August 30–September 2, 2004, Harbin, China.

20. "A Jewish Legacy Draws to a Close in North China," *New York Times*, February 27, 1983; "Russian Legacy Fades in North China," *New York Times*, August 11, 1985; Dan Ben-Canaan, e-mail to the author, May 17, 2020.

Epilogue

1. Mark Gamsa, "The Many Faces of Hotel Moderne in Harbin," in *East Asian History* 37 (December 2011): 30–31; "Jewelry Store Liquidated," *North China Herald*, December 25, 1935.

2. "The Jewish Cemetery in Harbin," Harbin Jewish Cemetery, accessed August 2, 2021, http://www.zegk.uni-heidelberg.de/hist/ausstellungen/harbin/cemetery.html/.

3. Noriko Uchiyama Valuev, "The Kaspé Case of Nikolai Martinov: The Full Story of the Case as Written by the Perpetrator Himself" [in Japanese], *Sever* 31 (March 2015): 83; Petr Balakshin, *Final v Kitae* [in Russian] (Munich: Sirius, 1958), 223.

4. "Biography of Lieutenant-General Michitarō Komatsubara," Generals.dk, accessed July 31, 2021, https://generals.dk/general/Komatsubara/Michitar%C5%8D/Japan.html.

5. Uchiyama Valuev, "Kaspé Case of Nikolai Martinov: The Full Story of the Case as Written by the Perpetrator Himself," 83; Balakshin, *Final v Kitae*, 223.

6. Uchiyama Valuev, "Kaspé Case of Nikolai Martinov: The Full Story of the Case as Written by the Perpetrator Himself," 100–101; Balakshin, *Final v Kitae*, 223.

7. Tetsuya Sunamura, *The Harbin Church Garden* [in Japanese] (Tokyo: PHP Publishing, 2009), 11–45, 46–78; Takeshi Nakashima, "The Kaspé Incident in Harbin, Russian Society, and Japan, 1933–1937" [in Japanese] *Humanities Bulletin* (Tokyo Metropolitan University): 490 (March 2014), 57; Alexandre Pernikoff, "Correspondence 'Bushido'," *Herald Tribune*, May 30, 1943.

8. Brian Edgar, "The Free French in Hong Kong: Louis Reynaud," in *The Dark World's Fire: Thomas and Evelina Edgar in Occupied Hong Kong* (blog), accessed October 20, 2021, no longer available.

9. Uchiyama Valuev, "Kaspé Case of Nikolai Martinov: The Full Story of the Case as Written by the Perpetrator Himself," 83; Balakshin, *Final v Kitae*, 223; "White Russians a Dying Breed," *Brownsville Herald*, September 30, 1984; Findagrave, accessed October 20, 2021, https://www.findagrave.com/memorial/89333650/alexie-shandar.

10. Alexandre Pernikoff, *Bushido: The Anatomy of Terror* (New York: Liveright, 1943), 222–84.

11. Uchiyama Valuev, "Kaspé Case of Nikolai Martinov: The Full Story of the Case as Written by the Perpetrator Himself," 83; Balakshin, *Final v Kitae*, 223.

12. Gamsa, "Many Faces of Hotel Moderne in Harbin," 31–32.

Index

Page numbers in italic indicate illustrations.

Kaufman, Abraham Josevich (*cont.*)
152–53; meeting with Morishima,
113; *Nash Put's* attacks on, 103;
police search of home of, 114,
147; protest against ban on use of
Yiddish, 19
Kazakhstan, 154, 159
Kempeitai: and ambush at Komissarenko's house, 94, 118; and
ambush behind railroad station,
96–97; destruction of records
of, 136, 137; detention of Jews
during Pu Yi's visit, 147; and
Eguchi, 72; imprisonment of
Vespa, 161; investigation of Kaspé
case, 64, 69, 87, 145; involvement
with Semyon's kidnapping, 120,
141; Komatsubara's promise of
assistance of, 87, 93; links with
Russian fascists, 72, 141, 143; and
Nakamura, 44, 77, 78, 87, 118; as
part of Harbin security, 42. *See
also* Nakamura, Konstantin Ivanovich "Kostya"
Khalkhin Gol, 159
Kirichenko, Nikifor Pavlovich:
assault on Shandar, 115; capture,
105; escape, 97, 98; exile, 159;
and Galushko's death, 140; and
Koffman kidnapping, 137; as
member of kidnapping gang, 77,
122, 139; and murder of Semyon,
96, 110, 119, 123, 141; ownership of
a brothel, 119; portrayed as victim
of Bolsheviks, 124, 125–26; recommended treatment of, 109, 125,
131; during second trial, 121–22;

during Semyon's captivity, 94–95,
104; sentencing of, 126–27, 133;
and White movement, 138
Kiselev, Aaron Moshe, 63–64
Klurman, Isaac, 148
Kobe, 151, 153
Koffman, Meir, 57–58, 63, 75, 77, 90,
137–38
Komatsubara, Michitarō, 87, 93, 142–
45, 159
Komissarenko, Dionisy Grigoryevich: abduction and confession,
76–77, 83; confirmation of
Nakamura's involvement, 137;
exile, 159; information shared
by, 82, 87, 88, 93, 94, 118, 123;
legal defense, 126; as member
of kidnapping gang, 75, 94, 96,
97, 138, 139, 140; portrayed as
victim of Bolsheviks, 124; recommended treatment of, 109, 125,
131; released on purpose, 104;
sentencing of, 126–27, 133; trial
testimony, 122
Korea, 6, 7, 8, 26
Kreutzer, Leonid, 33

Latvia, 148
Lazareff, Boris, 28
League of Nations, 51, 56
Lenin, Vladimir Ilyich, 25
Leonson, Mendel, 148
Levin, Lev, 114, 134
Liaodong Peninsula, 6, 8
Liaoning Province, 5, 40
Lithuania, 14, 148
Lytton Commission, 51–56, 59, 142

Mali, Leib, 148

Manchouli, 9

Manchukuo: and battle of Khalkhin
Gol, 159; envisioned role of Jews
in, 48–50, 142, 149–54; establishment of, 2, 40–41; Japanese
administration of, 42–43, 156;
Japanese recognition of, 39; legal
system, 106, 116, 125, 127, 128, 133;
and Lytton Commission, 51–56;
quest for international recognition of, 51, 59–60, 72, 112; and the
Semyon Kaspé case, xi, 115. *See
also* Harbin; Manchuria

Manchukuo Gendarmerie, 42

Manchukuo State Police, 42

Manchuria: geopolitical importance,
5; Japan's desire to control, 36;
multiethnic population, 8, 21;
during the Qing Dynasty, 6; rail
connections, 7–8, 9, 11–12, 156; in
regional map from 1928, 7. *See
also* Harbin; Manchukuo

Manchuria Daily News, 62, 64,
101, 146

Maoershan, 15

Martinov, Nikolai Andreevich:
arrest, 75, 97; background and
earlier crimes, 45, 119; and
Kaspé investigation, 68, 73;
legal defense, 125, 130; life after
imprisonment, 159; memoirs and
diaries, 136, 137; named as gang
member, 75, 77, 100, 141; prison
treatment, 115, 121; recommended
treatment of, 109, 110, 125, 131;
role in kidnapping, 118–19, 137,

138, 139; sentencing, 126–27, 129,
133

Maru, Saiji, 106–7, 115, 124–25,
130–31

Le Matin, 61

Mexico, 148

Mikhailovna, Lydia, 129

Ming Dynasty, 5

Moldova, 14

Mongolia, 7, 159

Morishima, Morito, 73, 110, 113, 114

Mukden, 15, 151

Mussolini, Benito, 23

Nagako, Empress, 146

Nakamura, Konstantin Ivanovich
"Kostya": and Galushko's death,
140; as head of Kempeitai in
Harbin, 69, 87, 93, 94, 141; links
to Russian fascists, 38; and Lytton Commission visit, 55, 56; as
mastermind of Semyon's kidnapping, 77, 84, 88, 94, 118–19, 137,
138; pedophilia, 43–44; postwar
life, 159–60; and Semyon's death,
97–98, 99, 140; use of spy at
Hotel Moderne, 78, 120. *See also*
Kempeitai

Nakashima, Takeshi, 136, 141

Nash Put (Our Way): accusations
against Josef Kaspé, 25, 62; attacks
on Harbin Jewish community,
146, 147; attacks on Kaufman and
Chambon, 101, 103; and N. E. B.
Ezra, 112–13, 113–14; on petition
to annul verdict, 129; reporting on
kidnappers' trial, 116, 121, 123–24,

leader of Russian Fascist Party, 23–25; links to Nakamura, 38, 43, 137; threats against Vespa, 120; trial and execution, 160; usefulness to the Japanese, 46. See also *Nash Put* (Our Way); Russian Fascist Party

Romania, 148

Russia: civil war, 49; control of railroads in Manchuria, 7–8, 156; return of Harbin Jews to, 147, 154; revolution, 18, 20, 21, 25, 62, 76; strategic interest in Manchuria, 5–8; treatment of Jews, 14–15. *See also* Russian Fascist Party; Soviet Union; White Russians

Russian Communist Party, 23

Russian Fascist Party: antisemitism of, 2, 25, 111, 138; approval of second verdict, 133; attacks on Chambon, 101–2; attacks on Josef Kaspé, 62, 108; links with Kempeitai, 141; petition to annul first verdict, 129; Rodzaevsky's leadership of, 23–26; role in Manchukuo, 46, 55; and Semyon's kidnapping, 73, 124, 137; terrorist actions, 38. See also *Nash Put* (Our Way); Rodzaevsky, Konstantin Vladimirovich; White Russians

Russian Orthodox Church, 25, 43, 44, 77

Russian Revolution, 18, 20, 21, 76

Russo-Japanese War, 8, 15, 36, 50, 150

Saito, Hiroshi, 113

Schiff, Jacob, 50, 150

Secret Agent of Japan (Vespa), 135, 141, 143. *See also* Vespa, Amleto Vintorino De Chellis

Semyonov, Grigory Mikhailovich, 129, 149

Sever, 136

Shandar, Alexei Yelievich: arrest, 97; denial of involvement in Kaspé case, 115, 122, 123, 125; and earlier kidnappings, 74–75; legal representation, 116; life after imprisonment, 160; and Martinov, 138; ownership of a brothel, 119; recommended sentence for, 109, 110, 125, 131; role in Semyon's kidnapping, 77, 94, 122, 139; sentencing, 126–27, 133

Shandong Province, 6

Shanghai, 145, 147, 151, 153, 154

Shanghai Ashkenazi Jewish Communal Association, 111

Shanghai School for Boys, 28

Shanghai Symphony Orchestra, 60

Shanhaiguan, 5

Shapiro, Constantine, 33–35

Shapiro, Isaac, 35

Shapiro, Lydia Abramovna Chernetskaya: family background, 2, 17, 32; life after Kaspé case, 160; marriage, 33–35; and Semyon's kidnapping, 61, 65, 69, 71, 92, 139; witness testimony, 123–24

Shapiro, Michael, 32

Sherel de Florence, I., 58, 63, 74, 75, 77, 118

Shimonoseki, Treaty of (1895), 6

Siberia, 7, 49
Soong Ching Ling, 28
South Africa, 148
South China Morning Post, 116
South Manchuria Railway, 7, 8, 9,
  36, 38
Soviet Union: and battle of Khalkhin
  Gol, 159; and Chinese Eastern
  Railway, 21–22, 147; efforts to
  undermine, 23; exodus of White
  Russians from, 19; and Fugu Plan,
  150, 153–54; and Japanese inva-
  sion of Harbin, 38; "liberation"
  of Manchuria, 154, 156; protest
  against second verdict, 134; return
  of Jews to, 148. *See also* Russia
Stalin, Joseph, 25
Stephan, John J., 25, 141
Straits Settlements, 148
Streicher, Julius, 25
St. Sophia Orthodox Cathedral, 12, 13
Der Stürmer, 25
Sunamura, Tetsuya, 136
Sungari River, 11, 42, 51, 52
synagogues, 17, 19, 113, 143, 147, 155

Taiwan, 6
Tianjin, 40, 103, 147, 151, 154
Time magazine, 39
Tokumu Kikan: during Fugu Plan,
  151; in Harbin security arrange-
  ments, 42; and "manufactured
  incidents," 38; and Martinov, 159;
  promised cooperation on Kaspé
  case, 87, 93; and Russian Fascist
  Party, 73, 120; unnamed chief of,
  48, 56–57, 119, 120, 142–45

Topas, Boris, 111
Trans-Siberian Railway, 8, 9, 46

Ukraine, 14
Union of Soviet Socialist Republics
  (USSR). *See* Soviet Union
United States, 23, 60, 148, 149, 150,
  153, 154
University of California at Berkeley, 32
Uruguay, 148

Valuev, Noriko Uchiyama, 136
Vespa, Amleto Vintorino De Chellis:
  forced work for Tokumu Kikan,
  47–49, 53, 119; on Galushko's
  death, 139–40; on Kaspé case,
  100, 119–20, 122, 137, 140–41; life
  after Kaspé case, 160–61; and the
  Lytton Commission's visit, 53,
  54, 55; on Osamu Eguchi, 72–73;
  on Rodzaevsky's role in Koffman
  case, 138; Rodzaevsky's threat
  against, 120; at Semyon's funeral,
  99; service to Zhang Zuolin,
  46–47; in Shanghai, 135, 145, 161;
  on unnamed chief of Tokumu
  Kikan, 142–44
Vladivostok, 6, 8, 9, 11, 138
Volgin, Oleg, 55, 78, 135, 138, 140,
  141, 161

Weizmann, Chaim, 56, 150
White Russians: abductions of Jews,
  148; antisemitism of, 2, 20, 49,
  57, 66, 111, 113–14; in Harbin, 2,
  19–20, 21; hatred of Bolsheviks,
  22, 137; and the Japanese, 39–40,

49–50, 134, 142–43, 150; Konstantin Nakamura and, 44; Nikolai Martinov and, 45, 137; in the police force, 45, 75. *See also* Russian Fascist Party
Wilden, Auguste, 62
Wise, Stephen S., 113, 153
Witte, Sergei Yulyevich, 14
Woliewski, Ataman, 63
Workers' and Peasants' Red Army, 21, 49
World War I, 18, 21
World War II, 154, 156, 157

Xiaoling, 93, 95, 98–99, 140
Xinjing, 116, 129

Yagi, Nikolai Nikolayevich, 44, 67–68, 69, 75, 101
Yalu River, 6
Yamaguchi, Tamizi, 130
Yasser, Josef, 28
Yasue, Norihiro, 149–50, 151, 152–53, 161

Yiddish, 14, 18
YMCA, 57
Yomiuri Shimbun, 136

Zaitsev, Yakov Kirillovich: account of kidnapping plot, 116–18, 119; arrest, 96–97, 140; denial of involvement, 115, 123, 125; escape from Soviet prison, 138; exile, 161; portrayed as victim of Bolsheviks, 124; prison treatment, 121; recommended treatment of, 109, 125, 131; revelations to Semyon, 141; role in kidnapping, 77, 122, 139; sentencing, 126–27, 133
Zarya (Rays of Sunlight), 61, 101, 116
Zeya, 76
Zhang Xueliang, 37, 38
Zhang Zuolin, 8–10, 22, 36–37, 45, 46
Zimin, Moisei G., 162
Zionist Society for Jewish Resettlement in Palestine, 19